THEATER OF ACCULTURATION

The Roman Ghetto in the Sixteenth Century

THE LECTURES THAT FORM THE BASIS OF THIS book were delivered at Smith College in the fall of 1996 when Kenneth Stow was the Ruth and Clarence Kennedy Professor of Renaissance Studies and a visiting member of Smith's Jewish Studies Program. The Kennedy Professorship honors two longtime members of Smith's Art Department who specialized in the Renaissance. The annual Kennedy lectures underscore the place of humanistic studies in the Smith curriculum. In this case they showed that the study of Jewish civilizations and cultures can deepen the understanding of how modern Europe developed and how civilizations and cultures, as a whole, evolve.

THEATER OF ACCULTURATION

The Roman Ghetto in the Sixteenth Century

KENNETH STOW

University of Washington Press, Seattle & London

Smith College, Northampton, Massachusetts

Library of Congress Cataloging-in-Publication Data

Stow, Kenneth R.

   Theater of acculturation : the Roman ghetto in the sixteenth century / Kenneth
   Stow.

       p.   cm.

   Includes bibliographical references (p.   ) and index.

   ISBN 0-295-98025-7 (cloth : alk. paper)—ISBN 0-295-98022-2 (pbk. : alk. paper)

   1. Jews—Italy—Rome—History—16th century.   2. Rome (Italy)—Ethnic
   relations.   I. Title.

   DS135.I85 R6637   2001

   945′.632004924—dc21   00-064822

"Every man has his mask."

— ERWIN SCHENKELBACH, PORTRAIT PHOTOGRAPHER, JERUSALEM

CONTENTS

VII

ACKNOWLEDGMENTS

IN APRIL 1963, Smith College held a symposium entitled "The Renaissance Reconsidered." One of the contributions described the reconstruction of Rome—physical Rome—by Pope Martin V following his return from the lengthy papal exile in French Avignon about 1419. The Jews of Rome may have benefited from that reconstruction; their life under Martin V was certainly predictable and undisturbed. The author of that study, published in 1964, was none other than Smith Professor Ruth Kennedy. It is thus highly fitting that thanks to the professorship endowed in Ruth and Clarence Kennedy's memory, the three 1996 Kennedy Lectures that I gave about the Jews of Rome in the much changed and turbulent setting of mid-sixteenth-century Rome, out of which this book grew, should also have been delivered at Smith. It is with pleasure and gratitude that I thank all those who made my tenure at Smith and these lectures possible, in particular Dean John Connolly and President Ruth Simmons—all in the hope that the original lectures, and this present enlarged study, in some small way carry forward the Kennedys' important work.

Following their delivery and on the way toward publication, the lectures benefited from the comments and observations of friends and colleagues at Smith too numerous to mention. Estela Harretche explained to me the intricacies of the interaction between theater and audience. I also thank Adam Teller, Katherine Beller, Laurie Nussdorfer, Deborah Jo Miller, and Robert Stacey. I was able to finish preparation of the manuscript while a member and fellow of a research group studying the Historicity of Emotions at the Institute for Advanced Study, the Hebrew University, Jerusalem. The work of this group, organized by Yosef Kaplan and Michael Heyd, led directly to significant additions. I also benefited from the incisive comments made after a close reading of the penultimate draft by Natalie Davis, herself a member of the group. Finally, I thank Naomi Pascal, Julidta Tarver, and Leila Charbonneau of the University of Washington Press for their faith in this book and for their editorial constancy. Anna Foa read the entire work more times than she would care to remember. Responsibility for the contents is, of course, mine.

KENNETH STOW
University of Haifa
1996 Kennedy Professor in Renaissance Studies, Smith College

THEATER OF ACCULTURATION

The Roman Ghetto in the Sixteenth Century

INTRODUCTION

The Jews of Rome and the Rhythms
of Roman Jewish Life

STORY, PLACE, AND SETTING

This study is about strategies of cultural survival. Its specific subject is the
Jews of Rome in the mid-sixteenth century: their persons, their families,
their neighborhoods, their formal and informal institutions. It is also a
study of how they found ways to preserve, and even enhance, their individual and collective identities. At the end of three hundred years of ghet-
toization (1555–1870), these identities emerged relatively intact. However,
what separated Jews from non-Jews in Rome was not only the obvious religious barrier of two permanently conflicting faiths. Jews and Christians,
especially the Catholic Christians of Reformation Rome, who are the Jews'
counterparts in this study, also differed on social and cultural planes.
These differences, sometimes only a question of attitude, were usually so
subtle that one is hard pressed to find them acknowledged. It is also
doubtful that the Jews of Rome would have realized that these minor variants of social custom and comportment might generate a permanent
state of low-key friction. Jews and Christians were attuned to the religious
gap distancing them one from another. They also knew the consequences
of remaining steadfastly Jewish. Yet, paradoxically, it was just these subtle

3

cultural differences, together with the obligato of low-key friction, and the ways in which these two were mutually reinforcing—that is, the modes and matrices of acculturation—that combined to both generate and sustain a Roman Jewish microculture, and thus to ensure Jewish cultural continuity.

The three essays at the heart of this study explain this unverbalized strategy of survival, a version of what the late Amos Funkenstein called the "dialectics of acculturation." So successful, in fact, was this dialectic that despite behavioral and cultural differences, Jews appear to have convinced themselves that they were as Roman as they were Jewish, as Jewish as they were Roman, and entitled to behave accordingly. However, the Jews were not oblivious to the gap—small or occasionally large as it may have been—between their convictions and actuality. This gap had to be bridged with respect both to the Jews' self-image and to the image they wished to project to non-Jews, especially ecclesiastical authorities. This they did by adopting measures that may best be named theatrical. This theatricality, as we shall see, became fundamental to Roman Jewish life.[1]

What I am searching out in these essays, therefore, is not a traditional portrait, a chronological recounting of events, institutions, and personalities. My aim is to describe and account for a series of often illusive behavioral modes. And it is in this spirit, reflecting what the historian Charles Beard pointedly called *an* (rather than *the*) Economic Interpretation of the Constitution,[2] that what follows is *an* interpretation of the Jewish past in the City of Rome. As such, it is selective, organizing one segment of the Roman Jewish past in a manner that allows me, as a historian, to paint a plausible portrait of Roman Jewish cultural survival. Admittedly, the protagonists of the drama, from the point of view of its direct effect on a large body of people, are few. And these three or four thousand Jews lived in an area of about seven acres, mostly during a thirty-year period (with respect to the specifics that will be discussed), from about 1536 to 1570—with important exceptions up to about 1640. In addition, the scarcity of parallel cultural studies prevents me from contrasting my arguments with what is known about Jews living contemporarily in other Italian cities, and the studies of Christian Rome for this period are principally institutional and intellectual, not cultural or social. The many studies of Italian society and culture at this time that do exist—and from which, for lack of alternatives, I have indeed drawn—concern Florence, and sometimes Venice.[3] Nonetheless, Roman Jewry in the mid-sixteenth century offers an excellent venue for seeking to answer the theoretical question of how a distinct and distinctive minority created the cultural tools to cope with a difficult, ambivalent, and sometimes hostile environment.

This last statement is true for technical as much as historical reasons. What I am referring to is the vast body of documentation informally known as the *Notai ebrei*, a collection of thousands of notarial acts drawn and prepared, mostly in Hebrew, by Jewish notaries in Rome during the sixteenth century. Since these documents reveal the patterns of Roman Jewish life, they are the building blocks on which this study rests.[4]

Yet before we turn to the *Notai ebrei*, a description of procedure and basic assumptions is in order. First and foremost, what follows is not a traditional monograph. Those who wish to pursue in great detail the contours and incidents of Roman Jewish life are invited to investigate the scholarly essays and documentary collections, including my own, listed in the intentionally thick notes and bibliography. The purpose of the present study is not to replace Attilio Milano's fundamental *Il Ghetto di Roma* (available in Italian and Hebrew, though regrettably not in English), which offers basic descriptions of times, places, structures, events, and even finances. Much of this forty-year-old masterpiece remains, and will remain, permanently valid. My intention here is to focus the reader's attention on the basic issues of Roman-Jewish cultural confluence without undue distraction, however enticing it might be to go on at length, especially in recounting some of the piquant episodes that the *Notai ebrei* bring to light. These episodes, in any case, are available in their full complexity in the two volumes of *The Jews in Rome, 1536–1557*, which I edited and annotated, and which reproduce or summarize the texts of the *Notai ebrei*. These volumes are also cross-indexed internally to facilitate pursuing episodes step by step.

A second and more difficult problem has to do with methodological underpinnings. The writing of cultural and social history is a frustrating experience. In traditional *histoire événementielle*—the history of events, diplomatics, politics, war and peace—the historian can present what readers may be lulled into accepting as a firm picture, the problems solved. This is far from being the case with the kind of historical writing found here. Ultimately, whatever is said has a patently obvious subjective aspect. The difficulties are twofold. To begin with, there is the problem of the documentary basis. Notarial acts represent people telling stories, giving witness in the way they want their stories recorded. Some notarial acts are straightforward, such as those concerning rentals, the amount of a dowry, a deathbed will. Yet even material of this sort can be opaque. Do people report their true ages, the real amount of rent, the actual value of their estates, the strategies underlying the decision to leave one family member the bulk of the estate at the expense of the other members?

We begin to intuit that even the simple can become difficult. How much the more in cases of litigation and the like? The historian may invent strategies of interpretation, seek codes, key words, and rhetoric in the texts. Quite often, for example, there are unmistakable references to Jewish law, the halachah, its observance, and, even more, to contemporary interpretation and reinterpretation woven into the language of those who appear before the notary. The historian must discover why the halachah is being used as it is in the immediate context. Or, alternately, what kind of situation is reflected when parties agree to settle their dispute through an oath rather than through litigation and arbitration. Yet strategies of interpretation can never be flawless, because even in their most literarily polished state, texts still reflect the complexities of real life. Nor may particular interpretative strategies be complacently and invariably invoked. In the long run, one can hope to be no more than the connoisseur spoken of by the great Dutch historian Johan Huizinga in his famous essay on the pitfalls and shortcomings of historical conceptualization, whose finely discriminating senses compensate, indeed, must compensate, for history's lack of scientific precision.

What is more, notarial records are sui generis, a form of documentation all to its own. To begin with, usually they are brief, but worse, they

rarely come together to reveal an entire episode. Teasing a story from notarial records is far more elusive than doing so from such sources as the
protocols and transcripts of trials, for the latter are often preserved more
or less intact and with great detail over tens of pages. The historian here
is also guided by the question, answer, and sometimes the tone, or voices,
of prosecutors and defendants; and the trials themselves that are most
studied are for criminal offenses, where issues are usually defined more
sharply than in the civil disagreements and litigations recorded by notaries. Moreover, criminal trials normally end in acquittal or a punishment that is almost always a fine, imprisonment, or execution. The
solutions in civil cases are frequently the product of agreement and rest
on nuance. Hence outcomes are generally unpredictable and often hidden
behind the simple and literal meaning of the documentary text. Which is
all to say that when confronting notarial records, the historian must
sometimes cautiously fill in absent detail, intuit the outcome, and, most
of all, be prudent. He or she may not recount or—dare I admit—invent
more than is at least reasonably justified. If, for example, in the story of
Joshua Abbina's funeral, told in chapter 3, the reader thirsts for detail, so
does the historian. The entire reconstruction is based on a single twenty-
line text. Other times, as in the stories of Ricca d'Aversa and Shem Tov
Soporto, also told below, we are documentarily better off, in the latter
case especially; the difference in storytelling will be evident. Yet, even
here, the story will not be complete, which is why, when working with notarial documents, what one historian interprets one way, another will interpret contradictorily.

This problem is compounded, for we are dealing with two sets of values, Christian and Jewish, not to mention the constant diversity between
what people do and what contemporary social theoreticians and commentators say they are supposed to be doing. A perfect case in point is the
famous line of the fifteenth-century Franciscan Bernardino di Siena that
999 of 1,000 marriages were of the devil because, wholly in disrespect
to Christian theology, the married couple were practicing some form of
birth control and engaging, for that matter, in unapproved sexual positions. By contrast, Jewish rabbinic authorities sanctioned some of those

positions forbidden to Catholics and at least debated the licitness of some forms of birth control. Yet, if Jewish couples were behaving in these matters just like their Christian counterparts, are we to assume that their motivation was ideological, that in sexual matters, or with respect to controlling reproduction, Jews differed from Christians? Or was it not, rather, a common popular conception of what to do in intimate relations between man and wife that determined the outcome? I suspect these questions can never be resolved to unanimous satisfaction. At the least, there is the trap of painting a portrait whose contrasts, lights, darks, and colors, are too sharply drawn. Along the way, furthermore, people will argue about just how one is to understand the intricacies of Jewish and Christian social theory and religious thought during the late Renaissance and early modern period. And they will rightly question whether principle and legal regulation, or even decision, reflect reality as practiced or perceived. Nonetheless, I personally will be satisfied to have initiated the debate, for a principal point of my enterprise here is that the perplexity in unraveling the skeins only emphasizes how Jews and Christians were always much alike but never truly the same. Which also means that to study Rome's Jews one must also study Rome's Christians, and vice versa. It is my hope that the paradigm of intercultural reciprocity that emerges from this study may be applicable to all "dialectics" of acculturation, whatever the specific setting or groups involved.

THE *NOTAI EBREI*

With these thoughts in mind, it is possible to turn directly to the *Notai ebrei*, the name commonly given to the collection of thousands of acts produced by Roman Jewish notaries beginning about 1536 and continuing until at least 1605, actually to about 1640, housed together in the Roman Capitoline Archive. Notarial acts, it must be realized, are legal instruments. The work of the classical European notary is not that of the familiar American notary public, whose essential task is to guarantee the authenticity of signatures. Classical notaries were but one step removed from lawyers and sometimes investigating magistrates. They drew contracts, took testimony, and registered agreements to accept arbitration—all according to strict and venerable formulae known collectively as the *ars dictaminis*, the notarial art—apart from drawing and recording various public acts. Notarial acts were also given universal credence. One would therefore expect that Christian authorities would not willingly allow Jews to perform this quasi-official function, in which the notary exercised, at least by delegation—and even more because of the authenticity accorded his documentation, both officially and, in fact, by definition—a touch of the independent jurisdictional power that authorities invariably denied the Jews. But for the one hundred or so years of the *Notai ebrei* this was not the case. Not only were Jewish notaries sanctioned, but the notaries themselves were rabbis who, until the end of the sixteenth century, wrote exclusively in Hebrew.

The *Notai ebrei* is thus extraordinary, a body of traditional notarial texts, yet, because of its authorship, one constructed in the language and terminology of tradition and law as both sought to accommodate themselves—as well as be accommodated—to the surrounding non-Jewish Roman world. These texts accordingly demonstrate how accommodation occurred and reveal the subtleties of its nature.

This accommodation was ubiquitous. For one thing, the rabbinical notaries indisputably thought in Italian, indicating the fluidity of the back-and-forth passage they and their clients—invariably Jewish, with notable exceptions—took between Jewish and Roman cultures. How fully their Italian-speaking clients understood the notaries' Hebrew translations is something we cannot know, although the vibrant expressions appearing on so many occasions suggest a high fidelity to original tone, affect, and even phraseology, not to mention to words themselves—even when the content of these words was the product of disingenuousness or even staging. Furthermore, the Jewish notaries of Rome achieved great refinement even though they were tyros with respect to the long tradition of the *ars dictaminis*; whether they had Jewish predecessors or parallels elsewhere, certainly in Italy, is doubtful.[5] Their road toward a Jewish, rabbinic *ars dictaminis*, to a notarial rhetoric, and to the establishment of documentary forms so precise that a careful reader may espy in them even patterns of formalized, public emotional structures, is thus a guide to a struggle for cultural accommodation. Yet because that notarial road was not an easy one, it is also a guide to acculturational lurches, hesitations, and, to be sure, failures.

That accultural accommodation entailed a constant, indeed permanent, struggle is brought home by the realization that unlike Jewish communities throughout the rest of Europe, Rome's was not one of immigrants. Jews had been there since before the time of Julius Caesar and most of Rome's other sixteenth-century inhabitants. One would have expected that the limits of accommodation were long established. They were not. At the same time, whatever its sticking points, the struggle toward accommodation that we observe through the acts of the *Notai ebrei* did not entail the pains of wrenching adaptation that, three hundred years later, were characteristic of such recently emancipated communities as those in eastern France (Alsace) and Germany. What we may intimate from the *Notai ebrei* is an almost calculated acculturational evolution, a solution so durable that it was shaken neither by the wave of Sephardi and Ashkenazi newcomers who arrived at Rome in the early sixteenth century nor even by the erection of the Ghetto in 1555. Indeed, the newcomers hastened to imitate existing practice. Such durability and adaptability are witnessed in the lives of the two who perfected the Jewish notarial art, the father and especially the son, Judah and Isaac Piattelli, members of the ancient Roman Jewish family bearing that name. For Isaac was linked by marriage to the Piccios, one of the leading newly arrived Sephardic families. The Jewish notaries thus not only recorded the minutiae of Roman Jewish life, but in their persons exemplified it as well.

What first attracts the student of their notarial acts, however, is not the grand themes of culture and acculturation, which the succeeding chapters will probe in depth. One is taken initially by the color and detail, the abundance of particulars the acts contain, opening a window onto the intimacies and intricacies of daily and personal life. Often the discussions are mundane, of rentals, apprenticeships, litigation, and occasionally communal and synagogal business. There are no grants of communal privilege and only rarely references to judicial proceedings before Christian authorities, which are discussed essentially because of secondary disputes growing out of primary litigation within the Jewish community. But there are numerous wills and testaments, records of matrimonial matches, divorces, accounts of family violence, and even the adoption papers of a little girl. There are mentions—usually oblique—of play, dance, gambling, barbershops, kosher meat, and of various items of clothing important for the history of dress.[6] *Neofiti* and their doings appear frequently. Regrettably, the matter of education hardly appears, and when it does, the topic is not the curriculum but the contracts made by fathers and teachers. There are, however, some interesting asides. Masters were not to strike pupils "too harshly," and teachers holding class in synagogues were to prevent students from damaging furnishings. One teacher accepted an obligation to prepare a youth for his bar mitzvah. And a certain youth contracted for dance lessons in anticipation of his wedding. Other pupils took music and poetry lessons; the number of sonnets they were to be taught was carefully specified. Someone contracted to learn how to swim. Notably, apprenticeship agreements often stipulate that apprentices must learn to read and write. Girls, too, apprenticed to learn *lavori femminili*, were taught the reading of Hebrew prayers.[7]

Jews, we learn, delighted in eating *tagliolini, la carne secca*, and chestnuts. There were Jewish caterers, who provided food and utensils for large receptions. Other Jews owned and sold fishing piers along the Tiber. Still others contracted with Christian farmers to buy crops of artichokes and pomegranates, or dried fruit, which were then resold at retail. There were butchers and their communally fixed prices, as well as scandal when attempts were made to sell meat from diseased (hence, nonkosher) animals. There were also women butchers, a reminder that women appear constantly and often as active protagonists.

Matters related to housing, above and beyond the simple issue of rentals, are ubiquitous. Negligent construction and overcrowding were a constant concern. Buildings sometimes collapsed, killing those trapped in the ruins, prompting the tenants of one structure to raise money to rebuild its crumbling foundations. Tenants also had to agree on where and how a well or a latrine was to be dug; small children had specially made appurtenances and chairs to aid them in relieving themselves. Even seats and chairs might stimulate litigation. Did a tenant who had rented a room have the right to place a chair on an adjacent porch? Or what recourse had a party whose window was opposite a neighbor's fireplace from which "noisome and disgusting smoke was forever issuing forth,"[8] blackening the wall if he opened his window, and making a distasteful blotch? Smoke made whitewashing stalls in the Jews' Market a frequent occupation. Considerable attention was paid to personal aesthetics, as seen in surviving inventories of barbershops and *stufe* (public baths), including locked drawers for clients' valuables while they were steaming off bodily dirt. Similarly interesting objects were possessed by the *hevrot*, the societies organized principally for charitable reasons. One owned a compass, a sand-clock, and a copy of Azariah de Rossi's controversial *Me'or 'einayyim*.

The *Notai ebrei* is, then, a truly private kind of documentation. It is not a mass of prescriptive texts, conciliar edicts, decisions of formal courts, or even theoretical legal discussion. Nor does it constitute a Roman Jewish version of the Florentine Catasto, the census of 1427, that has been studied so thoroughly by Christiane Klapisch-Zuber and the late David Herlihy.[9] The Jewish notaries made no composite lists of families, their wealth, their occupations, their ages, dates of birth and death, or their places of residence. The acts cannot be used to reconstruct the Roman Jewish population; statistical information must be teased out of the texts. But the *Notai ebrei* is virtually uninterrupted: there is barely a week or month for which there are no acts, especially those drawn in Hebrew. The acts were also prepared for a cross section of the Roman Jewish populace—people of wealth to the very, very poor—although the documentation is admittedly not complete. Lists of trousseaux, for example, had to be registered—likely for reasons of taxation—before a Christian notary, as is often alluded to by Jewish prenuptial agreements. But Jews registering trousseaux before a Christian notary sometimes forgot, or neglected, to have the parallel Jewish engagement agreement itself drawn up.[10] As a result, various receipts for the payment of a dowry are preceded by no matching Jewish/Hebrew prenuptial agreement.

Thus the primary subject of the acts is individuals: people promoting their own personal good, and often in preference to that of some conglomerate, whether family, neighborhood, or the formal Roman Jewish Community. Only, in fact, by concatenating individual lives into larger wholes can some sense be made of the collective private life of the Roman Jewish group.[11] The simplest two-generational nuclear families might become subservient to individual needs, as witnessed by Elia Passapaire, who stipulated before a notary in 1613 that during the coming Passover four months hence (the most familial of all Jewish festivals) his son-in-law Israel di Rosato "would come to Elia's home . . . with his wife and children, for a payment of 2 scudi . . . but with the provision that his son-in-law would behave properly and respectfully . . . otherwise . . . he might . . . be sent packing with no prior notice." (*stia in casa mia . . . con sua moglie et figlioli dietro pagamento di 2 sc. . . . con patto che suo genero li facci bon portamenti e li porti rispetto . . . altrimenti . . . possi . . . mandar via subito.*)[12] Nor was Passapaire's view exceptional. In 1584, the Council of the Community adopted a regulation that brothers living in the same building or apartment must pay their communal taxes as individuals. The Community itself, that is, easily perceived individuals as functioning both on their own account and in the smallest of possible units, the conjugal family—father, mother, children—and no more; these were units whose harmony, furthermore, was far from being a given.[13] This outlook had deep roots in a venerable Roman Jewish past.

THE ROMAN JEWISH PAST

What we know of the Roman Jewish past—the events themselves and growth of social structures that are the background for any further discussion—is sketchy. Even so, as preparation for understanding Jewish life in the sixteenth century, or at least to convey some of its flavor, it is well to review some highlights.

Jews settled in Rome as early as the second century B.C.E. They were considered supporters of Julius Caesar, arousing the ire of the aristocratic Cicero, who strongly opposed the "populist" Caesar. About one hundred years later, the historian Tacitus, also an aristocrat, described Roman Jewry's way of life as squalid.[14] The number of these Jews, in particular those who had settled on their own, may have reached twenty to thirty thousand; the number was swelled by captives brought to Rome after the Jews' defeat in the Great Rebellion against Rome in 70 C.E.[15]

Eventually, in the Roman Empire, and presumably in Rome, Jews were organized regionally into communities recognized as *collegia*, entities with corporate legal rights, including particularly the right of the community itself to inherit property. Legislation of the Christian Roman Empire canceled these rights some time between the late fourth century and the early sixth, abrogating ipso facto any measure of real jurisdictional autonomy the Jews had enjoyed, especially the right to ostracize communal members who violated disciplinary norms. This situation never changed formally, including in the sixteenth century. On the other hand, Roman Jews never lost their status as Roman citizens, which they had been since the edict of Caracalla in the year 212. They were also considered to enjoy the benefits of Roman law. Nonetheless, that law, which prohibited treating Jews arbitrarily and guaranteed the free practice of Judaism, also discriminated on religious grounds. Thus Pope Gregory the Great, for example, about the year 600, was able to order that Jews be compensated for confiscated communal structures, but without the satisfaction of having the structures returned, since they had been consecrated as churches in the interim.[16]

Gregory's actions set a thousand-year precedent. Roman Jews, like all other Jews of Western Europe, were going to be governed by a combination of secular and religious laws that never lost sight of each other and which, when observed, guaranteed the Jews' peaceful existence. This was generally the case for Rome, explaining in part why so little is known about Jewish life in Rome during this long period. What Jews had to fear was excess beyond the authorities' control; and outside of Rome, excesses did occur. More than once the Jews of Rome were approached by Jews elsewhere to present their case before the pope. And, following the law, and theology, popes often responded favorably. However, more than principle was sometimes involved. In particular, popes were impelled to aid Jews because of patron-client relationships. The most important of these was the one linking the Jews to the Pierleoni (a noble Roman family of distant Jewish origin), who seem to have used their influence on papal clients: first, Alexander II (in 1063), who declared that Jews were to be treated as peaceful members of society; and, second, Calixtus II (about 1119), who issued the fateful bull *Sicut iudaeis non*, which irrevocably guaranteed the Jews the benefit of "due process of law" (a well-known concept in the Middle Ages).[17]

It is certainly a myth created by the chronicler Ademar of Chabannes that, about the year 1020, the pope ordered a number of Roman Jews burned at the stake for desecrating an image.[18] Indeed, this alleged incident would have occurred about the time that Solomon the Babylonian (the nickname has never been explained) was writing liturgical poetry in Rome and shortly before Nathan ben Jehiel composed his Talmudic dictionary, the *Arukh*, which appeared in 1101 and is still used by scholars today. The diffusion of these works in northern Europe indicates that like Christian study, Jewish learning at the beginning of the second millennium was becoming internationalized. Both Christian and Jewish scholars crossed the Alps from Italy to France following time-honored commercial routes.[19] Through international travel, Roman learning and poetry reached the Rhineland, as well as France. The schools of Italy were the principal agent for transmitting to the North the wealth of learning that had matured in the Eastern Talmudic academies (*yeshivot*) of Babylonia (Iraq) and the Land of Israel.[20]

Scholars have often tried to extract realia from the diary of the traveler Benjamin of Tudela, who passed through Rome some time between 1159 and 1167. But factual retelling was the farthest thing from Benjamin's mind. His goal was Jewish glorification. He writes, for example, that the grandson of Natan ben Jehiel, also called Jehiel, enjoyed an administrative position under Alexander III. However, Benjamin's Jehiel was likely a literary Italian version of the well-known Jewish courtiers of the Kingdoms of Castile and Aragon; Jehiel did not represent the first in a line of Jews active in the papal court for reasons of finance or as physicians. We must be wary of Benjamin's statement that in twelfth-century Rome there were two hundred Jewish families, meaning a Jewish population of between 650 and 1,000.[21] Benjamin, after all, had spoken of the enormous glory and wealth of the (actually pauperized) Exilarch of the House of David, the "secular" head of Babylonian Jewry. For Benjamin, Jewish political power still existed—even if this meant portraying minor officials as figures of power.

In fact, it is Jewish political powerlessness that becomes clear in the reported burning of the Roman communal leader Elia de Pomis in 1298. It has been suggested that de Pomis was trapped in the war between the Colonna family and Pope Boniface VIII and that he sacrificed himself in order to save others. This explanation clarifies little.[22] On the other hand, it was in 1298 that Boniface VIII issued an edict forbidding the papal inquisition to prosecute Jews as "powerful persons," who were not entitled to know the names of their accusers. Possibly just such anonymous accusations had led to the trial and condemnation of de Pomis, most likely on the charge of encouraging the "apostasy" of Jews who had converted as a result of the near-violent (and still imperfectly understood) pressures applied during the early 1290s by Charles of Anjou, the ruler of the Kingdom of Sicily,[23] in league with a number of Franciscans. The bull *Turbato corde*, issued in 1267, had authorized the papal inquisition to try Jews for doing precisely this. No evidence points to any Jew other than de Pomis being executed; but inquisitors definitely sought such "offenders" out. About eighteen years earlier, Pope Martin IV had warned inquisitors against treating the simple association (*familiaritas*) of Jews with "baptized Jews" as grounds for incrimination.[24]

Such crises interrupted the normal calm. We are about to speak below of those moments where Jews and Christians in Rome shared a great deal in common. Yet alongside ongoing mutuality with Christian neighbors, patrons, and clients, there was a conscious and perennial sense of difference. Umbrian Jews, for example, were annually the targets of a "ritual stoning," reminding them that they were Christianity's (theological) enemies (Romans 11:28).[25] This yearly ritual seems to have been a prerequisite for good relations to resume—obligatory to place theory and contrasting practice in proper perspective. Yet one must not forget that so-called good daily relations also existed between Jews and Christians in places like the Empire (Germany), but that after about 1300 those relations were constantly interrupted by murder, massacres, and libels of blood and host desecration, so that by the end of the fifteenth century the Jewish communities of Germany were decimated.

From the later thirteenth century, conditions were not what they had been in papal territories either; it was becoming ever more difficult to determine where Christian "rights" began and those of the Jews left off. The special clothing prescribed by the Fourth Lateran Council in 1215—realized in the form of a "badge," a circle of yellow cloth sewn on the front of their garments for men and two blue stripes sewn on their shawls for women—was adopted in Rome by 1257.[26] It is not known whether these "badges," or eventually a *tabarro rosso* (red cape), were worn continuously. Yet a highly detailed papal letter from 1402 is most specific about distinctive Jewish dress, and the contents of this letter were reiterated on at least two occasions. The Roman civic statutes of 1363—notably composed while the popes themselves resided at Avignon—also insist that Jews wear a *tabarro rosso* over their outer garments.[27] The only ones exempt were physicians while practicing their art and communal leaders, whom Martin V (about 1430) permitted *sine dicto tabarro rubeo incedere possint impune et non ultra* while they held office and especially when they traveled outside the city to collect taxes Jews owed the papal government. There are also references in the late fifteenth century to Jews being punished for covering this garment.[28] However else Roman Jews were perceived, therefore, they were clearly seen first and foremost as Jews. They were also perceived, as early as the fourteenth century, if not earlier, as mostly inhabiting one specific Roman quarter, the Rione S. Angelo, within whose boundaries—explicitly spelled out in the papal letter of 1402 and subsequently restated—they were exempted from wearing the *tabarro*, suggesting that the Jewish area of residence remained stable.[29]

These controls and possible disturbances did not inhibit cultural life. The thirteenth century and early fourteenth marked a period of intellectual achievement—in fact, the last true intellectual moments Roman Jewry was to experience—notable for such students of Maimonidean philosophy as Hillel of Verona and Zerahiah Hen, followed somewhat later by Judah Romano. Immanuel ha-Romi (ca. 1270 –1328) composed his *Mahberot* (*Notebooks*) during this time, stories that share elements with the short adventures written by Boccaccio, although their genre, the *meqammah*, was used first by Jewish writers in the Islamic East, where it had originated.[30] Also compiled at roughly this time was the *Shibbolei ha-leqet*, the halachic compendium that formed the base of Roman Jewish practice; the compiler was Zedekiah di Abramo Anaw. Zedekiah's brother Benjamin composed the *Massa Gei Hizayyon* (*The Oracle of the Valley of Vision*), a moral discourse disparaging ostentatious wealth. But the scope of these works was limited. One must hesitate before speaking of a Roman Jewish renaissance. Jewish learning may also have been set back when, in 1320, Pope John XXII, reigning in Avignon, ordered the Talmud burned, perhaps in Rome itself for the first time.

Following the definitive papal return to Rome in 1418, Jewry policy seems to have acquired arbitrary aspects, sometimes explained by correlating periods of lighter restriction with the presence of a Jewish papal physician. However, conditions are rarely what they seem to be. The papal ear could be bent only so far. As always, the formal arbiter of Jewish life at Rome was not whim but Roman and canon law and theology, which balanced privilege with measured restriction. Thus in 1432, Eugenius IV instituted a strict-constructionist regime, suppressing special privilege and insisting that Jews benefit only from the rights extended them in *ius commune*, Roman law as then interpreted and applied in Italy.[31] However, a decade earlier Martin V had censured incendiary Franciscan sermons, because they decried the Jews' right to practice Judaism unhindered. This preaching, he said, countered conversionary efforts, which were better pursued through gentle suasion.

Martin's sincerity may be arguable; the popes had always been ambivalent about conversion. Their support for conversionary sermons did not extend to outright coercion, which was illegal.[32] But from the mid-fifteenth century, policy began to change. In papal letters concerning the payment of taxes, the Jews were no longer said to be tolerated solely for reasons of Christian Piety or Charity—a very serious matter, since Charity, *Caritas*, was the prime medieval Christian virtue, and thus Jewish toleration was integral to maintaining Christian morality. Rather, Jews were now said to be tolerated (in the word's true sense: accepted, privileged—and restricted) in the hope of converting them. What had been marginal was moving to center stage. Jews themselves would not become aware of this transformation, if at all, for more than one hundred years. In the later fifteenth century they were preoccupied once again with Franciscan preaching, which this time painted Jewish lending as a gangrene that was rotting society's foundations. The Franciscans also tried to co-opt Jewish loan banking, when in Perugia, in 1462, they promoted the first Monte di pietà (charitable foundation), offering small and, at first, interest-free loans to the lower classes. The history of these Monti is a checkered one. Eventually, they, too, began to charge interest to cover expenses, and there are examples of cooperation between the Monti and Jewish banks. At Rome itself, a Monte di pietà was founded in 1539, although it did not begin competing with Jewish lending until the seventeenth century, when it gained a near monopoly on small loans and hastened the Jewish banks' final closure.[33]

Franciscan preachers were also involved, directly and indirectly, in the fomenting of blood libels, the most notable of which was made at Trent in 1475, leading to the destruction of that city's small Jewish community. Nonetheless, there were limits to what such preaching could achieve. Taking up again the call of Martin V for restraint, if somewhat ambivalently, Sixtus IV bowed to pressures exerted by humanists and others in his curia (the papal court) and ratified the (demonstrably illegal) proceedings at Trent. But he also firmly warned that he would brook no repetition of the charge, reiterating at the same time the basic terms of Jewish rights.[34]

In fact, the fifteenth century and the early sixteenth were mostly times of rational, legally rooted governance. One prayerbook composed between 1447 and 1455 commemorated this situation by adding a prayer for the health and longevity of the current pope, Nicholas V (regardless of the charge leveled by some historians that Nicholas repeatedly limited Jewish rights).[35] Papal rationality also extended to matters of taxation. To offset, for example, the difficulties Roman Jews were experiencing in raising the 1,130 florins they were obligated annually to contribute to the papal treasury (a tax financing the annual pre-Lenten carnival games and named after the Piazza Agone—now Piazza Navona—and the Testaccio district where the games were held), in April 1402 Pope Boniface IX allowed Roman Jews to collect part of this tax from Jews living outside of Rome, at first from Jews living throughout the Papal States but eventually from the Jewish communities of Lombardy and Tuscany as well. Also noteworthy is that when, from about the mid-fifteenth century, the Jews were asked to contribute to an additional tax composed of a percentage of income and property, the so-called *vigesima*, ostensibly used to prosecute wars against the Turks, the tax was levied at a rate equal to that imposed on non-Jews. Higher rates were levied on the clergy, especially regular monks.[36] Considering the expulsions, riots, and mass forcible conversions Jews had endured during the hundred years or so beginning about 1290, the expulsion from England, Rome in the fifteenth century was a tranquil oasis.

Moreover, Roman Jews had managed to achieve a manageable coexistence with their immediate Christian neighbors. Jews and Christians frequently entered each others' homes,[37] and both spoke the same "Roman" language—although before the seventeenth century, Jews only occasionally wrote in Italian; even books of accounts seem to have been kept in Hebrew. Jews also maintained links with important Christian families in the Rione S. Angelo (the eventual site of the Ghetto, along the Tiber and directly opposite the Tiber Island, including the area of the present synagogue). Jews sometimes even summoned members of the Cenci and Boccapaduli families to arbitrate disputes.[38] The eventual Ghetto wall cut one Boccapaduli building in half, part of which was rented to Jews. These rentals forced Jews and Christians into close contact. As a rule, Jews did not own the properties where they lived or worked, even in the late fourteenth and late fifteenth centuries, as studies of Christian notarial records confirm. The *Notai ebrei*, too, never mention actual ownership of homes or land. Instead, the Jews operated a system of leases, or key-money, known (from its Talmudic origins) as a *hazaqah*, roughly "physical pos-

session." A relatively small forfeit guaranteed tenants the right of continued presence, in addition to which they paid an annual rent.[39] In the early
seventeenth century, papal officials codified this system as the *ius cazagà*
with the intention of eliminating rent gouging.

Jews had gravitated for commercial reasons to the S. Angelo quarter,
whose streets are mentioned in the privilege of 1402, no later than the
eleventh century, although some Jews continued living and working in
the Trastevere and others resided in the nearby Campo dei Fiori. The so-
called Piazza Giudea, at the center of the Jewish quarter, was a prime location on one of Rome's principal arteries, whether for commerce or
religious processions. There were two starting points, either Saint John
Lateran, Rome's diocesan church (the pope, of course, is also the bishop
of Rome), or the Campidoglio, the lay civic administrative hub. These
two spurs joined at the Portico d'Ottavia, the fish market close by the Piazza Giudea. The route then traversed the S. Angelo quarter, proceeded
through the Campo dei Fiori, and arrived at the Vatican. It was perhaps
no accident that the Ghetto wall cut Piazza Giudea in half, thus symbolizing the changes wrought by the popes in Rome's entire civic structure
during the fifteenth century, when they definitively wrested control of the
city from the old Roman and commercial aristocracy. The Jewish center
along this route was now isolated, and putatively (it never really happened
in fact) it was cut off. Indeed, traversing the city—whose population in
1500 was about 50,000, doubling to 100,000 by 1600—one perforce came
into contact with Jews,[40] whether as denizens, merchants, particularly of
foodstuffs, or artisans specializing in all the processes connected with the
production, working, and eventual repair of new and used cloth and
clothing.[41]

The integration of Jews into Rome's commercial life may also be in-
tuited from the records of Christian notaries, which show the Jews more
as debtors than as creditors of Christians; many of these loans must also
have been commercial ones.[42] Of course, Jews themselves lent. A dispute
in the 1530s ended with the so-called Twenty Old Lenders (the number
holding papal permits) losing their monopoly;[43] and, eventually, the
number of Jewish lenders and their assistants reached seventy. Each of

these lenders held a permit, *inhibitio foenerandi*, which prohibited anyone but the papal Camerarius in Rome from judicially interfering in their
affairs.[44] These permits thus legalized, de facto, otherwise canonically
forbidden interest, at least until 1682, when Jewish "banks" were closed.[45]
However, the grounds for this final closure were not patently theological.
They were theology cloaked in a mantle of mercantilism, indicative of the
secular aspects which often controlled politics in the Papal States even
more than did spiritual ones. This point is essential in understanding why
and how, apart from the strength of their own internal resources, Roman
Jews survived the disastrous sixteenth century.

SIXTEENTH-CENTURY CRISIS
AND THE ORIGINS OF THE GHETTO

Toward the middle of the sixteenth century, papal policy toward the Jews
changed course. Various results of this change and the reasons invoked to
justify it will be examined below. Its most visible effects were the Ghetto
and an increased flow of converts to Christianity; ultimately, the Jews of
Rome were impoverished. There were also psychological effects. The Jews
came to sense what they themselves referred to as their *ghet*, their divorce—punning on the word ghetto—from Christian society. At the
same time, private life continued much unchanged. Accounting for this
continuity was in no small part the pliability of both communal institutions and the rules of individual, familial, and small-group behavior,
many of whose intricacies will now occupy our attention. So pliable were
these institutions and rules that they facilitated not only survival in the
Ghetto but the successful absorption of hundreds of immigrants, who,
about 1500, entered Rome from all parts of the Jewish world.

Jews had always perceived their communities as self-contained, geographically sovereign units, governed by the halachah and its interpreters,
the rabbis, in conjunction with lay heads. The latter, however, invariably
sought—and usually managed—to dominate the former. This was certainly the case at Rome, where no formal communal rabbi or rabbinate
was ever appointed or chosen and where the closest to a formal rabbinic

official was the *Sofer Meta* (Civic Notary)—namely, the notaries Judah and his son Isaac Piattelli, the prime authors of the *Notai ebrei*. Moreover, whatever friction there was between rabbis and laity in Rome, it did not modify the community's perception of itself or its goals. Nor did it have much bearing on the ability of the city's Jews to control their own affairs. Theoretically, the Jews exercised the right granted to them by Roman Law of voluntary arbitration, which conferred upon the Jewish community juridical status. Yet this status was never one of primary jurisdiction. Sanctions like the *niddui* (distancing a member from the community) or fines to ensure that the results of arbitration were carried out always required the prior or post-factum assent of the true source of jurisdiction, the papal Vicar, who was also capricious.[46] How this anomaly affected practice will be seen below.

Until about the fifteenth century, the Roman community was roughly homogeneous in origin. By the later part of the century, homogeneity had yielded to diversity. Rome, by 1471, had at least six synagogues, each representing a different constituency such as the (non-Roman) Italians, the Romans, the Tedeschi (German or Ashkenazi), the Francesi, and the Catalans. There is also testimony about a synagogue of the women.[47] And, in 1600, a certain Anna d'Arpino was appointed—and indirectly paid—*dir* [daily] *l'ofitii alle donne* of the Scola Quattro Capi.[48] Women, in fact, regularly gathered for audibly chanted prayer. Reflecting a new diversity of the Roman Jewish population, the number of synagogues grew in the sixteenth century. There was a Castilian as well as a Catalan synagogue for the Sephardim. The Italians, apart from indigenous Romans (of the Scola Tempio), had founded the Scola Nova, the Scola Quattro Capi, the Portaleone, and the Scola Siciliana. Jewish immigrants had arrived from Provence, Germany, Spain, Sicily, and perhaps North Africa. However, many Jews with North African names such as Tripolesi were members of the Sicilian synagogue, and ancestors with this name were registered as members of Palermo's Jewish community as early as the first half of the fifteenth century.[49]

These immigrants, it must be stressed, were all Jews. Marranos—those shadowy figures whose real identity, whether Jewish or Christian, is so hard to fix and who were universally detested by Christians as arch-renegades—were not known in Rome. The chronicler Stefano Infessura mentioned "marranos" in 1492,[50] but he really meant Iberian Jews. A large group of true converts did arrive in Rome. But they were formally reconciled to the Church in 1498.[51] At Rome there was no ambivalent category, like that found on the Adriatic coast in cities such as Venice and papal Ancona, of (primarily Portuguese) Jews, forcibly converted in 1497 but later returned to Judaism, who were given papal charters to settle and carry on trade.[52] As former prefect of the papal Inquisition, Paul IV was enraged by these charters, and in 1556 accused twenty-four of the Anconitans of apostasy and burned them at the stake; fellow Jews, especially non-Portuguese ones at Ancona, cautiously kept their distance.[53] At Rome, no such accusations were leveled. Roman Jews of the sixteenth century were indisputably Jewish in both Jewish and Christian eyes—however divided, or undivided, these Jews were among themselves.

It is often said that early sixteenth-century Jewish Rome was an arena for so-called interethnic dispute. Evidence is brought by noting what various present-day historians have chosen to denominate Rome's many "ethnically" oriented synagogues, the word "ethnic" being a problematic translation of the Hebrew 'edah (literally, congregation, as in the Congregation of the Sephardim, Italians, or Ashkenazim). Most accurate with respect to contemporary usage would have been to translate 'edah with the Latin natio, for group of origin—not the modern nation. Also noted is the supposedly difficult arrival at Rome of (especially) Spanish Jews,[54] particularly since this arrival is described in the dramatic chronicle Shevet Jehudah, written toward the middle of the sixteenth century by the Sephardi exile Shelomo ibn Verga.[55] The indigenous Roman Jews, he wrote, offered a large bribe to the pope so that he would refuse entry to the Iberian refugees (said, by another source, to be camped on the Appian Way), to which the pope responded by mulcting the Romans and permitting the Sephardim to enter.[56] But Ibn Verga was invariably satirical and theatrical. He would have been surprised to hear himself described as a historian, certainly according to today's standards, and quite likely one of the things his tale of woe was intended to dramatize was the general unpreparedness and consequent overreaction that characterized the reception of Iberian refugees almost everywhere. Roman Jews were certainly not ready for this influx. They may also have feared that the arrivals included Marranos. But any such fear must have quickly subsided. Within a half-century the newcomers were integrated into the community and showing a steady increase in marital alliances. Accordingly, Ibn Verga's satire may thus have had a second, more intense, level of meaning: to point to the inter-ʿedah conflict among Jews that did not occur—or was quickly snuffed out, despite its possibility. His portrait of a paternal pope may be read as a biting commentary, depicting the opposite of what progressively typified papal behavior toward the Jews as the sixteenth century advanced.

On the other hand, Ibn Verga's tale may have been referring to a more substantial preoccupation: that a largely expanded, perhaps doubled, Jewish population in the city might generate anxiety on the part of both Jews and Christians about the overall Roman demographic balance. People are known to have reacted strongly to the enormous fluctuations in population caused by recurrent plague since the middle of the fourteenth century—a reaction no doubt sharpened in many places, including Rome, by the arrival of diverse foreign groups or rural migrants. To be sure, nobody knows just how many Jews arrived in Rome during the early sixteenth century. Perhaps their number expanded from about 900 to 1,700, but there are no hard data—just as there is no way to confirm how the Roman Jewish population grew from about 1,750, according to a (certainly not scientific) census made in 1527, to nearly 3,000 at about midcentury and to about 3,500 in 1593, according to another census. Yet, if the expansion of Roman Jewry was Ibn Verga's true concern, one suspects this expansion eventually had few repercussions. Any temporary disturbance in demographic balance that it caused would have been restored (if not at a continuously even rate) by the overall growth in the Roman population, which, despite plague and especially famine toward the end of the century, doubled from about 50,000 in 1500 to 100,000 one hundred years later.[57]

We must, of course, not deny the existence of intra-Jewish friction. It occurred particularly in the political sphere, where social amalgamation did not provide a sufficient cure. The formal Jewish Community, the Comunità or the Università, had long existed, headed by three so-called *fattori*, or *memunim* (chosen lay heads), who were assisted with the advice and consent of *VII boni iudei*, a Latin version of the Talmudic phrase "Seven Good Men of the City" and a term used throughout the Middle Ages. At Rome, the "Seven Good Men"—or sometimes fourteen of them—had evolved into a kind of ad hoc council, perhaps borrowing from Italian civic institutions.[58] More than homogeneity, however, this compact administrative mechanism presupposed underlying agreement on who the leading citizens were. With the arrival of newcomers, such a consensus was no longer self-evident. It took a papal intervention in 1505, followed by the *Capitoli* drawn up by Daniel da Pisa in 1524, to achieve what one scholar has called reconciliation.[59] From now on, one of the three *fattori* would be an *ultramontanus*, a (non-Italian) immigrant.

Apart from communal office, newcomers were able to achieve status within their separate synagogues. Indeed, in the early sixteenth century, Rome's synagogues began to function much like social confraternities, and papally ratified synagogal charters interchangeably refer to the synagogues by the Latin *communitas*, *universitas*, or *scola*, although their "corporate" privileges were extremely limited. It was stretching a point to have called synagogues corporations at all, even within the then contemporary sense of something as simple as a professional guild. Previously, synagogues were essentially places of prayer and houses of study. They were thus dependents of a larger community, a term which for Jews had an unequivocally spatial or geographical connotation. There could be no more than one "community" in any location. Communal ordinances, indeed, operated only within a spatially defined sphere, such as the centuries' old ordinance, the *herem ha-yishuv*, dictating who might live in a specific district. Other ordinances required the active consent or oath of all the district's members.[60] To be sure, Roman synagogues such as the Catalan or Castilian had taken the place of what were once geographically based communities that now, following expulsion, attack, or hurried emigration, no longer existed. But the rule perforce remained that in no single district could more than one community operate. Nonetheless, synagogal status could be enhanced, and thus synagogal officers were authorized to collect and distribute charitable funds, to give dowries to the needy, and to bear names like *parnas* once reserved exclusively for communal heads.[61] They were not authorized to compete with the Community itself, a point on which papal officials concurred. The statute issued to the Aragonese Synagogue in 1511, for example, confers upon the synagogue neither jurisdictional powers nor the right to collect (papal) taxes.[62]

Such limitations no doubt spurred the newcomers in Rome to seek the wider communal influence which they attained in 1505 and again in 1524 with the understanding that one of the three *fattori* would always be an *ultramontanus*. The reconciliation inherent in the *Capitoli* of da Pisa was thus essentially economic and political, not ethnic; what is more, the conciliar system that is the backbone of da Pisa's scheme seems never to have functioned on a regular basis.[63] In any case, the term ʿ*edah*, as used at Rome, was highly elastic. Sicilians, for instance, were considered *Italiani* despite the latter's distinctive dialect, liturgy, practice of marrying first cousins, and especially their former status as Aragonese subjects. The *ultramontani* included the French, the Ashkenazim, and all Sephardim, not what one might imagine as a natural, let alone united, ethnic arrayment.[64]

In the synagogues, too, ʿ*edah* was an elastic concept. The Italian synagogues were five in number, the Tempio, the Nova, the Siciliana, the Portaleone, and the Quattro Capi, and this division was jealously maintained. Synagogue members came from various Italian regions. Members of the Scola Portaleone most frequently came from southern Lazio. The names of congregational leaders also are constant, surely a function in part of wealth. Political advantage in the hands of the monied, therefore, not necessarily "ethnic" distinctiveness, supplied a prime justification for maintaining synagogues separate, Italian or otherwise. At the same time, synagogal membership was always in flux, with members sometimes crossing ʿ*edah* lines. Synagogues, such as the Castilian and Catalan, alternately amalgamated and split apart. Similarly—and most tellingly—the preamble to a registration of members made in 1571 by the Gemilut Hasadim (charitable and burial) confraternity states that individuals had to choose—once and for all—which identity, Italian or Ultramontane, they preferred. This sense of fluidity is reinforced by the membership lists that have survived from the various synagogues.[65]

Moreover, real problems between the ʿedot emerged when the dividing lines were blurred rather than sharp, especially when the so-called ethnic groups involved were more alike than not and when competition generated apprehension lest group integrity be threatened. Thus, in 1558, an attempt to amalgamate the Castilian-Francese synagogue with the Catalan-Aragonese failed the moment it was realized that the rites of both were nearly identical and amalgamation would have meant an end to ethnic specificity. It was again to protect a perceived threat to identity that the one real intergroup fight in Rome occurred between the Castilian and Catalan congregations, about 1520–21, and it flared up anew in 1539 between the now combined Castilian-Francese and Catalan-Aragonese.[66] Indicatively, the issue was which of the two schools' Talmud-Torah societies would have the right to deliver a public sermon on Shavuoth. When the other synagogues fought, the issues were usually mundane, such as the placement of staircases and windows in the single building the principal synagogues shared. Indeed, from the time that the Sephardi congregations, too, began to litigate in the manner of the Italian ones over walls and cement, one may say that they, too, had entered into the circle of normal Roman Jewish social patterns and structures.

Observing intersynagogal disputes thus reveals how the exploitation of diversity promoted cohesion. It also reveals methods that Rome's Jews adopted to promote survival in general. In 1558, the Scola Tedeschi litigated with the Scola Nova over back rent (owed the latter by the former)—after both had been closed for nine months, because a prohibited book, a commentary of Ibn Ezra, had been found in the Tedeschi. Even in moments of crisis, therefore, it appears that standard procedures and reactions were privileged over ones that might have been dictated by fear, or worse. Both sides seem to have decided that their common well-being was better served by litigation—pretending "business as usual"—than by silent cowering or concerted action to prevent repetitions of vicarial interference. Not changing pace before the implied threat of further closure—the Talmud itself had been burned in 1553—the members of the two synagogues apparently chose to defend themselves by resorting to what may seem to us pretense and avoidance. As we shall see, the often deliberate, indeed theatrical, recasting of events and processes to fit a palatable mold was a major tool of cultural preservation.[67]

In one sphere there was no need for pretense. When it came to social power and rank among Roman Jews, lower middle-class to middle-class parity was virtually the rule. With one or two possible exceptions, there were no Jewish patricians, and conversely, in the sixteenth century at least, there were few indications of the truly poor, at least in the notarial acts. The real common denominator, and the greatest social leveler—and one that brought the curtain down on potential interethnic friction— was the matter of "out-marriage" between various Jewish ethnic groups. Within but one or two generations of the early sixteenth-century immigration, Jews of all Rome's Jewish ethnic groups began to "intermarry" at a high rate. The sole, and notable, exceptions were the Castilians and the Catalan-Aragonese, the two ethnic groups which alone had reason to fear for their futures. Marriage between Castilians and Catalans was exceedingly rare. Before 1557, it seems to have occurred not even once.[68]

Another sign of homogeneity was clothing. Neither in law nor with one vague exception in practice toward the end of the sixteenth century did Jews dress diversely according to social distinction. Christians did. Jewish dowries were even more indicative of homogeneity. Even the greatest barely doubled the average. In Christian circles, large dowries were ten, twenty, and thirtyfold multiples of the norm. The relative homogeneity of Jewish dowries, by contrast, indicates that separating Jews from Christians and making Jewish life distinct were social, not solely religious, differences. Confusing the issue, however, was that these social differences were limited. For both Jews and Christians subscribed to a dowry system with all its attendant pitfalls. The Jews and Christians of Rome thus appear, and correctly so, to have been two likes that were not the same. This is a matter that will receive attention in the discussion to follow.

RITUALITY AND RHETORIC

But for the moment, how should we summarize? During fifteen hundred years of general stability, the Jewish community of Rome functioned reasonably well, yet not hierarchically; a community that was neither authoritarian nor highly empowered, yet one generally enjoying internal economic parity (within reason, to be sure); a community able to assimilate a large group of newcomers within no more than fifty years; and a community apparently so confident in itself that it could sometimes decide issues by acting as though outside factors were nonexistent or irrelevant, such as occurred with the closing of the Tedeschi synagogue. It was also a community—as we have implied—that gave individuals their respective due, though individual prerogative was firmly predicated on a consciousness of communal self and structure. It is this community that survived. But only by looking at the details, at how this community was enveloped within the Ghetto and how it used particular strategies for coping on both communal and individual levels, will we grasp how it survived.

What we will be looking for may best be described as a kind of rhetoric that sustained the rhythms ritualizing daily life, or what alternatively may be described as "the appropriate verbal [as well as nonverbal] context for sustaining the action or the ceremonial."[69] We want to know the codified forms people used to express themselves when they had to deal with each other and what we may learn from these expressions: in particular, how people viewed their family, friends, and adversaries, and how they perceived the world as a whole. We want to know what myths, metaphors, and images were created, however consciously, to give meaning and justification to current forms of existence, persuading Rome's Jews to maintain these forms despite the fate of living within a society that in theory, if not wholly in practice, was truly closed. And how, through these practices, did Rome's Jews convert—in their minds—physical closure into spiritual opening? As we will see, these myths and mechanisms, rituals and rhetorical molds, were well in place before the period of the Ghetto began.

At the same time, we must not forget that rhetoric—social rhetoric, in particular—and ritual are layered concepts reflecting the compound meanings and significance imparted to repetitive or programmatic actions that take place at ceremonies, festivities, and especially in times of crisis, but also everyday. All peoples, of course, have their indigenous social rhetoric and rituals, and these signify the basic structures of reality as well as symbolically representing reality's ideal image.

Among the Jews, the drive to create rhetoric and ritual was fueled by the repetitiveness of Jewish sacral acts. It has indeed been said that repetitive action is the essence, sometimes the very substance of Jewish sacrality—sacrality, that is, not rituality alone. For Jews, social rhetoric, ritual, and sacrality are virtually interchangeable. And all three are reified through verbal expression—especially that of individual prayer, even when praying within a group in the synagogue—and a seemingly infinite series of verbal benedictions pronounced over almost any imaginable activity. Or they are also reified through (mainly) private actions and procedures such as the dietary laws, *kashrut*, concerning the correct slaughter, preparation, and consumption of foods, the laws of family purity, regulating sexuality during the menstrual period, and of course the rules dictating what is permissible on the Sabbath and festivals. Study, too, is a ritual; for some, the most important ritual of all.

This Jewish devotion—better, dedication—to repeated verbalization and actions is not to be confused with a monastic brand of piety or, for that matter, with religion as an isolate. What is more, and this must be emphasized, we are not speaking of an ideal—clerical or otherwise.[70] Jewish rituality was a daily process for the large majority of Roman Jews, carried out, to be sure, with greater and lesser individual zeal and efficacy. The key word and goal, as in the meaning of the word *kashrut* itself, was correctness.

Yet correctness extended well beyond the sacral. Indeed, transferred from the sacred to the profane, it extended—as a modus operandi—to everything that Roman Jews did. Which meant, as we will see, utilizing, ingesting, restructuring, and, most important, amalgamating all that was available both from within and without the Jewish worlds. Nor was this process haphazard. It proceeded with a ritualized and rhetoricized consistency to create a cultural entity that was simultaneously at home in both Jewish and non-Jewish Roman ambients.[71] What was occurring, I stress, was not simply the taking in of extraneous elements, their masking, and the affectation—on the basis of simple declaration alone—that they were really Jewish. Such a solution might be apt for intellectual and aesthetic issues, but even then it was rarely adopted. More normally, it was the reverse that occurred. Jews might treat problems they shared with contemporary Christians as indigenously Jewish and then resolve them principally with recourse to the halachah, for example, in their firm conviction—as opposed to common Christian practice—that children were free to reject a parentally chosen marital partner.

In general, the process of cultural amalgamation was far more complex. It also involved a degree of illusion. Illusion but not delusion—for Rome's Jews seem to have constructed what might well be termed "virtual realities." As the Jews were no doubt at least vaguely aware, their construal of reality differed from reality as others construed and controlled it, papal authorities in particular, but at times the mass of Rome's Christians, too. Yet they had little choice, even before the establishment of the Ghetto. Fully to accept a Christian view of reality meant to acquiesce, in principle, let alone fact, to Christian domination and perhaps eventually Christianity itself. Under such conditions, amalgamation of any kind would have been impossible.

THE GHETTO AS THEATER

To best appreciate these virtual realities, we might liken the Ghetto to a theater, the cradle of illusion par excellence.[72] The Ghetto's physical precinct may certainly be likened to a stage. Yet, unlike most theaters, where the separate identities of actor and audience are always clear,[73] in the theater of the Ghetto, Jews sometimes acted solely for each other. So often in litigation, as the closing of the Tedeschi synagogue in 1558 once more testifies, the parties were intent on convincing one another that they, rather than forces outside, were in control. And as a result, Roman Jews addressed litigation as though—contrary to fact—they indeed possessed primary jurisdiction and were not dependent at all times on the whims of the pope's Roman Vicar. To be sure, there was a second audience, namely the arbiters and the spectators, Jew and Christian alike, each perceiving and appreciating the drama in his or her own way—including, of course, the Vicar. Yet occasionally the Vicar forgot both his powers and his position, and he became so absorbed by the masque that he took on the role of player himself, for instance by directing Jewish arbiters to apply Jewish law instead of magisterially imposing his own solution. But in most cases those outside remained there, left to reflect on a drama that revealed the fine points of distinctively (Roman) Jewish behavior. We may only speculate on the Jews' appreciation of this dramatic message.

However, even a minimal awareness, or purposefulness, does not vitiate the figure of theater, which in fact may be further articulated. Orchestrating, as it were, the testimony in litigation, the notary might be considered the director; and advocates like Abramo ben Aron Scazzocchio, who appears in this guise and as an arbiter in close to 150 separate notarial acts, may be assigned a constant leading role.[74] In what I have called elsewhere "halachic dramas," and the late Victor Turner would have called "social dramas"—where the staging truly verges on the intentional—Abramo, indeed, Rabbi Abramo, might be seen as the actors' coach, or even a playwright. His assignment, as in the social drama, was to defuse social disturbance and crisis, to reintegrate social behavior gone awry—or as it might be put in Hebrew, to recreate *shalom bayyit*, to restore peace within the house, household, and community. At least once he was described by a woman litigant as *ha-pashran*, "the mediator," or, more broadly, the coordinator of litigation between parties. Ghetto theater, its dramas, and its attendant emotions thus did much to shape the contours of what may be called Jewish public space.

But we should not mistake this ritualized drama as signifying a society closed in on itself, unbending and unwilling to modify venerable ways. Roman Jewish society emphatically was not like that. It had absorbed far too much from the outside. Nevertheless, it was cautiously conservative. What was taken in from the outside was taken in slowly and selectively.

As a result, what became part of Roman Jewish "civic ritual" was not easily jettisoned. Conversely, we may infer from this delicate process that it would fall victim to its own inertia. For although the Ghetto period opened with the Jews manipulating their surroundings, taking advantage of their complex—virtually intercultural—culture to create tools for survival, in the long run, a kind of inertia, or the conservatism of a fixed rhetoric and ritual, put the tools of manipulation ever more out of date. And rather than expediting new adjustment and change, these tools ground Jewish cultural development to an increasingly visible halt.

This cultural stasis was not without virtues. Paradoxically, it became an essential tool in allowing the Jews to perpetuate not only their own identity but also a vision of the world that included the dual convictions of "freedom" and of being as Roman as they were Jewish. These convictions would serve as the levers of Jewish social integration—admittedly more rapid in communities other than Rome, especially those of the North, and Turin in particular—when the Roman Ghetto fell and Rome became the capital of a secular Italian state in 1870. And no matter how "out of date" they had become, unlike the Jews of Eastern Europe, the Jews of Rome did not integrate socially into a world in which they found themselves confronting "codes of modern political discourse [that were] all but opaque," not to mention its spoken and written language. For also unlike what has been said of Eastern European Jewry, the Jews of Rome were not "trained mainly in the traditionalist Hebrew idiom. [Nor was it for them] a quantum leap in vocabulary and terms of reference, no less than in consciousness and ideology, to make the transition to modern, secular, political [social, and cultural] thought."[75]

What, then, was the specific content of Roman Jewish social rhetoric, especially at the more creative and flourishing start of our period; what were the elements of Jewish civic ritual?[76] One might think to search these elements out in the rhetoric of historical memory; and Jewish histories at this time were indeed composed, albeit not specifically in Rome.[77] Moreover, what these histories convey primarily is a sense of hesitation. Change of any kind, when it occurred, was partial and halting. But this mirrors perfectly the kind of change that took place in sixteenth-century

Roman Jewish social practice and behavior. The two spheres of codified memory and social behavior were interdependent: hesitation in one reflected, if it did not reinforce, restraint in the other.

Such hesitancy is also evidence of constancy—a fixed set of principles, a single and unified plot. Hence, the simile of "Ghetto as Theater" is so appropriate. The name of the drama is "The Roman Persuasion." The theater—the stage which has alternately been called the "arena," or a "sociological wall"—is the Ghetto itself.[78] And the audience is duplex, including both Jews and Christians. Catharsis—this is of course a comedy, not a tragedy, because the Jews, however shabbily, survived—was achieved by Jews convincing each other or the external Christian world that the abnormal was perfectly regular. In particular, they seem to have convinced both themselves and all of Christian Rome that the Ghetto, which the popes probably intended to be a temporary solution, an antechamber to mass conversion, could endure as a permanent Roman geographical and social feature and, what is more, sustain continuing Jewish cultural life.

The plots were varied. Those employed in litigation were built on what appears to be a consistent, if not necessarily intentional, role-playing bent on restoring ruffled social order, hence qualifying as classic "social drama": ritualized acting to reestablish shaken equilibria. One may also discern plots and theatricality in the everyday. An essentially unconscious role-playing was couched in what I would like to call rhythmic rituality. In the Ghetto's palpably artificial atmosphere, every activity required structured roles—roles that became so ingrained, so natural, that people were most often unaware that they were playing a perpetual game of "Staging one's ideal (read, idealized) self."[79] Synagogue heads could thus make the synagogue look like a center of power or an autonomous institution by litigating, constantly and for decades, with members of other synagogues (all housed in a single structure) over such issues as the removal of a staircase or the site of a new window. To litigate thus became the normal mode of synagogal coexistence. The perhaps "intentional" social drama of the original litigation had become inextricable from daily life, an unconscious role-playing that had become endemic, even in times that called for greater sensibility and awareness. Put otherwise, the acute crises that normally evoked social dramas had become chronic ones; the dramas these crises spawned continued nonstop. To mark this distinction and to emphasize their continuous, rhythmic, and ritualized nature, I would like to call these dramas collectively "social theater." [80]

Other scenes, masques, and rituals which made up the stock in trade of this Roman Jewish social theater are sometimes more difficult to sight. There was the sacral coloring the notary bestowed upon clients, who normally identified themselves using their common Italian names; these the notary invariably translated in his register into the (standardized) Hebrew parallel, the name used in the synagogue, at a boy's circumcision, at the funeral, and on the four occasions during the year when memorial prayers were recited in public by a group numbering no fewer than ten (men). [81] Here a Jew was simultaneously both Jew and Roman; this usage applied to women as well. Continuous and unconscious role-playing also underlies the turn to Italian as their formal language by the rabbinic notaries about 1600. They were not forced into this change (as all Jews were with their books of account); nor was this a paradoxical "closure that led to opening," as it has been phrased; [82] nor do I believe it was produced by Hebraic ignorance. The notaries were always somehow rabbis. Rather, similar to the nocturnal use of coffee that will be discussed below, this change was a tacit declaration, born admittedly of necessity, that they, the notaries, were not irremediably closed in.

It was also in this vein—where the signs inherent in language are sometimes the most accurate—that the Jews spoke of the Ghetto as their *ghet*, the bill of divorce, which notably is given by the husband and placed directly by him in the hand of his now former wife. [83] The Jews had been "divorced" (from Roman society, as the popes intended), but like any divorcée, they were entitled to consideration and support for their offspring—an offspring, following this second metaphor, which they had in common with the Christian husband, its identity being a shared Roman past of more than a millennium's duration. On the other hand, perceiving the artificiality of such tableaux, Jews in various other cities celebrated the Purim of the Ghetto, pretending to themselves—of course, in the

Purim spirit of *carnavalesque* inversion and satire—that the Ghetto heralded liberation, that enclosure was good.[84] In fact, at the most, the Ghetto walls described a "sacred precinct." The traditional term for the Jewish community, the *kehillah kedoshah* (holy community), thus took on precise physical and spatial dimensions, just as during Ascension days, the forty days after Easter, rogations and "the beating of bounds"—processions with a monstrance and the consecrated host worn around a priest's neck—demarcated a similar holy precinct for Catholics, often new fields, but also the parish community itself. In this concept of the *kehillah kedoshah* there was a certain solace, a certain sense of security, even of existential autonomy.[85] Yet was not this very solace the fruit of the type of illusion I meant when speaking of creating virtual realities: consciously endowing the institutions of the community with an aura of sanctity, thus to remake them—and the community itself, as it were—into the kind of patently artificial structure, spoken of by Victor Turner, that "has to be constantly maintained" in order "to keep out structure,"[86] in this case, of course, the potentially threatening structures and ways of Christian Rome?

But the ability to construct such marvelous self-images, regardless of their precision, had its limits. For to sustain these images, the characters had to remain unflaggingly believable to both portrayer and portrayed, actor and audience. Over time, therefore, role-playing and drama had to be ever more firmly enhanced, verging sometimes on the extreme. Jews thus might nearly riot when a Christian miller provocatively drove his wagon of flour at breakneck speed through the Jewish space of the Ghetto; nor did they hesitate to engage in a rock-tossing match with a band of Christians or voluntarily turn over to papal civic authorities two Jews guilty of aggravated breaking, entering, and burglary, who surely would be sentenced to hang.[87] Such actions were part of Roman Jewry's need to persuade—both itself and others—of normality and internal self-control.[88]

We must not overstretch the metaphor of life as theater and as perpetual social drama. Nor should we artificially seek out role-playing and a precise sense of drama at all times. On occasion, our information is too limited to allow real drama to be singled out. Nonetheless, in the awareness of the Ghetto's intrinsic anomaly and of the formal break it had made with a millennial past, we must imagine Jews perpetually creating strategies for coping—strategies that over time became repetitive and ritualized. And it was this repetitiveness that conferred on them a dramatic, if not dramaturgic, theatrical character, expressive of the meanings with which actors invest their roles. Emotions, too, such as anger, love, and joy, especially in their public—official—expression, might be harnessed to these ends; so often, as we shall see, what appears to be emotion was only a masque. Drama was ubiquitous, and it is this dramatic character, this theater, this rhythmic ritual that we should keep in mind in the following essays as we observe the Jews contending with the problems of acculturation within the framework of Ghetto life.

Yet there is a need for one last preliminary word. In my estimation, Ghetto drama eventually became itself a tool of cultural, social, historical, but especially social memory—the codified repetition of behavioral patterns that functions to remind society's denizens of precisely who they are.[89] Thus, Ghetto drama reified memory, rhetoricized and formalized nostalgia. It is not by accident that Rome's Jews today identify going to buy and consume the cakes made in Rome's one true "Jewish bakery," located at about the site of the Ghetto's principal gate, as an act of pilgrimage, far more ritualized than visits to the roughly adjacent—modern—synagogue. At the end of our story, we will return to this site. On the maps, it appears simply as the intersection of two streets. Roman Jews call it simply *piazza*. No place could be more fitting for some closing thoughts.

1 / The Jew in a Traumatized Society

ROME, THE ETERNAL CITY. It was also a Holy City—not quite *the* Holy City, Jerusalem, but nonetheless a serious contender. As late as the sixteenth century, Rome's borders were defined not by walls alone, but by rogations, holy processions demarcating the limits of civic sanctity, the limits of the civic holy body perceived as an earthly personification of the Holy Body of Christ and watched over by his Mother, the Virgin.[1] Such bodily metaphors were not unique to Rome; but elsewhere, in Venice, for instance,[2] they had acquired a laicized, civic accent. In Rome during the sixteenth century, the century of Protestantism and Catholic Renewal, these concepts came to stand for a replenished and restored aura of sanctity in a city whose mores and morals had once earned the censure of Catholic rebels and deserters. By 1600, orators spoke of Rome as "a theater of unheard of piety" or "pristine piety." Others called it the perfected society, like the Church itself, whose members existed in "the perfect bond of peace." A society in order; and so, the preachers said, Rome had been since the earliest times—despite the reality of a sordid past. Even toward the close of the fifteenth century, Savonarola had called Rome the whore of Babylon. But a few decades later, the city was being called the New Jerusalem; and popes, like Sixtus V in the late 1580s, sought to reify this holiness by placing crosses on pagan buildings, much as the Pantheon had been consecrated centuries before, an act that not only sanctified but exorcised the spirits of evil. A holy city following the heavenly archetype, Rome in the sixteenth century acquired a central role in the march of Christianity toward the realization of salvation by way of the Church Triumphant.[3]

What, then, could Jews possibly be doing in Rome? Were they not, by their very presence, both spiritually and physically polluting its Holy Precincts?[4] And had not such an anxiety been verbalized at Venice when the sixteenth century began, during the debate whether Jews should be allowed permanently to settle in that city, a debate that was resolved through a tenuous compromise? Jews would be permitted to settle, but in the Ghetto—the old iron foundry on a tiny island in a corner of the city—quarantining them, in effect, to limit the potential Jewish civic and social threat.[5] Yet this compromise, too, was questioned until the mid-seventeenth century. For even in what today we would call civic politics, there was myth, and that myth bound social well-being—civic stability—to a rock-solid confessional foundation. As put by Guido Ruggiero with respect to Venice: "what we might call 'civic religion' offered the promise of rule that was legitimate because it was based on Christianity and was concerned with creating a truly Christian and moral society."[6] If Venetians could think this way, how much more the Romans, certainly Rome's ecclesiastical rulers? And should not the anxiety in Rome have been even greater, however hypothetical any Jewish threat might be?

Yet unlike Venice, Rome had harbored Jews for centuries.[7] Both sides, Jews and Christians, had found modes of accommodation, and their behavior had a great deal in common. This was so much the case that when the accommodation was upset in July 1555 by Pope Paul IV's ordering the establishment of a Ghetto, which was to endure for over three hundred years, the Jews appear to have downplayed, for themselves in particular, the Ghetto's significance. They should have been traumatized, as eventually was Roman society as a whole, and surely would have been if they had allowed themselves fully to appreciate the vast changes that Paul IV had wrought in their lives. Yet their initial verbalized reaction to the dashing on the rocks of a thousand-year-old equilibrium was a measure of perplexity—perhaps in part the product of the nearly traditional terminology Paul IV adopted in his directive *Cum nimis absurdum,* which ordered the Ghetto walls built.

The restrained Jewish reaction paralleled that of Rome's Christians, whose sole known observation about the new policy toward Jews was that Jewish commercial activities in and around the city had been ordered to cease. And for Christians—even the papal court—this order created innumerable problems. Initial confusion reigned for both Jews and Christians. Moreover, they both thought Paul IV's policies would not last. For that matter, any Jewish anger at these policies was matched, if not surpassed, by the increasing anger of Rome's Christians. For the radical policies of Paul IV had begun to raise havoc with Rome's centuries-old way of life. The sigh of relief was universal when the election of Paul IV's successor, the Medici Pius IV (1559–65), augured a return to "feasts and many other happy times." The language with which Pius IV's first acts were applauded ("The whores are beginning to go out in their coaches as was their custom, in fact, with greater respect than ever") was a deliberate attempt both to encapsulate complaints and to deride Paul IV's oppressive asceticism and inquisitional zeal. It was indeed in this spirit of derision that the rioting crowd celebrated Paul IV's death in 1559 (or to be more exact his death throes, so anxious were Romans to burst out in revenge) by placing a yellow hat on the head of the statue in his likeness, erected only a few months previously on the Campidoglio, Rome's city hall. The action was in "memory of his having placed this yellow hat on the Jews," but we should read into it neither love nor disrespect for Jews, only anger at having custom and practice disturbed. The anger was so great that the rioting continued with a mock execution—the head of the statue was lopped off—and the inquisitional archives were sacked and the records burned. By contrast, Pius IV had joyously "returned to Rome its former liberties."[8]

Jewish joy would not be so complete. Pius IV did relax some of Paul IV's commercial restrictions. But he did not exempt Jews from wearing the yellow hat. Nor did he abolish the Ghetto, although there are indications that at least some of its walls were demolished. The Ghetto thus was to remain. There was to be no return to the past. Repairs to the walls were made, in fact, very close to the start of the reign of Pius V (1566–72), the immediate successor of Pius IV, who, like Gregory XIII (1572–85) who succeeded him, renewed explicitly the rigor of Paul IV. Gregory XIII also compelled the Jews to attend conversionary sermons, actually a violation of canon law. Even the reign of Sixtus V (1585–90), who, with some slight justification, is often considered a benefactor, brought no respite. Indeed, it was during Sixtus's pontificate, thirty-five years into the Ghetto period, in 1589, that the Jews finally began fully to grasp their predicament, saying for the first time that they were living in their *ghet*, their state of divorce from the broader Roman society.[9] Metaphor aside, Rome's Jews were finally admitting—to themselves—that their intimacy with that society had been seriously disrupted. At the same time, like so many truly divorced spouses, they were at a loss to explain, or accept, their new social and emotional reality, although by beginning to grasp what had happened they were expressing a resolve to cope with this novelty successfully.

Yet before we enter into this complex world of accommodation (and reaccommodation after 1555), a world of the similar and dissimilar in Jewish and Christian behavior, a world in which the Jews of Rome (vis-à-vis Rome's Christians) were at once both "in" and "out," we should examine the Jews' physical surroundings. We should have a clearer image of especially the Ghetto, founded as it was in the quarter called the Rione S. Angelo (along the Tiber, a little more than a mile down the river from the Cathedral of Saint Peter) where nearly all Roman Jews had lived for generations and whose establishment, I believe, symbolized Rome's final submission to exclusive papal control.

The Ghetto was small. The present synagogue occupies about 30 percent of its surface. You could walk from end to end in less than two minutes, and in the spring, when the Tiber regularly flooded, you would probably be walking through mud. About 7 acres in all—trapezoidal, 250 yards at its base, 170 at the top, and 150 in between—it housed an average of 4,000 people, some of whom had money only to rent a corner of a room, some of whom could not afford to marry, not only for want of money but for want of space in which to make a home.[10]

The pictures and drawings following page 54 speak better than the proverbial thousand words to give us a sense of what the Ghetto was like: the narrowness of the streets, the closeness and height of the houses, the ground plan of the Ghetto's first floor, a veritable beehive; the way people dressed, at least in the late nineteenth-century watercolors of E. Roesler-Franz on display today in Rome's civic museum on Corso Vittorio Emmanuele; the view from the Tiber with the houses abutting the river, inviting inundations, bringing mud and disease; the way the sections of the Cinque Scole, or the Five Synagogues, were nested one on top of the other in a single structure; the smallness of the entire area. The photograph showing the new (1904) and present-day Tempio Maggiore and the Cinque Scole building after it burned in 1894 and before it was razed in about 1908, with the rest of the Ghetto already razed, gives a view of the majority of the Ghetto surface. The superimposition drawing shows what existed then compared with what is there now. And the Portico d'Ottavia, that structure going back to ancient Rome with the fish market underneath, must be mentioned, though in truth, and despite the nostalgia it continues to generate even today, it lay just *outside* the Ghetto wall.

To complement these pictures, we can do no better than to offer a brief selection from the noted historian Ferdinand Gregorovius, writing in 1853, six years after the walls had been torn down, and seventeen years before the Ghetto's final days. Gregorovius's eyewitness description is inimitable:

The ghetto is reached either from the city, by way of the Theater of Marcellus and the Porticus of Octavia through the Via Savelli, or from Trastevere, by way of the Tiber island and the Bridge of Quattro Capi. This bridge affords a most striking view of ancient and medieval Rome, a picture so strange and enchanting as can hardly be paralleled in this city of memories. . . . [D]irectly ahead are the ghetto houses in a row, tower-like masses of bizarre design, with numerous flowerpots in the windows and countless household utensils hanging on the walls. The rows ascend from the river's edge, and its dismal billows wash against the walls. It is only a few steps from the bridge to the ghetto, whose level is extremely low. When I first visited it, the Tiber had overflowed its banks and its yellow flood streamed through the Fiumara, the lowest of the ghetto streets, the foundations of whose houses serve as a quay to hold the river in its course. The flood reached as far up as the Porticus of Octavia, and water covered the lower rooms of the houses at the bottom. What a melancholy spectacle to see the wretched Jews' quarter sunk in the dreary inundation of the Tiber! Each year Israel in Rome [Gregorovius here plays on the idea of Israel, in bondage, in Egypt] has to undergo a new Deluge, and like Noah's Ark, the ghetto is tossed on the waves with man and beast.

The physiognomy of the ghetto environment struck me as penetrating the atmosphere with gloomy imaginings. . . . [The darkened aura of] the Porticus of Octavia . . . its ruined and blackened arches gaping upon the stinking Pescara, that crowded and dark fish market where the Jews' fasting fare is laid out on stone slabs . . . [or] The Place of Tears where stands an old palace [that of the Cenci]. . . . Before 1847, a high wall separated the Palace of the Cenci from the Jews' Square. . . . Here was the principal gate of the ghetto; wall and gate are now torn down, and part of the rubble still lies scattered about. If we now enter the streets of the ghetto itself we find Israel before its booths [another play on words, this time referring to the fall harvest festival of Sukkot, or Booths], buried in restless toil and distress. They sit in their doorways or outdoors, on the street which affords scarcely more light than their damp and dismal rooms, and tend their ragged merchandise or industriously patch and sew. The chaos is . . . indescribable.[11]

There is nothing left of the original Ghetto. Even locals imagine it larger than its true dimensions. Roughly conterminous with the traditional Jewish quarter, it was, as the photographs leave no doubt, too small from the beginning to house Rome's Jewish population, some of which had previously begun to move outside. It took about four months to finalize the Ghetto's perimeter, and rental contracts made during those months were equivocal, containing clauses like: "I will rent the house, but only if it is included in the area permitted to the Jews."[12]

It cannot be overemphasized that the people segregated in the Ghetto were not strangers in Rome. Neither were they foreigners, like those who sometimes had enclaves in various Italian cities. Nor, because of their modes of comportment and the rapidity with which those Jews who had entered the city during the first decades of the sixteenth century had integrated socially, could they be likened to the troops of immigrants and migrant workers who made their way to Rome at much this same time. Rather, numbered among the city's most ancient residents, Roman Jews looked and for the most part talked, dressed, and lived like any other Romans.[13]

For centuries, the worlds of Roman Jews and Roman Christians had been roughly one, and the eventual closure in the Ghetto was not air tight. The world that sought to alienate the Jews was ambivalent, far more curious about the Jews and even attracted to their ways than it made itself out to seem, including on the level of learned culture. Those two particularly Renaissance phenomena of Christian Hebraism, the study of Hebrew and rabbinic literature, and kabbalistic investigation intent on proving Christian truth by exploiting the mystical Kabbalah's own exegetical tools, proceeded well into the seventeenth century. In reverse, there was a Jewish attraction to such things as Christian magic and alchemy, although both of these had certain autonomous Jewish roots; and Christians for their part, including the future Paul IV, Cardinal Caraffa, were avid to possess the secrets contained in a Jewish *operam divinationibus et incantationibus*, a book of magical formulae. The Jewish study of secular philosophy, Italian and Latin literature, and formal Italian grammar continued (even in Rome) until the Ghetto's very end.[14]

Yet, despite similarity and commonality, there was a subtle difference. And it was the subtleties that ultimately separated Christians from Jews. Superficial likeness does not necessarily imply identity. Jews and Christians in Rome thus met in taverns, usually Christian, but Jewish ones as well,[15] where they drank, gambled, and sometimes ate together. Occasionally, they ate the same foods: *alici, sarde, tonno*, and *carne salata e secca* (anchovies, sardines, tuna, and dried and salt meat). Their tables surely looked alike—today, true Roman food is considered to be Jewish food. For their part, Jews drank Christian wine as a matter of course, despite rabbinic protest (at least of many Ashkenazi and Sephardi, as opposed to Italian rabbis, who did not object).[16] But here similarity ended. In their homes and in their communities, what the Jews ate was kosher: the meat ritually slaughtered, inspected for illness, and punctiliously prepared; not to mention that Jews refrained from pork and from the seafood so beloved by the Christian Roman palate. *Kashrut* was no ideal, not the reserve of the few. The communally quashed scandals when corners were cut in the kosher butcheries, as well as the communally supervised lists of meat prices that have survived, leave no doubt on this score.[17]

Thus in similarity there was also diversity. Apart from what was consumed and apart from the manner of animal slaughter, there were two different food rituals with two different underlying principles. For Christians, the principle had to do with time—when one ate or refrained from eating certain foods. For Jews, the principle was a question of what was perennially permitted or forbidden.[18] In addition, the holiest of Christian meals, the Eucharist, was prepared and presided over by a male priest. For the Jews, every meal, no matter how insignificant, was a holy meal, with its prescribed set of pre-meal benedictions and the lengthy "last blessing" if no bread was eaten, or pages-long "grace after meals" otherwise; and meals were the province of individuals and solely their own responsibility. We should not neglect to mention the weekly Sabbath meals, with special blessings over wine, or the meals of the festivals, especially the elaborate and exceptionally ceremonial Passover Seder, with its complete liturgy as found in the Haggadah, the retelling of the Exodus, and its host of prescribed, unleavened, foods. These meals were also a time of family reunion, certainly in Jewish Rome, as the Jewish notaries attest.

The preparation of food, too, was a family matter, although the individuals who most often took charge of this aspect of ritual propriety were women. Yet, along with spouses and children, these women were acting within the ambit of that very biological, conjugal family that Jewish writings idealized as an intrinsic vehicle of holiness: that special Jewish brand of holiness whose essence is "propriety," living according to Jewish law, the halachah, rather than the devotional or transcendental kind of sanctity associated with such as Christian saints. Even the menstrual cycle with its associated "laws of family purity," including the self-policing by women of their personal ritual cleanliness at menstruation's end—which in fact obligates spouses to engage in sexual relations—was a font of sanctity, again as Jews understood the term.[19]

By contrast, Edward Muir's magisterial synthesis of ritual and its meanings, especially in the early modern period and primarily in Christian, especially Italian, society, never discusses the family as the seat of ritual, whether sacred or profane, and especially not at the table. Indeed, for centuries the Christian biological family was considered the antithesis of the (clerically articulated) Christian familial ideal. A spiritual family composed of the hierarchy and the body of the faithful took precedence over the biological family, in which sometimes spouses were encouraged to renounce sexuality outright.[20] The biological family gained legitimacy in clerical eyes only when, from the fifteenth century on, it began to be pictured as embodying the virtues of the Holy Family; the family of Christ was now envisioned with a young Joseph playing the role of Mary's real consort rather than the part of an aging, fatherly man. Legitimacy also demanded that the Christian family increasingly, if sometimes hesitantly, accept the scrutiny and discipline imposed by the (renewed office of the personal) confessor and dispenser of sacraments known as the director of souls.[21]

That this clerical ideal of the Holy Family was also congruent with reality has been cogently argued with respect to changes in testamentary practices in seventeenth-century Siena. As membership and devotional practices multiplied in both men and women's pious confraternities—practices with roots in the sixteenth century—so, too, did donations and other gifts to religious establishments multiply at the cost of both financial strength in the family lineage and the unmitigated loyalty that had been a trademark in families throughout the social spectrum in previous centuries and in various Italian regions. These devotional confraternities also situated ritual activity outside the home and family.[22] Thus, when Jews and Christians said they inhabited a holy community—in Hebrew, a *kehillah kedoshah*—they were referring to contrasting sacral ideals, and, to no little extent, practices as well.

This contrast also extended to the ways in which sacrality was expressed. Judaism has hardly any demonstrative ceremonial animation; one would be hard pressed to call the observance of *kashrut* a ceremony. In Christian social rhetoric or ritual, it is ceremony—public ceremony in particular—that is often central, and certainly the most visible. The best example of this, perhaps, is the sense of Christian wholeness, unity, and sanctity, whether actual or symbolic, realized through the annual Corpus Christi procession, in which nearly everyone (at least in smaller towns) participated, thus representing civic seamlessness, the aspiration to *imitatio Christi*, the imitation of Christ, and the likening of the town, and its unified corps of believers, to the perfected divine body of Christ and its oneness. In addition, Jewish rituality, whether ensconced in verbalization or achieved through correct procedure—all enshrined and elaborated in rabbinic teaching and literature—took place within a rhythmic Jewish conception of time. This Jewish time was divided by a series of daily, weekly, and festive repetitions. Christian liturgical time and the Christian liturgical calendar were predicated, as is much of Christian piety, on replicating and revering in annual cycles the major events of Christ's life and death.[23]

Moreover, wholly unlike the highly individual, highly privatized Jewish version of verbal rhetoric, that of Rome's Catholic Christians was almost exclusively the province of priests. Not only that, but at Rome, in particular, the one surviving Jewish priestly ritual, the one demonstrably Jewish ritual of animation (aside from the truly minimal animation of the Torah procession, the carrying of the Torah around the synagogue before and after its reading, or the waving by individuals of the *lulav*, a frond of three leaves, and the *etrog*, a citron, during the Sukkot Festival of Booths) was and continues to be usurped, or at least compromised, by the family. I am referring to the Priestly Benediction. This is an elaborate affair, pronounced with the priests barefoot (the *Kohanim*, a class distinction passed on by fathers telling sons; a strictly male caste, to be sure), their heads covered by the *tallit* (the prayer shawl), their fingers held apart two by two, and their hands washed by Levites (again a distinction passed on by father to son). This benediction is made normally only on the Sabbath and festivals, and at Roman Jewish weddings. But in Rome this benediction is also made with families gathered, to the extent possible, under the *tallit* of the nominal family head—or *taled*, as it is pronounced in Judaeo-Romanesco. It is he who confers the blessing, embracing the family with his outstretched arms and hands, as though it has been relayed through him, from the priests, to his kin. This practice is visible even today. Yet at weddings the blessing is often conferred by a matriarch, completing the transference of the ritual's essence, and efficacy, from priest to family—thus advertising Jewish ritual's uniquely individualistic and familial nature. At the same time, one wonders whether the visibly sacramental qualities of this complex ritual could ever have come into being were it not devised literally—nobody knows exactly when—in the shadow of the Catholic Church.

What these contrasts and shadings suggest is that we, as historians or as plain curious people, should no longer be trying to answer the traditional question asked about Renaissance Italy: Did Jews and Christians live harmoniously, sharing a common culture, until a certain point during the Renaissance, after which social and theological reaction brought the harmony to an end and mandated cultural closure (whatever these often inflated terms may really mean)?[24] Rather, following the instructive lead of recent histories of the Jews in such places as nineteenth-century Germany, we should spurn neatly tailored commonplace antinomies such as "assimilation" versus "seclusion," or an "open" versus a "closed" society;[25] we should search instead for a Roman Jewish subculture that was at once Roman—attentive, appreciative, and receptive to the non-Jewish Roman world—and Jewish in its deep-seated essence as well. What we will find is a culture that was defined by a broad range of distinctive, and emphatically neither derivative nor exclusionist, individual and communal behavior. This was a culture that went beyond explicitly Jewish ritual, practice, and thought, and—not coincidentally—played a role in bringing Jews and Christians together, but also keeping the two apart, creating a state best described as tense intimacy.[26]

What, then, defined the Jewish subculture—or microculture—at Rome, and how did it fare after the Ghetto was established? What were its resources for coping, successfully as it turned out, so that for over three hundred years the gap between Jews and Christians never became unbridgeable? By subtlely—sometimes consciously, but equally often unawares—reinforcing existing cultural bulwarks, the Jews of Rome managed to entrench both their Roman and Jewish identities. This is an achievement that would serve them well during the Ghetto period, and also after the Ghetto was abolished in 1870.

Apart from the intrinsically Jewish in personal and familial ideals and in ritual practices, the Jews had their own special concept of space.[27] The holy space of the *ghet* was not the same as the holy precinct of Christian Rome. Although both Jewish and Christian spatial sanctity originated in the wall constructed around Jerusalem by the biblical Nehemiah, putatively five centuries before Christ, in order to create a ritual precinct,[28] what really defined a Jewish ritual precinct was not so much a wall, or even rogations (reminiscent of Joshua's siege of biblical Jericho, as well as of Nehemiah), but the people therein. Accordingly, Nehemiah followed his construction of a *ritual* wall (a jackal, it was said, could leap over it) with a census tallying the rightful members of this ritual city. No less important, he followed the census with a public reading of the statutes, the Torah, and a public oath in support of moral behavior. Jewish holiness thus depended principally not on a three-dimensional sacred space, nor on an inner personal reception of grace or a system of priestly sacramentality, much less on the sacralizing presence in Rome of Peter and his successors. It depended on what the Jews—individuals as well as the group—did, or thought.[29] This spatial concept, moreover, might spill over into reality. In a dispute between two synagogues, one replied to an interrogation by a rabbinic notary that it would never think to harm its opponent! For were not its members holy, constituents of the synagogue whose very name was "The Fearers of the Lord"—those who obeyed God's laws and commandments?[30]

There were similar distinctions with respect to time and sound. Besides the already mentioned differences in the annual ritual calendar, ritual time itself was perceived in different ways. Its particular activities and restrictions aside, for example, the Sabbath was the preferred day for reaching prime Jewish communal decisions, with the Communal Council convening in one of the five Roman synagogues. Yet, Jews were not tied exclusively to the Jewish calendar. Nonchalantly, they called December 25 *Natale*, Christmas, thus living comfortably within the two systems of time. They were comfortable, too, with Christian music, especially Catholic sacred chant, which consciously or unconsciously they adopted. Adapted would be more precise;[31] their creations of special tropes and music are still heard in Roman synagogues today. So close were the Jewish and Christian forms of chant that even clerics could not always tell them apart. In Modena, in 1604, an inquisitor asked the Jew Leo whether some Jewish boys playing a game had not been singing "a song in the Christian manner." No, said Leo: "We were singing as Jews do." Leo "then began singing in the Jewish mode, asking whether this was not similar to what had been heard. He sang again in the Jewish mode," commented the inquisitor, "not . . . dissimilar to our [chant]."[32]

The knowing ear, of course, can tell the difference. And there is a difference of perception as well as of instrumentalities: the Sabbath legally, halachically, prohibits the sounding of an organ, but the Roman (Italian) sounding of the shofar, the ram's horn, on the Jewish New Year, Rosh haShannah, is unparalleled, distinguished by its undulations and unbroken notes. This is in sharp contrast to what is heard in synagogues, certainly Ashkenazi ones, elsewhere. Nor should we forget that no shofar is ever sounded in a church. Jewish life, consequently, had its own sphere, its own pace, its own sounds, its own Jewishness—an aura that generated a life style distinctly the Jews' own, one part of which was to reject Christianity. Such rejections were not well received.

Most Jews refused to convert, of course, but some refusals were like burrs in the Christian side. A poignant example is the story of the condemned Jewish thief in the seventeenth century.[33] Comforted by the society of S. Giovanni Decollato, he agreed to convert before being hanged (if only to avoid a painfully slow death). But he really agreed because he knew that canon law insisted on a three-day wait before baptism to discover whether the convert was sincere; in other words, he agreed to convert in order to earn himself a three-day reprieve from the gallows.[34] And thus our poor thief managed to postpone his execution time and again, offering to convert, only to repent of his decision at the end of the three days. Firm in his Judaism, he was led back and forth to the gallows, where, at the last moment and as the rules required, he was asked anew to save his soul. But even the churchmen finally had enough, and hanged the thief.

Contemporaries can hardly have failed to see in this drama that so-called Jewish *duricia*, the hard-heartedness that ecclesiastics had bemoaned for centuries. Nor could they have failed to link the events to what they viewed as Jewish perversity. The Jews were fulfilling their carnal stereotype as described by Paul and Augustine more than a thousand years earlier.[35] And on a distantly abstract level, they were vicariously reliving the murder of Christ, this time through derision, pretending to accept him for the worst of reasons, to avoid loss, including the loss of life, or in order to endure a less horrible death.[36]

Yet did not the perceived spiritual perversion of this last-minute rejection also remind beholders, the members of the ministering confraternity of S. Giovanni Decollato at least, of the Jews' patently *Jewish* social categories and religious priorities? Rather than being preoccupied with a cure for their souls, two other condemned Jewish felons, shortly after the start of the eighteenth century, asked to see a notary. In the Italian familial tradition, they were most concerned about bequeathing their few worldly possessions, in this case to their fiancée and offspring respectively.[37] But this privileging of mundanity also reminds us that the world of the Jews was one in which anticipating certain Protestant models—marriage was not a sacrament. This was a world that saw marital sanctity expressed in the behavior of spouses toward each other, not in the Catholic concept of marriage as a sacramentalized symbol of faith and of unity with Christ and the Church.[38] Jewish private life was not given over to the direct supervision of the clergy—as some claimed it should be for post-Tridentine Catholics—though frequently it might outwardly seem to have been.[39] Rabbinic and priestly roles, moreover, should never be confused. The rabbi is a font of halachic opinion and teaching, exercising moral but never sacerdotal or sacramental authority. This provided all the more justification why Jews, again much like the despised Protestants, should perceive as civil institutions what to Catholics were sacral or sacramental.

This clash of contrasting ideals seems to have been well understood; and the Catholic clergy countered by condemning aspects of Jewish marital behavior. In particular, Jewish sexuality and Jewish women had long been the subject of open grievance—as well as of no little fantasy—among ecclesiastics, who complained that Jewish men took second wives to satisfy their sexual desires while their first wives were pregnant.[40] Jewish women themselves, traditionally heroines in tales of Jewish martyrdom—particularly in a twelfth-century Jewish historiography that on the subject of martyrdom was singularly ungendered—were made out by horrified Christian chroniclers to be monsters who would go to any extreme rather than see their children saved in Christ.[41]

Yet, these fantasies, especially the sexual ones, stretch the truth more than they pervert it. Jews were, after all, told by rabbinic authorities that marital sexuality was a virtue, not a concession in which sin always inhered.[42] In addition, on very rare occasions, a Jewish husband whose first wife had been sterile for at least ten years of marriage might receive permission to exercise his halachic privilege to take a second wife—although, to be sure, the consent of the first wife was prerequisite. This privilege was not granted automatically. One husband petitioned (to papal authorities, since it required an exemption from civil law) to take a second wife only after he had been married for fifteen years. But perhaps most significant with respect to uniquely Jewish practice was the right legally to divorce and, more important, remarry afterward. With reference to the sixteenth century, this was a tentatively embarked upon novelty, even among Protestants (specifically in Calvin's Geneva).[43]

What most disturbed the Catholic clergy was that Jewish leaders of all stripes unconditionally lauded the conjugal family, thus preserving the ancient model of the conjugal family as a pillar of society, the very model that the Catholic clergy by deemphasizing the biological family firmly eschewed or about which it remained irredeemably ambivalent. By contrast, the centrality accorded the Jewish family was present even in the words of

the family-centered Jewish Passover ritual (citing Exod. 13:8), instruct-
ing: "And you shall tell your sons [of the Exodus]." The "you" vouchsafed
each and every household head, not clerics, nor even rabbis, with the
duty of passing on one of Judaism's fundamental myths. Even though
in practice the Jewish family unit was often insufficiently cohesive to
play the role theoretically assigned to it, this role would never have been
assigned were the family not envisioned as constituting Jewish society's
central core.

This Jewish model may have proved even more disturbing, since the
concept of the family as structurally central had been revived and lauded
by fourteenth- and fifteenth-century Florentine civic humanists. In the
words of Leonardo Bruni, in 1427: "the fundamental union, which by its
multiplication makes the city, is that of husband and wife. Nothing can
be accomplished when this union does not exist, and this love alone is
natural, legitimate, and allowed."[44] Bruni and compatriots like Coluccio
Salutati (1392) were, of course, bestowing an ideology on long existing lay
concepts and practices, in particular the laity's constant preoccupation
with ensuring that male lineages survived. That this preoccupation was
shared by all social classes may have troubled the clergy even more, providing at least one explanation why—spurred on by the momentum toward Catholic internal reform in the late sixteenth century—it made
such efforts to draw men and women into devotional confraternities, encouraged pious bequests, and promoted the desire on the part of many to
be buried in confraternal vaults in preference to those of the family. The
clerically directed spiritual family was being relaunched under confraternal auspices.

Concomitant with the increasingly devotional role, the traditional
public role of the Christian lay confraternity was being reduced, again
through clerical manipulation. Yet, at just this time, the public role, especially as a forum for arbitrating disputes, among Jewish confraternities
was being enhanced, as we shall see below in detail. Power in Jewish Rome
was diffused, if not fragmented, among various entities. Jewish society, as
it viewed and operated itself, was an aggregate of individuals and of au-
tonomously distinct units; it did not picture itself, as Catholic thinkers

1 / Map of central Rome. The Ghetto (unmarked) sat just opposite the island on the Tiber's bend.

3 / *Aerial photograph showing the modern structures whose outline is super-imposed on the Ghetto plan in the previous plate. Portico d'Ottavia is at the upper right.*

2 / *Superimposition of the outline of current structures over the floor plan of the Ghetto. The largest structure is the current synagogue and its gardens (lower right). The extension at the top was added in 1824. The Portico d'Ottavia (upper right) is outside the Ghetto. Piazza Giudea (upper left) is actually two squares. That within the Ghetto is also known as Piazza Mercatello. The Cinque Scole are mid-left (large square). The current so-called piazza is roughly at the upper right corner of Piazza Giudea outside the Ghetto walls.*

6 / *Piazza Giudea fuori le Mura, outside the walls, with the main gate of the Ghetto on the right. Drawing by the eighteenth-century artist G. Vasi.*

4 and 5 / Two views of the Ghetto from the Tiber. Bridge of Quattro Capi linking the Ghetto to the Tiber Island (top photo, right). On the island is the hospital of the Fatebenefratelli, founded in the Middle Ages and still operating.

7 / Saint Peter's Cathedral, located a little more than a mile by straight line from the Ghetto and the current synagogue. Standing on a bridge crossing the Tiber, one sees the cupola of Saint Peter's in one direction and the dome of the synagogue in the other.

8 / The new synagogue, the Tempio Maggiore, 1904, viewing also the shell of the building of the Cinque Scole, the Five Synagogues, burned in a fire in 1894 and razed about 1908. The open space is the bulk of the Ghetto razed after 1885 for reasons of public health and urban renewal.

9 / Drawing of the Cinque Scole housed in a single structure. One can easily imagine the conflicts between the synagogues over space.

edificio delle 5 scole

 S. TEMPIO S. NOVA □ S. CATALANA □ S. SICILIANA □ S. CASTIGLIANA

10 / *Photograph of the Cinque Scole and the piazza, or square, of the same name, toward the end of the nineteenth century.*

11 / *Via Rua, the Ghetto's main street, with the Portico d'Ottavia and a preaching friar, as depicted in the late nineteenth-century watercolors of E. Roesler-Franz. These watercolors are the major remaining images of what Ghetto life may have looked like.*

12 / *Photograph of Via Rua, with garments for sale extending along the walls. Space was rented by the meter and centimeter. Late nineteenth century, as are all the photographs.*

13 / *Via Rua near Piazza Giudea within the walls.*

14 / *Via delle Azzimelle, north end. This street ran the length of the Ghetto, toward the river. Via Fiumara ran in front of the houses abutting the river. Via Rua ran from the Portico d'Ottavia to Piazza Giudea.*

15 / *Via delle Azzimelle, detail.*

16 / *Piazzetta delle Azzimelle.*

17 / *Piazzetta delle Azzimelle as depicted by Roesler-Franz.*

18 / Arco delle Azzimelle as depicted by Roesler-Franz.

19 / Piazzetta del Pancotto.

20 / Vicolo Capociuto as depicted by Roesler-Franz.

often pictured Christian society, as a corporately unified whole mirroring the Holy Body of the Church.[45] Nor was there a unifying Jewish—sacral—corporate head: the pope. Thus the modest powers of the formal Jewish community were shared by synagogal groupings, but also by confraternities. Perhaps even more than the synagogues, these confraternities reinforced qualities of voluntarism and lay leadership, such as once typified medieval Christian confraternal life. But these qualities were now ones that the Church and its ministers were trying to expunge, which they did by turning confraternal life toward primarily pietistic directions and by gaining control over the confraternity through the "creation," as one historian has put it, "of a bond between the practice of charity and the frequent use of the repeatable [eucharistic] sacraments of the Church."[46] Jewish confraternities enjoyed—at their "will"—the services of the "adjunct" *rav melamed*, the teaching rabbi. They also were never allowed to displace the family from its role as the guardian of children and the focus of children's loyalty.[47]

Indeed, again contrary to Catholic clerical desires, it was not priests but the children's fathers who were charged with overseeing the education of their offspring, especially sons. And as the Jewish notarial acts attest, what Jewish fathers repeatedly specified that their sons be taught, even those sons being apprenticed, was the biblical text along with the range of basic classical Jewish biblical commentaries.[48] This was at the same time that the Catholic Church was exerting itself to remove biblical materials from the hands of the faithful and keep them exclusively in clerical possession. Thus the Jews supported a culture, especially a familial culture, that was most unlike that *imagined* for its faithful by the Catholic Church. This distinction was all the more pressing because in so many areas, especially those of practical aspirations, the attitudes of Catholic families were more often akin to Jewish ones than to those the Catholic clergy were urging their flocks to espouse.

Priestly control of Christian behavior, too, was anything but perfect. What priests condemned, the laity might well overlook. Theological nicety and subtle distinctions surely were not on the minds of Christian spouses as they quarreled or made love. The heads of bourgeois Italian families also did their best to marginalize priests and the Church with respect to the ceremonies and processes of matrimony. In other words, actual Christian behavior, not only attitudes, often was far more similar to Jewish behavior than to what Catholic theology demanded.

However, although Jewish and Catholic laity may have seen eye to eye on many issues, there were others on which they did not. We will see this below in discussing divergent Jewish and Christian approaches to the thorny problem of marital choice, irrespective of the emphasis that the Christian laity attached to the familial unit itself. Rejection of certain aspects of Jewish behavior could also be direct, verbal, and crass, such as the increasingly frequent public mockeries of Jewish ritual, especially weddings and funeral corteges. Both of these became subjects of satirical drama. Yet perhaps the purpose of the mockery and satire was to project Christian misgivings onto others. In one such drama, admittedly from a later period, the Christian author has the young, beautiful Jewish Gnora Luna married off to a decrepit octogenarian, whose demise she demonstrably hastens. No doubt this dramatist was simply transposing from Pietro Aretino's sixteenth-century satire on marriage, the *Sei giornate*, in which Aretino has one of his heroines, Nanna the whore, matched by her mother with "an old man, who only lived because he was still eating." The predictable result was adultery and then the fulfillment of her husband's wish: "to have me for his wife or die." Nanna, accordingly, "buried a little knife that I had in his chest and his pulse beat no more." [49]

Mockery thus may well have grown on a suppressed current of identification and a denied realization of common foibles. But it also rested on ambivalence. And it was in this spirit that Christians constantly entered the Ghetto, did business there, shopped, and sometimes partook with Jews in a glass of wine, sharing sociability as well as social etiquette. For their part, Jews, on the festival of Purim, might pretend to be Christian police. The realms in which Jews and Christians concurred and behaved alike were thus many. But it has also been justly said that Jews were "intimate outsiders." [50] Alike did not mean identical, which was especially true with respect to the ways in which Jews and Christians consciously perceived their behavior. If, for example, the vast majority of Christians did not follow Bernardino di Siena's admonition to pray in preparation for intercourse, they had heard him admonishing them to do so in the same public squares where he had often moved them to fervor and repentance. It is hard to imagine that the visions Bernardino conjured up did not subtly modify his listeners' behavior. The same applies to Jews, whose masculine image, among other things, instilled through repeated rabbinic teaching and writing, has recently been said to be the contrapositive of the Christian one.[51]

DISTINGUISHING THEORY FROM PRACTICE is not solely a matter for historiographical retrospection. It was also a crux for Christian authorities, whether ecclesiastical or secular, throughout the medieval and into the modern periods. Within the matrices of Christian theory, these authorities asked themselves how best they were to govern the Jews and set appropriate limits on Jewish activity. The medieval solution had been an equilibrium based on limited and legislated segregation. This was far more complex than the simple realization—as is so often inadequately put—of the biblical verse first adduced by Augustine that Jews should not be killed, lest God's name be forgotten (Ps. 59:12). Augustine himself had explained this verse as: let not their "memory" be destroyed.[52] The true origins of attitudes toward Jews were propounded by Paul, who inextricably linked Christian salvation at the End of Days with the Jews' integration into the faith; he also could not imagine society without a Jewish presence. After all, in the Epistle to the Romans, did not Paul emphasize that he himself was a Jew? Such pronouncements left no alternative. Some solution, some balance, had to be achieved—albeit one permanently tilted toward Christian advantage and against the Jews. And in the putative (institutional) unity of the medieval world, this balance worked, within limits, at least for the Church. Secular society lacked the tools to sustain such an equilibrium, and it alternately expelled or massacred its Jews in large numbers.[53]

Yet the source of this violence was again the writings of Paul. For in Galatians (chaps. 4 and 5), Paul had warned that contact with Judaism (note: not with Jews) might pose the same danger to salvation and faith that yeast left to ferment too long might pose to a rising lump of dough. By no later than the fifth century, and repeatedly thereafter, Christian commentators saw the danger coming from the Jews themselves. So deeply did their interpretations seep into Christian thinking, that by the ' later thirteenth century, on the eve of the expulsions from England and France and the great German massacres of the early fourteenth century, medieval lawyers began to ponder whether Paul's words (which conclude by referring to the expulsion of the biblical Ishmael) might be used legally to justify a Jewish expulsion. They indeed could, these lawyers decided— if Jews threatened the fabric of social harmony beyond repair.[54]

The extent to which thirteenth-century kings and others took note of this decision is moot. However, irreparable damage to the social fabric is exactly what Jews were accused of doing by Franciscan preachers like Bernardino da Feltre in late fifteenth-century Italy, who charged that Jewish lending was like gangrene consuming the holy body of Christ's faithful—a gangrene which, like the lenders themselves, must be cut out in order to save the body as a whole. Others said that Jews conspired to destroy the Christian order by killing Christian children—not simply to repeat the murder of Christ, but to gather Christian blood for perverse and magical reasons. Miraculously, it was the Virgin, who, traditionally in such tales of ritual murder, saved at least the soul of the child, hence protecting the Eucharist itself that symbolized the sanctified Christian social body.[55] The moral is self-evident: Driven by an existential fear, leading forces within the Church determined to overturn the centuries-old equilibrium that had made life possible between Christians and Jews. This, and more.

At the turn of the sixteenth century, a mix of forces and events made it clear that Catholic society could not continue as it had: these were the Protestant Reformation, a self-generated internal drive for Catholic reform, which had a major conversionary aspect, and the discoveries of New Worlds peopled by untold numbers of the unsaved said to be thirsty for salvation. Perhaps the time to convert the Jews, too, had arrived. The Spanish and Portuguese had failed in their attempts to do this. So many

New Christians had reverted to Judaism. But the Spanish and Portuguese had used expulsion and even illegal force as a means, for which they had been castigated by Pope Paul III and Cardinal Pier Paolo Pariseo in the 1530s. Now, under Paul IV, the argument would be taken up again through demonstrative action. Closed in the Ghetto and subjected to the strict enforcement of law (what some contemporary theoreticians of Jewish conversion called "pious lashes"), the Jews would finally recognize that they were being justly punished for their theological stubbornness. At long last, willingly and wholeheartedly, they would convert in droves.[56]

Completing this conversionary ardor were flashes of millenarian expectation: Did not Paul IV in 1556 write to his sister that he had been chosen to hasten the millennium's advent?[57] Even humanists played a role in this revision. Sigismondi de' Conti da Foligno, an adherent of the papal Curia no less, accused the Jews, but especially Marranos, of spreading the germ of syphilis, then a new, acute, and murderous disease. This accusation reminds us that humanists had also spearheaded the charge of ritual murder so devastatingly leveled at Trent in 1475.[58] The Jew who was once feared as a source of spiritual danger and as a font of social ferment had thus been transformed—by representatives of the intellectual elite at that—into a well of physical infection, from which, and from whom, maintaining distance was an imperative.

Notably, this infection was associated not only with Jews as Jews but with the Marranos, that transmutation one legist called the *pessimum genus hominum*, neither Jew nor Christian, perhaps atheists, whose existence signaled—more than anything else did—the perils of insecure faith, that most menacing of all enemies in the highly threatened and anxious early sixteenth-century Catholic world.[59] The Marrano was living witness to an incomplete rite de passage, one who had left the old but failed fully to integrate into the new. The bearers of such potential insecurity and imprecise identity were not to be sustained.

Yet there was also a question of justice. Were all New Christians (the technical name for those who had converted in Spain after the riots of 1391) actually Marranos, many of whom were often impostors who, at their convenience, feigned Christianity to some and Judaism to others?

Or were not large numbers victims of mass forced conversion at the hands of the Portuguese king in 1497, hence entitled to return to Judaism—albeit such a return signaled a Christian defeat? These questions were asked and debated hotly by canonists, high curial officials, and even by Popes Clement VII and Paul III themselves.[60] Thus, added to all the other issues concerning Jews was this new, particularly devilish one: who was a Jew in the first place, and where did the line dividing Jew from Christian begin and end?

All of this created a formidable challenge, enlarged still further by the secular needs of the solidifying body politic of the Papal State, which was far more than a papally headed religious entity.[61] For example, to expand the Papal State's commerce, Portuguese merchants—who practiced Judaism but were also fugitives from the events of 1497 and thus arguably Christians—were invited to Ancona in the 1530s and 1540s to develop that city's international port.[62] Similarly, longtime Italian Jews had for centuries provided loans to the poor, and the new alternative to these loans, the Franciscan system of Monti di pietà, was often ineffective. It did not strike firm roots in the Papal State until the later seventeenth century. As late as 1585, the Franciscan Sixtus V relaunched Jewish banking in tens of small towns throughout papal domains.[63] Moreover, irrespective of any benefit the popes may have hoped to achieve from Jewish activity, they were bound to uphold the Jews' time-honored legal status, that of *cives*, roughly "citizens," entitled to enjoy the same legal privileges as all others in the Papal State, at least with respect to civil and criminal justice. Canon law, too, forbade depriving Jews of due legal process: established by the canon *Sicut judaeis non* five hundred years earlier, in the early twelfth century.[64]

The Jews, as we have observed, were also integrated into Rome's ongoing commercial and occupational structures. Sometimes Jewish enterprise was independent. At other times, Jews were clients of major commercial families such as the Boccapaduli and the Cenci, in whose midst the Jews also lived and to whom they often paid rent as tenants within the system of the *hazaqah* described above.[65] It was not, however, necessary to be a client in order to hold a *hazaqah*. Christian notarial records contain the names of a large number of Christians in whose properties the Jews dwelled. These arrangements obviously generated interdependence.

Christians were further dependent on Jews as providers of services. The Jewish share in services was out of proportion to the Jews' three percent presence in the population. But unlike elsewhere in Italy or even in the towns of the Papal State, the principal service Jews provided in Rome was not lending. Only about seven or eight percent of Rome's Jews, the fifty to seventy of them who operated as lenders, could claim the title of banker, and even they lent principally on a small scale. Most Jews worked as suppliers and producers, whether as provisioners of grain and other foodstuffs or as artisans, especially as tailors and producers of fine lace.[66] So visible were Jews in this latter sphere, that in the early sixteenth century an attempt was made to create a combined guild of Jewish and Christian clothworkers, for which statutes were actually drawn up. Tellingly, however, and with respect to the contrary direction in which events were to move, already in 1552, Rome's Christian clothworkers petitioned that Jews be excluded from selling new goods.[67] The innovative prohibition ordering Jews to abandon the traffic in new clothing introduced by the papal bull *Cum nimis absurdum*, the bull in which the Ghetto was ordained, may have been in part a response to this petition. However, Paul IV was also no doubt motivated to introduce this novelty in the context of his overall Jewish policy, in which restriction was bound up integrally with conversionary expectation.

The clothworkers were surely thinking of commercial advantage. Indeed, in the seventeenth century the guild of Christian clothworkers brought suit, contending that Jews were producing and selling new garments in disregard of the bull. That papal courts—after decades of litigation—finally ruled in the Jews' favor gives us an inkling of how phlegmatic and at cross-purposes with itself papal policy toward the Jews sometimes might be.[68] Yet it must be appreciated that these zigzags were the result of the principled character of papal policy. Restriction demanded justification. Even the eventual closing of Jewish banks in Rome in 1682 was preceded by a precisely reasoned legal polemic.

When, accordingly, Paul IV instituted a Ghetto at Rome in July 1555, he was reacting to both stimuli and constraints far broader and more complex than those that moved Venetians to found the first Ghetto in 1516.[69] The Venetians had sought a middle way between serving the commercial needs of their city and those of their souls—as they themselves put it. The pope, too, was looking for such a compromise. But beyond that, beyond the unique demographic and social status of Roman Jewry, and beyond the religious upheavals and conundrums of the ensuing forty years, Paul IV—this fanatic octogenarian, noted for fierce discipline in all realms—had his own private expectations. For, persuaded of a quickly approaching millennium, he had already, in his former post as prefect of the papal Inquisition, ordered the Talmud burned alongside other Hebrew works that were said to anchor the Jews in their disbelief. No such order had been issued by a high ecclesiastical authority in over two hundred years.[70] Paul IV also advanced the interests of the House of Converts established at Rome in 1542 by the founder of the Jesuit Order, Ignatius Loyola. And he pointedly adopted the method of fostering conversion through financial pressures, which had been espoused first by Pope Gregory the Great late in the sixth century, by turning a reasonable system of Jewish taxation into an instrument of punitive burden.[71] In a word, Paul IV had embarked on a mission to convert the Jews en masse—and in his own days. However surprising it may seem, this is something that no previous pope had ever entertained doing. The Ghetto, confining the Jews into a social and spatial limbo, from which they could emerge only upon their baptism, played a central role in this program.[72]

The Ghetto decree, moreover, came at the very start of Paul IV's pontificate. What sparked it? Was he reacting directly to a blood libel, quickly found to be false, but which still agitated the Roman populace?[73] Was he responding to the recent spread of already crowded Jewry into the choicer quarters of Rome, likely along the newly constructed Via Giulia adjacent to the Jews' traditional neighborhoods, even today one of central Rome's most prestigious streets?[74] Or was he thrusting out at everything together, with millenarianism as his driving force, not to mention his conviction that harsh, but legal, discipline would yield spontaneous mass conversion? Add to this an intangible dramatic element, of the kind that surfaces in the closing story of Shelomo ibn Verga's always opaque and often satirical (near contemporary) history of Jewish tragedy: the story of an archbishop who falsely accuses a single Jew of stealing a sacred image, arousing papal wrath. The Jews are ordered expelled and their children forcibly baptized—an order, however, that is swiftly rescinded when, that same night, the offending prelate and his retinue are the sole victims of an earthquake that shakes the entire city: "I suspect," says the pope, "that it was on account of the Jews that the Archbishop met his fate [that is, in the Jews' place]."[75] About the Jews, therefore, about the Church's obligation to them and about their obligations to the Church in return—so I read Ibn Verga's message—there was endless uncertainty. Reality had become so entangled that the Jews could be made the subject of quasi-farcical satire or, alternately, fear and consternation, requiring extraordinary political measures.

But whatever the conglomerate of motives that pushed Paul IV to take these measures, the Jews did not seem properly to appreciate them. Who, after all, had more day-to-day experience with the popes than they? Some popes had been more difficult, there had been trying periods, but all in all the canons had been observed.[76] Was it not a combination of a Jewish request and a solicitous patron, the Pierleoni, who used their influence on the popes in both 1063 and 1119 to have the protective bull (and eventual canon) *Sicut iudaeis non* first issued?[77] So why—however anxiously—in reaction to the Ghetto decree, the bull *Cum nimis absurdum*, should the Jews say anything more definitive than: "the pope [Paul IV] has ordered the Jews to sell our homes . . . [and] to live together?"[78] Perceived in these terms, this decree neither embodied novelty nor augured revolution with respect to the papal-Jewish past. Or perhaps the Jews did understand, blasé as they pretended to be: their traditional areas of residence were restricted, including those in the districts of Ripa and Trastevere, where not only had some Jews lived for centuries, but where Jews had been exempt from wearing the *tabarro rosso*, the Jews' red hat.[79] During the Ghetto period, the red hat, now made into a degrading yellow, was, it seems, universally obligatory; rare exemptions were granted only to those setting out on a journey. Its wearing was also so much the more easily supervised, as in fact were all of Paul IV's restrictive edicts. To this, add the more immediately palpable aftermath of the Talmud burning, the increased emphasis on conversions, *Cum nimis absurdum*'s other, commercial limitations,[80] the fines being levied right and left in lieu of heretofore reasonable taxation, and the anxiety generated by reports that many had opted to convert or that others had left Rome in despair. There is also the fearsome account of general Jewish consternation composed by one Benjamin ben Elnatan of Civitanova (in the Marche of Ancona) after his escape from an Inquisitional jail during the riots following Paul IV's death in 1559.[81]

Yet, however extraordinary it appears, for the Jews of Rome in 1555 these events and decrees seemed mostly another crisis. There had been crises with the popes before, and surely this one, too, would pass. That it would not, nobody could know. Jewish anxieties may also have been falsely allayed, because, unlike the Catholic kings of Spain in 1492, the popes of Rome had not instructed the Jews to convert or leave. Instead, the Jews of Rome were told to convert or stay—within, to be sure, the Ghetto's limits. It is thus no wonder that Rome's Jews took over thirty years even to *begin* to admit that—determined either to convert them or isolate them until they did convert—the popes had permanently changed the rules. This was a situation no Jewish community had ever confronted. All of this the Jews admitted only grudgingly and with doubtful conviction, to judge from their day-to-day behavior. The initial impact of the Ghetto may have been lessened by the possibility of leaving the Ghetto area during the daytime, and of dealing with Christians commercially (in the few remaining unrestricted spheres). Jews even continued the occasional use of Christian arbiters in purely Jewish litigation.

But the rules had changed. Nor was the issue solely one of the papacy challenging Jewish religious belief. There was also the matter of Jewish social culture. For if the Jewish subculture, especially where it stood at cross-purposes to Catholic (clerical) culture, was a source of friction, then any pressure the existence of the Ghetto exerted on the Jews to change their faith had to bring in its wake a demand to modify the Jewish cultural essence. Isolation in a ghetto thus forced the Jews to confront not one, but two forms of integration. Until they rejected not only Judaism but also the distinguishing signs of Jewish subculture, they were condemned to remain physically isolated. This was a dilemma not unlike the one faced by Jews living in Western Europe two centuries later. They too—as a prelude to social integration—would be pressed to reconsider the bases of their social existence.

In the sixteenth century, however, this social issue was something nobody—neither popes, nor Romans, nor Jews—could consciously articulate. If for no other reason, this was not an epoch that privileged cultural and social issues over matters of faith. Nobody was capable of saying, as indeed would be said in the nineteenth century with respect to Jewish social integration, that the Jews' social diversity was as unwelcome as their religious uniqueness.[82]

How much the more difficult it was then for the Jews in the sixteenth century to respond directly to the new challenges they faced. In addition, on a social and cultural level, despite the Ghetto, the Jews themselves did not significantly change—nor did they see a need to change. Their past behavior had allowed them to be as simultaneously Jewish and Roman as they desired; and Roman Christian society had agreed to this duality—to be sure, provided that the Jews accepted canonically restrictive norms. Hence, Jews could not appreciate that paradoxically it was a cultural—alongside the traditional religious—issue that was making their problems so acute.

Fortunately, however, in sixteenth-century Rome such misapprehension became a virtue rather than a vice, as did the lengthy denial of having been excluded. For the truth is that regarding their own best interests, not simply out of inertia or obliviousness, it was preferable for the Jews of Rome, on social, cultural, institutional, and even intellectual levels, to ignore the Ghetto's cultural challenge and keep marching in place. And this is precisely what they did, certainly during the Ghetto's opening decades, and, judging from the textual record, for even longer. If we look at their daily behavior, at their Jewish lives, even where on an everyday basis they came into contact with pontifical authorities, we will see hardly any "fear and trembling." What preoccupied them were issues that no one, by any definition, would call traumatic. In response to the Ghetto—and by way of well-codified patterns of response—Jews persisted in that which was rooted in their social and cultural structures and memories. As we will now see, it was this constancy, this tacit persistence, and this commitment to their own Roman-Jewish culture—or Jewish-Roman culture, if you will—which did so much to ensure that Roman Jews would survive with their identities essentially intact.

2 / What Is in a Name?
or, The Matrices of Acculturation

JEWS AND CHRISTIANS in sixteenth-century Rome, we have said, were two "likes" that were not the same, a predicament that seems to have eluded even the Jews themselves. Jews had always known of the religious gap distancing them from Christians and of the consequences of remaining steadfastly Jewish. But they never could have realized that the subtleties of social comportment and custom that were theirs alone might generate palpable friction with society at large, especially Rome's ecclesiastical leadership. Ironically, it was just these subtle behavioral differences and the ways they were maintained—the modes and matrices of acculturation, and the settings in which they were acted out—that combined to create a Roman Jewish subculture and also functioned to ensure this culture's continuity.[1]

To wit: In 1554, Elia and Joab, sons of the prominent rabbi and advocate Abramo Scazzocchio, swore to neither gamble nor eat in any *osteria* located in Rome or less than two miles away, irrespective of whether "the owner was a Jew or [as it was invariably said] a *goi*." The central issue was gambling, a kind of Jewish disease in Italy; one has only to read the autobiography and letters of the famous Venetian Rabbi Judah Aryeh di Modena.[2] Nonetheless, if Elia and Joab Scazzocchio dined at an *osteria*, it is

67

not at all clear what they would have eaten, for this was more than simple accommodation. At issue were matters of mixing and coping in a potentially alien world, as well as the retention of Jewishness while finding avenues of social participation—and survival. Accordingly, this was a question of acculturation, adding to one's cultural identity through adoption, adaptation, and modification, rather than a question of assimilation, blemishing one's cultural essence through negation and abandonment, and leading, often, to outright denial.[3] Jewish acculturation in sixteenth-century Rome thus required that Jewish behavior be rooted in a set of time-honored principles simultaneously distinguishing Jews from others, yet also sufficiently elastic to make Jews comfortable both at home and in Roman society as a whole.

Child-adoption, for example, was not new in the sixteenth century. It is spoken of in Tuscany, in previous centuries, but what it constituted is another matter. We know of foster-parenting, God-parenting, even taking in unrelated children and making them heirs. Full adoption in the modern sense may also have occurred. These phenomena have been studied in detail for this period in France, and the parallels are instructive. The formal law, it seems, shunned adoption as not in the natural order of things, especially when property was bequeathed to those not related by blood. Yet something akin to full adoption did take place, using the notary to draw up the contracts. These contracts often specified that adoptive parents were "to love the child as their own" and to act as though the child had been "born of their own bodies." The reason for adoption often seems to be simply that the parents were childless, and girls were adopted as easily as boys. There might also be *donationes inter vivos*, "irrevocable gifts," to ensure testamentary bequests.

When Jews in Rome adopted—admittedly, there are but two examples of this—here, too, the notary was the intermediary. The reason for adoption was also childlessness. Thus Angelo q.m Salomone di Scazzocchio and his wife Diana were not young when in 1569 they adopted the girl Tutto Bene, whose mother had died and whose father now gave her up. Angelo and Diana were also directed to love the child as though she was their "real daughter," and Diana was told "to love and care for her as though Diana had given her birth." Yet, in the halachah, at this time at least, legal adoption did not exist. The solution the notary proposed was that Tutto Bene be adopted as an "irrevocable gift," a classic halachic term; it would be too risky to speculate whether the notary, Isaac Piattelli, had taken his cue from the *donatio inter vivos* of (Christian) Roman Law, with the donation now being the child, not the property the child was to inherit. Yet however Piattelli reached this solution, it is clear that although Jews shared goals and motivations with Christians, including parallel terminology, their mode of effecting and legitimating adoption had to be made to rest on indigenous Jewish roots and legal fonts. This was acculturation in full flower. There was also a practical addition that was strictly Jewish, perhaps unique to Roman Jews. For as a sign of affection, and to complete the adoption, Angelo and Diana changed the child's name from Tutto Bene, that of her natural grandmother (this was the Roman Jewish naming practice), to Graziosa, the name of her now adoptive grandmother. This mode of acculturation through faithfulness to Jewish roots was the rule.[4]

Still, acculturation in Rome was specially facilitated, for it moved along a two-way street. For example, in 1554, Agostino Spagnolo registered a complaint before a Jewish notary that a certain Jacobo called Tatò had taken possession of his apartment without permission, by promising the owner a higher rent. Probably intentionally, Agostino was invoking the centuries-old, yet recently reissued (1554) ordinance of one Rabbi Jacob Tam, prohibiting a Jew from renting a house whose Jewish tenant had fled after the rent had been abruptly and sharply raised. The appeal by Agostino, a Christian, to this internal Jewish protective legislation—this resort by the majority to minority procedures—could only have quickened the pace of Jewish acculturation, persuading Jews to believe that Roman society had received them well, and easily. Some Christians were familiar enough with Jews to have learned elements of Judaeo-Romanesco, which they erroneously referred to as *hebraico*.[5]

With a reciprocal ease, the Jews adopted Italian grammatical usages, even into the formal Hebrew of notarial texts—and sometimes with what to us may be humorous effect. For instance, in rental contracts, notaries consistently seem to ignore whether the owner was a man or a woman and refer to dwellings as *habayyit shelah*, her house—as opposed to the normative Hebrew, which distinguishes between *habayyit shelah* and *habayyit shelo*, his house; that is, the notaries were following the Italian rule, which like French insists that nouns and their pronouns agree in gender.[6] Nor was this all. *Bayyit* (house), in Hebrew, is masculine. The origin of the feminine pronoun in *habayyit shelah*, therefore, is its agreement with the Italian for house, the feminine *casa*. It is clear in which language Roman Jews framed their thoughts—even to the point of unwitting distortion. *Lehitqadshah*, says one notarial act, for the Italian *sposarsi*, to be married, a form that in Hebrew, in this context, would be "to marry oneself"; more, the notary has tacked on a feminine pronoun: "to marry *her*"; the limits dividing Hebrew from Italian have been blurred beyond recognition.[7]

Italian usages were also consciously adopted. In 1552, Rabbi Abramo Scazzocchio described an engagement by saying that the parties had reached the stage of *teqi'at kaf* and *qinyan*. There was nothing new in Hebrew about *qinyan*, a symbolic act of purchasing signifying that a betrothal had taken place. However, *teqi'at kaf*, the "planting of a hand," a public handshake by the contracting parties to seal an engagement agreement, translates—and imitates—the ritualized Italian *impalmamento*.[8] Clever translation justifying novel practice thus enabled Jews to assimilate parts of Italian matrimonial procedure into their own.

Epitomizing adoption and adaptation, of course, are the notarial acts that inform this present study—acts drawn by notaries who were rabbis, writing in Hebrew (and eventually Italian) between 1536 and 1640, but who were also learning and borrowing forms from Christian counterparts. This extraordinary effort allowed Rome's Jews to transact business previously carried out before a Christian notary—in particular, the formal registration of rentals, partnerships, and the like. More important, these acts bespeak a consolidation, if not an unprecedented institutionalization of Jewish modes of arbitration: the internal adjudication of disputes, particularly those concerning marriage, wardship, inheritance, and intracommunal affairs. Without the notary, a social intermediary whose activities substituted, I would argue, for those of otherwise lacking or weak Jewish institutions, the shape of Jewish life might have been quite different.[9] We will examine these problems closely in the coming chapter.

The principal notaries, the father and son, Rabbis Judah and Isaac Piattelli, were also members of one of those five select Roman Jewish families tracing their origins in Rome to the time of the Caesars. That these probable defenders of the status quo nonetheless pioneered the development of a Jewish notarial art (*ars dictaminis*) illustrates the measure of Roman Jewish acculturation. No less important is this development's lateness, generations after the notarial art had become finely honed among Christians. Late, too, was the development of the professional Jewish advocate or lawyer, personified by Abramo ben Aron Scazzocchio, an ubiquitous figure throughout the notarial acts.[10] This delay, or lag, in Jewish acculturational rhythms has great significance, as we shall see.

Beyond the information the notarial acts convey and the situations they describe, they reveal the social and cultural principles on which Roman Jews built their lives. And more than any other source, they betray the dramaturgical rituality of the everyday, such as the tearful plaint of a certain Ricca, which was really a sophisticated exposition of legal principle taught to her by her lawyer,[11] once again, Abramo Scazzocchio. These notarial acts thus reveal a set of social codes. A prime example is the use of names.

A certain Elia di Jeruham was referred to by the notary as Elia di Haninah. This was no scribal error. For another Han(an)iah, we are told, was commonly called Clemenzio. But Clemenzio—that is, God's mercy —is precisely what all three names, Hananiah, Haninah, and Jeruham, mean. Writing in Hebrew, the notary always preferred the Hebrew name; he added the Italian, if at all, only for added identification. By contrast, the people who came before the notary spoke Italian and regularly called themselves by the vernacular name they used naturally and commonly on the street. In the case of Elia, therefore, his almost certain response of "Clemenzio" when the notary asked his father's name was automatically translated: once as Haninah, and a second time as Jeruham.[12] A Roman Jew thus had two names: a Hebrew one, used formally by the notary and ritually in the synagogue, and a vernacular one, the one he or she used in public.

What, then, is in a name? A great deal, for this double Italian usage smacks of the advice of the nineteenth-century Russian *maskil*, or Jewish Enlightener, Judah Leib Gordon, who urged his fellows to be "a Jew at home, a 'man' on the street."[13] Clemenzio (or his son Elia) certainly had no intention of going that far, with the implication that in public Jews should leave their Judaism behind. Clemenzio-Jeruham's double persona distinguished rather between sacred and profane. With respect to the latter, Clemenzio was an Italian—more properly, a Roman—side by side with his being Jeruham the Jew. Yet he would no doubt have balked at having his essentially Jewish identity mistaken. For however much, as an individual, Clemenzio felt himself at home in Roman secular society, the people around him, the non-Jews, he unfailingly called Goim, the Goi, or the Goyah. Never is a Christian identified with anything but his or her "caste" name.[14]

Nonetheless, Jews lived with these Goim, drank and gambled with them, did business with them, and even used them as arbiters. Food too—as we have seen with reference to the ubiquitous Roman taste for anchovies, sardines, tuna, dried meat, table and spiced desert wine, and such spices as pepper, cloves, cumin, and nutmeg, *noce moscatta*—created significant commonplaces.[15] Yet food is also a key to subtle distinction. For do not food and how it is consumed signify groups, memories, and identities, and reflect social image, status, and the relations between genders? And does not food also help to define boundaries between the sacred, the profane, and those entitled to perform sacred or sacramental acts? "What is in a meal?" asked the noted anthropologist Mary Douglas,[16] trying to fathom the taxonomy of the Jewish dietary laws—laws that, despite common tastes, did distinguish the Jew and limit Jewish-Christian table fellowship. Obviously, reflecting on this point, the answer to Douglas's famous question is "far more than we observe on our plates!"

Thus exhibiting perhaps second thoughts, one convert had his sister, still a Jewess, bring him regularly the traditional Sabbath stew, cholent.[17] At the other extreme, to defend a bishop who had cast doubt on the veracity of the blood libel at Trent in 1475, it was said that as a Christian his record was unblemished; it was known that he never violated the ancient canonical prohibitions and dined with a Jew.[18] At Rome, a fifteenth-century extension (it would seem) of these perennially reissued canons set Saturday as the market day for Christian merchants. Jews—both *Judaei* and *Judaeae* are explicitly mentioned—were to set up their stalls on Fridays alone.

Yet, here, too, there was a fine balance: Jews formed over half the spice merchants in the provincial towns outside the Roman capital. Did they sell their wares only on alternate days?[19] Moreover, if at Rome the statutes fixed a Jewish and a Christian market day, they said nothing about the customers' identity; thus the statutes' ostensibly original intention was facilely flouted. Indeed, should we portray for ourselves Jews and Christians indifferently jostling each other in the market and selling food one to another—a practice the papal bull *Cum nimis absurdum* deliberately sought to purge—we may better perceive why, as we have already seen, one Roman Jewish woman apparently chose to ignore this restriction and succinctly summarized the entire bull by saying: "the pope has ordered us [Jews] to sell our homes," or as another Jew put it, "the pope has ordered us to live together."[20] This manner of speech surely betrays the same ambivalence as Clemenzio's double Italian-Hebrew name. The new regime, they are apparently saying, has decided to limit where we Jews may live, and the other clauses of the bull *Cum nimis* have little import; except for the question of domicile, they scarcely affect our daily lives, our way of doing things, and the kind of person we meet at home or in our work. Indeed, the economic effects of the bull would be sensed only decades later.

In the twentieth century we might call this attitude denial. There is no question that Roman Jews sought to cope by avoiding outright confrontation. But that does not mean they censored their speech, for they were experienced with the moods and meddling of the papal Vicar and with the officers of the Apostolic Chamber, the papal treasury. On the other hand, few may have had direct experience with the interrogators of the Holy Office, the Roman Inquisition. Roman Jews thought they knew

exactly what they were doing.[21] Their modes of expression before the Jewish notary were thus molded to avoid pitfalls, but not out of fear. Nor do
we hear echoes of the kind of episode narrated by the chronicler Benjamin ben Elnatan, writing five years later about his arrest in Civitanova,
his difficult journey to Rome, his imprisonment in Rome's inquisitional
jail, and about the flight, conversions, and bankruptcies among Jews in
the Papal States outside of Rome in the wake of the bull *Cum nimis*.[22]

Was Rome, then, a singular safe haven for the Jews? Psychologically,
it seems that it was, even if they were obligated to make peace with duality. They frequented the Jewish notary more on Sundays—when business
with Christians was out of the question—than on other days; yet they had
no compunction to stipulate in the acts that they would pay their rents (as
did all Romans) by *natale*, Christmas—the word written, to be sure, in
Hebrew transliteration.[23] Jews also had no problem referring to locales in
Rome as San this or San that, albeit often in a Hebrew that dropped the S,
leaving "'An" this or "'An" that, a usage suspect enough to make the Inquisition at Bologna about 1568 ask whether rather than being an abbreviation for San, "'An" was not an abbreviation for the derogatory *agnello*,
or lamb. And the answer given was evasive.[24] But that was in Bologna,
where Roman *gergo* (jargon) and pronunciation, especially the suppres-
sion of consonants and the elongation of vowels—common to all Romans, whether Jews or Christians—was possibly unknown.

In Rome, a number of Christian practices had percolated into Jewish
behavior, including ritual behavior. Christian matrimonial practice had
noticeably modified that of the Jews. Throughout the European Jewish
world since the later Middle Ages, the custom was to engage a child, wait
a period of time, then perform the betrothal and the wedding ceremony
together—as it is done today—or just hours apart. The betrothal was the
kiddushin, giving a ring and plighting the troth (in Renaissance Christian
terms, the *matrimonium*); the wedding, the *nozze*, occurred standing under the *huppah*, the Jewish wedding canopy. In Rome, customs were different. There, like Roman Christians, Jews became engaged, waited a short
time, were betrothed, and only months later celebrated the wedding. We
have already seen how the Jewish attachment to Christian marital proce-

dures led to the use of the Hebrew *teqiʿat kaf* to translate *impalmamento*, the ceremonial handshake that sealed engagement bargaining.[25]

At the same time (reminding us that what was "like" was not truly the same), the lawyer who introduced this usage also said that the *impalmamento* accompanied an act of *qinyan*, a betrothal. His aim was to demonstrate that his client, the groom, had gone beyond the engagement and effected a betrothal, or true marriage. In which case, since the match was later broken off (albeit before the pair stood under the wedding canopy), the bride would require a costly—to her—bill of divorce. She could have walked away from an engagement merely by returning a few low-valued engagement gifts. The reasoning here was strictly Jewish. Consequently, even in the procedures of matrimony, where obvious imitation may well have convinced both Jews and Christians that their behavior was essentially the same, there were differences. Jewish and Christian societies were propelled by distinctive, if similar, cultural ideals.

This distinctiveness comes to the fore when contrasting the rights and privileges enjoyed by Jewish and Christian women as opposed to those enjoyed by men. In Renaissance society as a whole, women's (Christian women's) powers and privileges differed from city to city. For example, upper-class Venetian women had greater freedom than Florentines to manipulate their dowries and make bequests. In Florence, women's rights over property—especially to designate heirs—steadily declined from the fourteenth through the sixteenth centuries. Nonetheless, as put by one scholar: in both Venice and Florence, *potestas* was not *auctoritas*; that was reserved for men alone. Even Venetian women who owned property, principally their ever-increasing dowries, and whose husbands were perhaps dependent on this property to maintain their standard of living, were not free to initiate economic pursuits on their own. This limitation notwithstanding, already in the fifteenth century the economic clout of Venetian patrician women seems to have raised their esteem in the eyes of husbands; it may even have stimulated affection, husbands speaking of their *consorte*, the one who shared their fate. In Tuscany, with certain variations between Florence, Siena, and Arezzo, it was only in the seventeenth century that women again were granted greater freedom over their property and sometimes received legacies from their husbands that surpassed the obligatory restitution of their dowries. For by this time, it has been said, men had become less concerned with maintaining male lineages, the raison d'être for excluding women from legacies in earlier centuries.[26]

What of the Jews? Jewish women certainly did not enjoy the same privileges as men; nor should we entertain illusions about women's equality. Much as their Christian counterparts, Jewish men generally saw themselves as women's guardians and thus vouchsafed with the power to rule over them privately in marriage, and publicly as communal officials. But whatever its precise nature, that rule was heavily moderated. Jewish women in Rome often played the role of protagonist—economic protagonists, in particular—precisely as even patrician women in Venice could not. This was true irrespective of social class, although admittedly the wealthiest Roman Jew was a pauper compared with the Venetian, Florentine, or Roman merchant prince. Jews in Rome were essentially members of the middle to lower middle class; even bankers' daughters never received dowries that exceeded twice the average dowry bestowed upon other Roman Jewish brides.[27] Roman Jewish women could also manage their late husbands' estates, sometimes even in the presence of adult male children, and often without the stipulation that remarriage required them to relinquish control over either their children or the estate.[28] Christian women, too, sometimes were so empowered—Venetian patricians from the fifteenth century, at least, and Tuscans from the seventeenth century—but mostly to ensure that agnatic relatives, those on the husband's side, would not divide a single large patrimony into many parts. Yet these women were often prohibited from remarrying.[29]

Ironically, the Christian women most restricted seem to have been those of Rome. As late as 1680, a statute reissued by Innocent XI excluded Christian women from inheritances (beyond the restitution of their dowries) unless they could demonstrate in court why this local statute should be vacated in favor of the statutes of *ius commune* (Roman law as applied in Italy), which did allow women to be heirs. Moreover, when Roman

Christian women made such appeals or were party to a contract, they were not free to represent themselves. A statute of 1580, whose consistent application has recently been studied, made it obligatory that any contract women entered into be countersigned by a male guardian, known sometimes as a *mundualdus*. This law, to be sure, could be—and was—used to protect women. Even years after a contract was signed and executed, women sometimes went to court to insist on a reversal, usually meaning the restitution of monies, claiming that the contract was illegal, since it had not been countersigned. Nonetheless, formal dependence on a male guardian put women at what was minimally a technical disadvantage. It certainly provided a basis for substantial concessions.[30]

By contrast, Jewish women did not require a "guardian." What Christian women obtained as legal exception or as male concession, Jewish women obtained, at least on the face of things, by legal right. In an obviously permissive manipulation of earlier restrictive legislation, the early twelfth-century Rabbi Eliezer ben Natan (the Raba"n) declared that women may freely undertake negotiations: they may *nos'ot ve-notnot*. Indeed, "women may themselves be guardians (*apitropsot*) and owners of businesses; they are entitled to contract, to borrow and lend, to pay and be paid, and to give and accept pledges."[31] How Roman Jews, not only Jewish women, coped with this transparent incongruity between Jewish and local Roman law, at least after 1580, cannot now be said. Perhaps Rome's Jews tacitly agreed among themselves never to question a contract that a male had not countersigned. These were civil contracts, after all. Improprieties would surface only should a contract be challenged or if, for some reason, it had to be registered before papal authorities. On the other hand, beginning toward the end of the sixteenth century, Jewish women seem often to contract in the company of a male, whose precise role the notary does not specify. Were Jews then accommodating themselves to the law, or does the unspecified male presence suggest they were attempting to compromise, vaguely conforming, yet equally seeking a way to allow women to go on contracting independently as in the past?

In Jewish notarial records up till this time, women contracted independently, or were made to guarantee a contract's performance. This was precisely the case with Diana, the adoptive mother of Tutto Bene/ Graziosa. For she, rather than Angelo her husband, swore to uphold the terms of the adoption. Angelo was required only to consent. Since both were active adopting parties, one might have expected the oath to have been administered to both. There was a viable middle ground here, too. Rabbi Leon Modena of Venice wrote, in his autobiography, about his late grandfather, who nominated an uncle and his wife (the mother of four children) joint—and equal—trustees and guardians of the grandfather's estate. This was in the early decades of the seventeenth century. In 1560, one Dolcebella was made the sole *apitropsit* of the orphans of Mordechai di Rossetta.[32]

Jewish women enjoyed the prerogative to remarry following divorce, which indeed they enjoyed exclusively until it was introduced, and then only tentatively, in newly Calvinist (sixteenth century) Geneva. Jewish women might also, seemingly with little or no impediment, leave bed and board, never to return. Christian women might achieve "separation from bed and board," but this was sufficiently exceptional to have required a special clause in a father's will. Or they would have to approach a tribunal, as in Venice, beginning late in the sixteenth century. In Calvin's Geneva as well, separation entailed a lengthy judicial proceeding. In Jewish Rome, a simple notarial declaration (irrespective of behind-the-scenes negotiations) seems to have sufficed; the abandoned husband might even agree to pay his wife a regular allotment.[33]

Although a Jewish girl usually did not choose her husband outright, she did have the recognized right to "refuse" (*me'un*, as it is called in halachic texts) a prospective parentally selected partner she disliked.[34] It was considered a victory for patrician Venetian women if mothers could postpone marriage from about thirteen to sixteen so that a girl could make her vocational choice more maturely: a choice between the marital bed— and a future of caring for the home—and life in the convent.[35]

Entitled to carry on business affairs on their own, Jewish women in Rome were sometimes most enterprising. One of the Ghetto's major butcheries was owned by a consortium of women as late as 1619. Some Jewish women ran shops, contractually divided profits, and sued each other, often as full partners, not as their husbands' dependents. By contrast, Italian Christian middle-class women had been eased out of the workplace, except in the sale of food or as an assistant in a spouse's atelier.[36] In the home, too, Jewish women differed from Christian counterparts, directly responsible as they were for that body of ritual that takes place only within the home. We have noted that women supervised the household's ritual purity,[37] and that they were no less responsible for the ritual purity of their own bodies, giving them significant control over the timing of sexuality. Manuals on menstruation and ritual purity urged that sexuality's basis be mutual consent between husband and wife. This was consent not only to the act itself but to modes of performance, not to avoid sin or to reciprocate the conjugal debt, but to achieve what the manuals openly called marital sanctity. However, the authors of these manuals surely did not anticipate the clever tactics of Marchigiana Tartaglia. To avoid sexual relations entirely with her unpleasant and unwanted husband Beniamino, she simply refused to go to the *miqveh*, the ritual bath, thus remaining ritually impure and sexually unavailable to any man.[38] Jewish women were also not excluded from directing public ritual. The women's section of the synagogue (traditionally, Jewish men and women pray apart) often was the site of a parallel prayer service with a woman—we know the name of at least one in Rome and of others in Germany—leading the women's responses. The convert and former rabbi Giulio Morosini wrote that parallel to the men's service in all large Italian Jewish centers, women prayed in rooms attached to the synagogue and known as *scole delle donne*.[39]

Jewish women were not burdened by what Christiane Klapisch-Zuber describes as the syndrome of the "cruel mother," the norm—at least in upper-class Florence—that forced widowed mothers to decide whether to remain unmarried, living with their children under the same roof, or, should they wish to remarry, to desert these children, who then became wards of the late husband's surviving relatives.[40] Among Jews, there was no such norm, despite the frequent efforts of male relatives to take charge. These efforts, apparently related to the "cruel mother" syndrome, remind us that with the notable exception of the right of Jewish women to be their own independent legal agents, the Jewish distinctiveness we are now engaged in describing was foremost one of degree, not essential nature. At the same time, however much Jewish male relatives were motivated to intervene in imitation of Christian practice, they were also motivated by their perception of Jewish law. The halachah assigns sons to the custody of their fathers, who are obligated to supervise their sons' education directly. Various Christians texts argue that fatherly instruction instills bad manners, poor morals, and encourages violence. Direct supervision of education is again the justification for assigning Jewish daughters to the custody of their mothers. And many daughters were indeed educated, seemingly at a higher rate than Christian girls.[41] A number of contracts apprenticing Jewish girls to learn *lavori feminile*—meaning principally fine embroidery—also specify that the mistress was to teach Hebrew *reading*.[42]

These general rules concerning custody, however, were regularly observed in the breach. The influential legal authority Moshe Isserles commented that every day divorced mothers were seen with custody of young sons; fathers arrived in the morning only to assume their educational responsibility, accompanying their sons to school. Isserles was writing in Eastern Europe, but his description applied to Rome, too, where fathers also customarily returned with a midday repast.[43] The needs of the child as an individual, what rabbinic texts explicitly called the child's "best interests"—but clearly those of the mother as well, balanced with those of the father—were here taking precedence over consideration of unrelieved patriarchal control.[44]

Those "best interests" did not come to a halt when children married, especially daughters, who were not merely transferred from the jurisdiction of their fathers to that of their husbands.[45] In those, notably few, cases of battered wives that reached the stage of litigation, fathers regularly appeared to argue their married daughters' part; Judah Scazzocchio, in particular, expressed "compassion" for his daughter Vittoria. Judah's is the strongest expression of real (not formulaic) emotion in the entire *Notai ebrei*; but, it turns out, Judah's own mother had herself been repeatedly beaten.[46] Even so, Judah's practical concern was to secure his daughter's divorce and the return of her dowry. The complex notarial acts in cases of beaten women seek optimistically to restore "marital peace," but also leave room for an eventual, equitable divorce, without forcing wives to return in the meantime to husbands they had left. These texts reflect a cycle of beatings, sometimes provoked by or following public insults and curses on the part of wives. Divorce was usually contingent on either or both of the parties being unable to modify their behavior.

In theory, striking wives was at once permitted and highly censured. Abramo Scazzocchio said that "most men do exactly this [strike their wives]—albeit there are those who hit and those who [only] chastise." But Abramo should not be taken at his word, since he said that while defending Sabato di Jeruham Capone, a known abuser. With respect to striking wives, Roman Jews from various backgrounds had to find a way of meshing discordant traditions. The appearance in the notarial texts of vague phrases such as "a mild castigation" seem to reflect both an Ashkenazi tradition, which was uniformly opposed to striking, and Eastern and Spanish traditions that were more imprecise. We should also note that sometimes the tables were turned: a husband berating a truly overbearing wife whose son had struck him, and a wife instigating her father and brothers to beat her husband, as well as the wife who may have done the hitting on her own. But it is the beating husband, such as Sabato di Jeruham Capone, who more often appears in the texts. Capone was even incarcerated following an accusation by his mother-in-law that his beatings had caused the death of his first wife, her daughter Speranza. Nor were Capone's excesses forgotten. Once the truth was discovered, the brothers of his prospective bride, Rosa di Jehudah, intervened and aided their (twenty-two-year-old!) sister to break her engagement.[47]

Typical of notarial texts, we know at least half of this story only because Capone hired Scazzocchio to claim that Capone had been betrothed, not merely engaged. No doubt Capone's hopes were the less than laudable ones of forcing concessions before granting an (obligatory) bill of divorce. These hopes were dashed. Yet over a year passed before the case was finally settled, and we know nothing about what happened in the meantime. One of the things we *can* know, however, is that the active role of the brothers in this episode, as well as of fathers in protecting married daughters in other instances, should not mislead us about the formal standing of women in court.

In the matter of litigation, too, Jewish women were considered their own independent agents. Scazzocchio made a point of "protesting," lodging a formal claim against Rosa di Jehudah herself and a separate "protest" against her brothers. Jewish women were halachically exempt from that most complex institution, the *mundualdus*, the male testator or guardian, without whom Christian women in various cities could sign no contract, conduct no independent business, and, most of all, not represent themselves before a tribunal. This last is precisely what Jewish women did. Perna Capone, for example, in fact the sister of Sabato di Jeruham, initiated litigation on her own about who should properly inherit her late brother's estate, fearing that her nieces were being prejudiced in its division. In 1538, Mazal Tov Zamat sued her own father over monies she said he owed to an orphan. And in 1541, she sued her sister-in-law, Fresca Rosa, over three rings her late brother, Fresca Rosa's husband, had given his wife in 1527, the year of Rome's great sack, during which the rings had disappeared.[48] It was also on her own, in 1556, that Ricca d'Aversa employed Rabbi Abramo Scazzocchio as her legal representative. He represented her and her alone, Rabbi Abramo said, in her desire to break an unwanted engagement to Menahem da Pisa made many years before by her late father.

Ricca's was a match that the parents, but neither of the spouses, seem to have wanted. She made no attempt to hide her apparent dislike, telling the notary: "He never smiles at me; in fact, he spurns me. This match was made strictly for money. To which Gentildonna, Ricca's mother, responded by erupting in anger: 'My child, I don't like what I'm hearing. As far as I'm concerned, what is right is for you to go with your mate. . . . After all, he is from an illustrious family, . . . [and] this [match] was God's doing. . . . Unite with your intended, and make me happy.' Nevertheless, Ricca refused [saying] 'I spurn him, I do not want him, nor do I desire him. Besides, I've endured all kinds of vilification and slurs from my intended, so I've not the faintest doubt that all he did was for money. I tell you three times over that even were I to be given a thousand thousand thousands, I'd never ever marry him.' . . . [Not to mention that] since he left Rome, he's never once written me, not even a single line."[49]

Ricca was about eighteen, an average age for a Jewish woman to marry; men married at about twenty-two or so. One suspects that Ricca was cosponsored, perhaps by her fiance Menaham, who himself apparently wanted out. Ricca quoted him as saying "to my mother, and even to my face, that 'My father [Salomone da Pisa] acted hastily to make a match for me so quickly; I'd rather want another ten years before taking a wife.'" The cosponsor could have been Rabbi Abramo himself, who had a score to settle with Ricca's prospective father-in-law, or might even have been Ricca's mother, despite a seeming fit of motherly wrath at her daughter's rejection of marriage with a scion of Italy's richest Jewish family, for this was the Roman branch of the da Pisa family. Isach Rignano, whom Ricca married within six months of the dispute and to whom she remained married for over twenty years, may have been in fact a more favorable match. Indeed, all three may have cosponsored Ricca, banding together to pay her fees.

As Scazzocchio emphasized, however, these cosponsors, if they existed, remained always behind the scenes. What is more, Ricca won her case handily—and despite the threat of her prospective brother-in-law to approach the papal Vicar's court—on the basis of its intrinsic merits, which were encapsulated in the Talmudic dictum that daughters have a right "to choose their husbands" and, more, "to refuse." It was this idea that Scazzocchio instructed Ricca to echo so dramatically in her apparently tearful plea before a panel of Jewish arbiters. But Scazzocchio also had her say that her fiance had not written a single letter after leaving Rome. Not by chance, this same, seemingly frivolous claim had formed the basis of another successful plea made in 1519 by Donnina Zarfati, daughter of the late Rabbi (and papal physician) Samuel Zarfati, to end her engagement to Judah Corbito. She had "never been satisfied" with this engagement, Donnina said; indeed, in the eight years(!) of its duration, "Corbito had never sent her a letter of greeting, much less given her gifts." Ricca's pouting that da Pisa had never written was thus to cite cold and hard legal precedent. Just as Donnina had been freed because she refused the match, so was it necessary to free Ricca, too. Moreover, just as Corbito had sent no engagement gifts, so, by extension, the gifts that Menahem's father said he had sent were not gifts of betrothal, whose receipt would have entailed a full divorce; they were only gifts of an easily reversible engagement. There had also been no ceremony in the presence of ten male witnesses, a prerequisite in Jewish Rome for a legal betrothal to take place.[50]

Yet apart from Scazzocchio, the advocate par excellence, no man ever appears alongside Ricca, not even her brother, whose very existence is known only from a random act having nothing to do with this case. Indeed, notwithstanding the case's inordinate complexities, Ricca did all her pleading on her own. And the male-controlled Community accepted her pleas, if only by tacitly sanctioning the proceedings, and thus its procedures.[51] The Community also did not cavil at women who made engagement pacts for their sons while fathers were still alive, as well as those who managed their children's inheritances in the case of consecutive marriages. One second wife made her husband include a clause in their engagement pact prohibiting a (divorced) first wife and her children from freely entering the house of the second; nor was the first wife to remove anything from the house without the second wife's special permission.[52]

Jewish women also appeared on their own before the notaries to take oaths in matters concerning marriage, inheritance, litigation, and simple business affairs. Most extraordinary was a certain Rosetta, a banker, who stipulated that if her son left Rome to establish a business, she would follow him and so would her new husband, should he desire to remain her mate.[53] All of this took place in Rome. Possibly, there were variants in other Italian cities, such as Florence. One wonders whether bit by bit Jews residing in Florence took up that city's restrictive policies toward women—albeit, in nearby (also Tuscan) Siena, Jewish women remained social protagonists. It was there that a Jewish youth, as late as 1612, told a matchmaker that his widowed mother had consented to his match with a young woman from Rome (the matchmaker, too, was a woman), for without his mother's permission he said he "would have done absolutely nothing."[54]

Jewish women thus continued to be privileged and to maintain their rights. And this was so if only because, as was the case with Ricca at Rome, the Jewish Community believed this posture to be correct. It should be added that fathers and mothers apparently sometimes saw advantages— as perhaps did Ricca's mother, Gentildonna—in breaking one engagement to allow a second, more favorable one. Thus it is hard to tell whether we should give full credence to the claim of a certain Contessa that she rejected her fiance when she saw how badly he behaved, even though her claim was seconded by her father, who said that the prospective groom was unfit and uncouth. Irrespective of who was pushing for the break, the right to "refuse" seems to have been unquestioned. This was a real right, really exercised, not the canonical privilege that parents often pressured their children not to use. Consent, too, was real—*retsonah*, "her will," not that formal consent embodied in the so-called mutual *verbum de praesenti*, "agreement in the present moment" by the two spouses, constituting a canonically valid marriage. Accordingly, Rabbi Menahem Azariah da Fano, in the Italian north, validated as an intrinsic right the decision of one young woman to "refuse" and break an engagement. And, instructively, her father was told that should he insist on the marriage, he would be guilty of "forcing" his daughter. The ones urging the "refusal" were none other than the young woman's mother and a circle—be it noted—of her mother's women friends.[55]

Parents, to be sure, relied on daughterly obedience. But nothing guaranteed it. One rejected suitor was told merely that he would have to prove himself a better suitor—the second time around. He might have consoled himself, nonetheless, because in the sixteenth century Italian rabbis decided that so proper was it to allow young women to reject an unwanted match that they extended this right of "refusal" to men. Heretofore, men had theoretically less to say about their prospective marital partners than women did. This willingness to consider children's marital preference suggests that Roman Jewish practice fully concorded with Judaism's traditional accent on the conjugal family as a distinct unit. Alternate models—patriarchal, hierarchic, multigenerational, or extended—carried little weight, as indeed they had not among European

Jewish families since at least the high Middle Ages. Reminding us of the world in which Jews had developed their family models, as well as ideals, is the plea of David Arbi. Insolvent, and unable to pay his daughter's dowry after a three-year engagement, he beseeched that the engagement not be broken off: for "What God has joined, let no man put asunder." In moments of stress, anything was apparently legitimate, even citing the Gospels. Yet prompting Arbi was no doubt the Jewish midrashic concept that "matches are made in heaven," originally taken to mean that man should not interfere to break them up. The line dividing Jewish from Christian thinking might sometimes be razor thin.[56]

But this is also to say that on occasion what might at first look like borrowings were really indigenous; that what had been taken in from the outside was no more than superficial. Indeed, regardless of family strategies, girding the rights and privileges of Jewish women at Rome were the canons, and contemporary interpretation, of halachic justice. These rights and privileges were also predicated on common consent to the halachah's frequently figurative—if not clearly contrary-to-fact—application; the role of rabbis here was moot at best.[57] To illustrate: one absolutely regular engagement, followed six months later by the payment of the dowry and a wedding, resulted in a scandal and then judicial censure when the groom claimed that his bride was not a virgin.[58] The claim was false; a group of respected women, including the bride's mother-in-law, eventually testified that they had seen the blood of virginity on the bridal sheet.

This episode is the only one of its kind (in these notarial acts). But our concern is not whether the widespread Mediterranean custom of exhibiting the bridal sheet was the Roman Jewish norm, as some rabbinic discussions suggest it may have been (throughout Italy).[59] What interests us is the potential shame and shaming of the groom, Shem Tov Soporto. For on his wedding night, Shem Tov (good name!) had been impotent. He claimed he was cursed, "knotted" into impotency, the popular name for this nearly universal superstition.[60] This disgrace Shem Tov confided only to his intimates. However, the entire episode came to light, because the halachically driven Jewish Community would not safeguard the groom's honor at the expense of the bride's.

The Community, in fact, launched a thorough investigation, during which the following sometimes ribald testimony was taken, first from Moise Cohen, then from Haim Anubo, and last from Gemma Bonanno. According to Moise Cohen di Ancona: "I met Shem Tov q.m Isach Soporto on the street called Bank Street, and I asked him where he had gone, since I had not seen him for a number of days. Shem Tov answered that he had celebrated his *huppah*, but he had been 'tied,' until the third night, when he was cured by an old man, to whom he gave a few coins. After having labored for two nights, he at last was able to do the job. He was happy and in good spirits, thank God." Haim Anubo di Moise of Rome then said that fifteen days earlier, at the exit of the Sabbath, he was in the house of Shem Tov, "and Shem Tov told him: 'Do you not know what happened to me?' . . . He had been 'tied,' and he could not [take his wife's] virginity. Shem Tov recounted that 'he had been tied by a [close] friend, whom he would never have suspected. The knot was undone by a *goi*, who led him to the river where there was a ladder made out of millstones, and there [he had Shem Tov] urinate following instructions. And he was healed; and on that very night, he took [*qiniti*] his wife.'" Finally, Gemma, the elderly widow q.m Giuseppe di Bonanno, testified that the day after the wedding she had gone to see if Ricca was *scoperchiata* (her lid was off). It was not; Ricca was a virgin. "So she asked Shem Tov if he had come to her [in the way of a husband], and if he had touched [had intercourse with] her. He replied that he had. To which she retorted: 'You came to her? Certainly not.' The next day, they called her [again]. And Shem Tov told her 'that now he knew that this was from God, for "they [his genitals] laid down [or had gone quiet]" on him.' Gemma was again called on Saturday, the next day, that is, . . . and they showed her a robe soiled with the blood of *betulin*," and she also saw the bloody sheet, although "she herself said she did not need to see it, because, praise God, she did not have an evil tongue."

Once this testimony of Shem Tov "cure" was taken, and it had become public knowledge that Shem Tov had consummated the marriage, the Community forced Shem Tov to admit the false charge in the presence of an extraordinary panel of "rabbis, rabbinical Judges, and arbiters"; indeed, the very intervention of the Community as Community was exceedingly rare. As a penalty, Shem Tov was told to double the additional sum, the so-called *tosefet*, normally paid by the groom (a percentage of the bride's dowry or wedding portion) and invariably considered a woman's possession or that of her heirs. In this specific case, the bride's possession of the *tosefet* was also stipulated in the engagement contract.[61] Women's rights, it would appear, were bound up in a system of communal propriety and a balance between men's and women's honor that insisted upon privileging the woman when to do otherwise would have irreparably tarnished her name. Shem Tov's exoneration would have meant a shameful divorce for his wife and effectively erase all chances of a respectable future remarriage.

Yet, more strikingly, the decision to defend explicitly women's honor led to a solution with uniquely Jewish aspects. To be sure, Christians did not leave betrayed or impugned women undefended. As has been documented for Rome, in particular, no adventurer could hope to take a women's virtue without compensation, often a dowry to ensure a legitimate marriage, assuming, of course, that the woman and her family lodged a complaint. In Venice, such complaints were assigned to a specific tribunal, the Esecutori alla Bestemmia. The Jews moved somewhat differently. For one thing, Jews normally confronted charges of virginity's absence by making it virtually impossible, short of pregnancy, to prove halachically that the signs of virginity had truly been lost. However, there was also the matter of redressing tarnished honor itself, and among Christians the honor needing redressing was often considered that of the luckless maid's father. Various charges of corrupting young Christian women made in Venice are specific on this score. And, accordingly, just as the Bible (Deut. 22:19) gives the collected fine to the father of a falsely accused daughter, Venetian authorities assigned fathers, rather than their daughters, the fines that were levied. For Jews, as the case of Shem Tov Soporto illustrates, the honor sullied and in need of redressing was that of the daughter, the bride. Thus they privileged the biblical injunction (also found in Deut. 22:19) that "it is improper to defame a virgin of Israel" by falsely claiming that she was not a virgin, and they doubled Ricca's *tosefet*. That is, to make their point and to redress honor as they considered proper, they were willing to take the extraordinary measure of modifying a biblical injunction and transfer the fine from father to daughter.[62]

This essentially halachic solution is not the only part of the episode that is distinctly Jewish. For to have his "knot untied," as he put it, Shem Tov had turned to an elderly *non*-Jew, who instructed him to urinate on a millstone (a symbol associated with "knotting" in at least Jewish exegesis as early as the twelfth century). But would a Christian have turned as easily to a Jew? Christians had approached Jews for magical formulae or for love potions, elixirs of love, as outraged Bishop John Chrysostom tells us they were doing as early as the fourth century (and no doubt earlier) and as the canon law repeatedly prohibited. Nor had such practices ceased. An unnamed Christian in a case brought before the Inquisition in Venice in the seventeenth century was charged with asking the Jew Abramo to discover who was responsible for his, the Christian's, wife being possessed by a devil for as many as eighteen years.[63] Nonetheless, even were Christians willing to approach Jews for the kind of magical, or near-magical, healing associated with the "knot," they would certainly not have followed Shem Tov's example and admitted freely before authorities, whether lay or religious, that they had turned to a Jew for this advice. For as we have just seen, Christian authorities would not pass over such behavior in silence.

One doubts with respect to the "knot" that Christians ever would have approached a Jew. For in this instance, what apparently was purely profane to Jews—for both Shem Tov and the Jewish Community and its institutions, for whom it was immaterial whether he was cured by Christian or Jew—was attributed by Christian authorities with sacral or sacramental overtones. A synod in Apulian Oria, in 1641, thus threatened with excommunication those who "rendered newlyweds unable to couple." The laity, too, linked "knotting" to the sacral. In 1723 (the case is late, but not the procedure), Anna Sanasi, frantic about her son's impotence, turned first to a priest, actually a Capuchin friar, Fra Gregorio Lupo, then to a "cunning" lay healer, and finally to Antonella Seppi, the *magara*, or woman magician, who was suspected of having "tied" the victim to begin with. Yet, even Seppi's proffered amulet was rejected, on the grounds that it was sacred; and proper sacrality required the intermediacy of a priest. Indeed, sacrality, or what might well be named countersacrality, the anxiety that the sacral will be misused, has been called a central concern in Christian rituals of healing and in the way these rituals were perceived by Christian layfolk.[64]

True commonality of interests hence ceased with the anxiety Jews and Christians jointly shared about the subject of "knotting." However much Roman Jews and Roman Christians had common cultural values, however much their outward behavior was similar, that behavior was affected directly or indirectly by variations in underlying confessional principles and outlooks. The Jews' firmness—yet elasticity—in safeguarding such principles was instrumental in conserving a specifically Roman-Jewish culture.

Moreover, within sixteenth-century society, the effect of confessional principles was ubiquitous. They were influential not only in shaping religious practice and private life, but also in molding public life and political attitudes. For example—and with no reference to the real issue just discussed of a daughter's virginity at marriage—Jews lacked the spiritual female role model of the Holy Virgin, so central in Christian society and social thought. Thus they were not taken up with such complexities as Mary's own immaculate conception (her unique freedom from original sin), and they had no prompting or need to idealize women's bodies as inviolable sanctums, as did Christian thinkers and especially preachers.[65] This was an excuse, of course, for placing women fully under men's tutelage and control, whether the guardian be father, husband, brother, male relative, or priest.

Jews also did not resort to the image of the body, whole and impregnable, such as the Corpus Christi, to define or symbolize political entities united and whole. Jews never developed, let alone took literally, as did

Christians, the metaphor of the Body Politic. Theoretical Jewish political perceptions, even of such concepts as representation and representative bodies, were in fact so underdeveloped that Jews seem never to have learned properly to distinguish between public and private domains. Christians had trouble doing this in practice, too. They were constantly changing their minds, for example, about which issues should be categorized under the rubrics of public or private law. But at least for Christians, theory and an ever increasing concept of the sovereign state and true political bodies existed. Attempts were also constantly made to implement these concepts in fact. For Jews, the theoretical concept of sovereignty was virtually nonexistent.[66] The consequences with respect to specifically Jewish modes of internal governance, to the extent this governance was possible, will be seen below.

This blurring of the public and private had more than political effects. The late David Herlihy argued that such blurring promotes wide-ranging behavior and initiatives in women, and also their participation in public life;[67] and this argument seems to apply well to Roman Jewish women. Nonetheless, it is the political ramifications that are the most intriguing. In my view, the utter transparency of borders between Jewish public and private domains goes a long way toward accounting for the resiliency of Roman Jewish society when Paul IV established the Ghetto— and the resiliency of its political dimension, in particular. The ability freely to pass back and forth between public to private lent that which needed to be public, the structures of Jewish arbitration, enormous flexibility; and on these structures Ghetto conditions did not impinge. Accordingly, Jews could think—I believe correctly—that the Ghetto neither violated nor structurally weakened their political order. Jews even came to see the Ghetto wall as a boundary encouraging a sense of spatial holiness. In another context concerned with overlapping cultures, such boundaries have been called "sociological walls," barriers that are simultaneously and selectively both porous and protective, hence allowing the community to take advantage—as the Roman community did within the Ghetto's spatial perimeter—of a fluid organizational structure. Individuals, for their part, could perceive in the Ghetto a safe and elastic arena, within which they might securely operate and from which they might repel assaults on their Roman-Jewish identity.[68]

Thus, Ghetto confinement may have severely stunted cultural growth, but it did not cut acculturation off entirely. In the early eighteenth century, Anna del Monte was uninhibited to name a woman convert who had pressed Anna herself to convert a *rash'ah*, an evil one; and Anna also had the strength to emerge a Jew after she was dragged into the House of Catechumens and held there for thirty days. Yet Anna retold the tale of her confinement and trials primarily in colloquial Roman [Italian] speech.[69] This fact emphasizes forcefully what we have been saying all along: the Jews of Rome were as distinctly Roman as they were Jewish— and as Jewish as they were Roman—and so they remained even in moments of crisis.

ONE FINAL ASPECT of this bifurcated process of Roman Jewish acculturation requires our attention. In so many instances, acculturation occurred after a significant gap in time. I am not referring to the obvious—that, by definition, one acculturates to "something" that already exists. I mean a demonstrable hiatus of decades and even generations prior to adoption, adaptation, and absorption. Furthermore, in many instances, Jewish behavior, notably with respect to such things as the rights of women both to inherit and to determine heirs, often seems to have exhibited patterns that some Christians once, but no longer, observed—indeed, patterns that Christians, at least statutorily, had openly rejected.[70] Hence, Jewish acculturation was selectively conservative, often restrained, among other things, by a concern for Jewish law or traditional practice. Put otherwise, between Jews and Christians there existed an acculturational gap. I caution that this gap measures the distance between "what was" and "what is." It does not refer to issues such as "modernization" or the flight from it.

This "acculturational gap" or "selective absorption" created unease among Christians. But selective absorption also had implications for Jewish stability. For what this process illuminates is that central consequence of Jewish acculturation at Rome: rather than fueling assimilation—cultural negation and disappearance—it promoted a viable subculture. In their collective mind's eye, so to speak, the Jews were not accommodating to the ways of the dominant (Christian) society. They were first selectively adopting individual practices and then domesticating them by subtle modification so that they could be inserted into, and under, the rubrics of Jewish law and custom.

Yet, however Jews understood the process of selective absorption, it must be appreciated as one of cultural creation, of converting the external into something Jewish, something part and parcel of normative Jewish practice, such as on those rare occasions when Jewish lawyers cite specific Jewish laws in their briefs, which they do opaquely, with the intent of making an opposing party, lawyer, or even a judge despair of tracing the citation's source. This device was ubiquitous among Christian lawyers of the day.[71] The Jews' "Romanness" had thus become an adjunct of even their *scholarly* Jewishness, and vice versa, which thereby enhanced, albeit somewhat perversely, Jewish cultural integrity.

Conversely, such selective absorption persuaded the Jews that their behavior conformed to the standards of their neighbors, even while the halachic wrapper in which they enveloped their actions assured them that the seemingly extraneous was intrinsically their own. By extension, therefore, no matter how much the Ghetto physically separated the Jews from Christians, psychologically the Jews never perceived it as hermetically sealing off the outside. At times, it seems that the Ghetto did not affect Jewish attitudes or behavior at all. Did it not take thirty-five years for the Jews to invent the pun-metaphor of the *ghet*, the Hebrew bill of divorce, to describe their newfound state? And who knows whether even Roman Jewry's great impoverishment after its loan banks were closed in 1682 awakened it to the full dimensions of the gap separating the Ghetto Jew from the Roman Christian—assuming, which is not at all certain, that a true caesura ever existed.[72]

In other words, because Ghetto enclosure per se did not substantially alter Jewish behavior, it became possible for Jews to convince themselves that what was Ghetto segregation, or even "divorce," was neither final nor without relief. In many ways, the situation of the Jews as a whole was akin to that of the first wife (met above) who, like a desired guest, would have come with her children into her former husband's home, had not the second wife stipulated otherwise. Thus Jews in Rome could almost casually go on playing the compound role of Clemenzio-Haninah-Jeruham and consider their presence in Rome a natural one, whose continuity, whatever papal policy specified, was never in doubt. The stage was set for a drama in which Jews could blur, or sometimes even ignore, the differences between themselves and their non-Jewish neighbors, yet recognize that as Jews, which they most definitely wished to be (as was the case with Anna del Monte), they must punctiliously foster their own, Jewish ways.

This was an advantageous bipolarity. Even in the darkness of the eighteenth century—especially after about 1750—when the popes sought to revive the direst of sixteenth-century discriminations, Jews were still studying, even writing, tracts of Italian rhetoric. That the quality and Italian style of these tracts were neither high nor up-to-date is irrelevant.[73] Ghetto confinement may have stunted cultural growth, therefore, but the Jews were convinced that they were most comfortable with a blended Jewish-Italian mode of comportment. And this conviction remained firm. Of Trieste in the late eighteenth century—admittedly a different environment with a far shorter history of ghettos, yet a history of ghettos just the same—it has been said that the Jews there had a "tradition of acculturation," an "ease and familiarity with non-Jewish realms," a "positive evaluation of the high culture of Italian Gentiles," and a perception that "neither Torah [Jewish culture] nor general culture had to yield in order for the other to have a place." This ability to balance cultures, in Rome as well as in Trieste, was, I submit, a product of selective absorption and conservative acculturation.[74]

So much for the Jews. But what of the Christians? They were not silent partners in this process, and we would like to know more. About some things we can speak with assurance; about others we may only speculate. Our best guide is perhaps the Giudiate, the mocking imitations of Jewish ritual practices that took place during Rome's raucous Carnival season before Lent. The Giudiate mocked weddings, but, even more, these ploys mocked the Jewish funeral. As we shall soon see, the Jewish funeral was demonstrably hybrid, a true example of selective absorption. And it was this hybridization that seems so to have irritated Christians. For the Jewish funeral in the sixteenth and into the seventeenth century, at least, retained practices, especially loud mourning, that Christians no longer deemed acceptable. It perpetuated behavior that lagged behind and reminded Christians of discarded modes of comportment—comportment that apparently was now embarrassing. Moreover, irritation could also be a prelude to violence. Regularly, at Carnival time, the popes issued edicts *Di Non Molestare gli Ebrei.*[75]

Selective and conservative Jewish absorption, the Jews' acculturational lag, was thus as potentially annoying as it would be to wear last year's coat to a fashion-conscious gathering, which by the way, Renaissance and early modern society often were with respect to clothing designated appropriate by law.[76] However consciously variants in Roman Jewish behavior were perceived, such as the broader initiatives exercised by Jewish women or the ability of Jewish children to reject a potential spouse, these variants were surely no less disturbing than such major and obvious differences as the nature of Jewish belief. These variants could also be extremely subtle. Slowly but surely, for example, the names of Christian women, once primarily descriptive (such as Dolcebella or Belladonna), were, under the influence of Catholic reform, becoming preponderantly those of saints.[77] Free from this influence, Jewish women continued to bear names like Dolce, Ricca, and Caracosa, the kind of non-biblical names they (as opposed to Jewish men, whose names were traditionally biblical) had borne for centuries.

Authorities, moreover, must have been uncomfortable with the Jewish notarial art, developed at least two centuries after this art was perfected among Christians, which enabled Jews to enjoy considerable de facto autonomy in settling affairs through arbitration—indeed, far more than the papacy was willing to grant and was even seeking to curtail. To compound the problem, Jewish notaries were drawing their acts in Hebrew, a language known by only a limited number of Christian savants. Isaac Piattelli, the central Jewish notary, continued drawing his acts in Hebrew until his death in 1605, and other notaries began writing in Italian only about 1580. One wonders whether this ultimate shift was purely voluntary, or was it also by order of the popes, just as Paul IV had forbidden the continued use of Hebrew in banking ledgers in 1555.[78]

Even more unsettling for the clerical hierarchy, but possibly for pious laity as well, may have been the impregnability of Jewish lay confraternal bodies to the fundamental change toward priestly spiritual direction that marked post-Tridentine organizations of this type. Jews did enhance confraternal pietism, making (often kabbalistically oriented) prayer into a central confraternal activity.[79] But a rabbinic presence was at best ancillary, meaning that the Jews developed their own brand of "interiorized piety" without a parallel to the priestly "director of souls" so central to the early modern Catholic pietistic endeavor. It was as though, through selective absorption, the Jews were implicitly questioning the structure of contemporary Catholic religiosity. One might even cautiously say that the subculture created by Roman Jews was tacitly challenging Roman culture at large as much as it was imitating it and forwarding Jewish integration. This, I believe, gives us reason to pause.

SIMULTANEOUS CULTURAL IMITATION and confrontation was not a pattern limited to sixteenth-century Rome. Pointedly, it has been argued recently that the so-called Liberals and the Liberal movement in early nineteenth-century Germany originally opposed Jewish emancipation, the granting to Jews of equal civil rights, just because these Liberals—who constantly linked issues concerning both Catholics and Jews—were convinced that Jewish culture was detrimental to Liberal political goals. This was wholly apart from the question of religion and religious belief. In the words of Dagmar Herzog, the Liberals "perceived Jews [not Ghetto Jews, but acculturated, German-speaking and educated Jews, ostensibly integrated into German society], to be the ones who were peculiarly illiberal, resistant to modernity, and uncompromising." In the words of these Liberals themselves: "[Jews were the] 'most stubborn devotees' of 'stagnation.' "[80] It requires only the substitution of "selective absorbers" for "stubborn devotees," and "conservative acculturation" for "stagnation," to realize that with respect to subculture and integration the essential terms had changed little. This was true on both sides of the fence—irrespective of how new were the specifics: historical, geographical, ideological, and, most important, the modes of expression.

For what *grosso modo* the nineteenth-century Liberals opposed was the kind of Jewishness embodied in the syndrome of Clemenzio-Jeruham. What they wanted, much as Pope Paul IV had wanted three hundred years before, was legal discrimination, if not political and social segregation, until the Jew became fully a German, meaning a liberal German, and preferably a Christian one, too.[81] To which challenge, enlightened German Jews responded, as effectively sixteenth-century Roman Jews had done before them, by denial, by reemphasizing their commitment to German culture, yet simultaneously integrating that culture into intrinsically Jewish expression. One example is the *History of the Jews* written in the 1850s by Heinrich Graetz, with its praise of (German) philosophical rationalism, its criticism of the Catholic Church, and its loyalty to secular rulers.[82] Jews also developed their own version of *Bildung*, the humanistic German educational ideal, as well as an explicitly woman's mode of Jewish life informed not only by traditionally Jewish comportmental modes but by essentially German ones, too.[83] Yet, in this behavior, Jews were unknowingly questioning and distancing themselves from German culture as much as they were absorbing it. For *Bildung*, the aesthetically enlightened and universalistic culture espoused by such as Wilhem von Humboldt toward the close of the eighteenth century, had been superseded at the start of the nineteenth. As George Mosse has written, "through their [the Jews'] consistent commitment to Humboldt's [brand of] *Bildung* rather than to that nationalized and romanticized concept of self-cultivation which had managed to pervade popular piety and culture . . . there was danger of isolation."[84] In short, the Jews were caught in the crossfire of an acculturational lag.

This German pattern may help explain the course of events in the late nineteenth and early twentieth centuries in Italy, where the exit from the Ghetto of Jews who had been acculturated and Italianized for centuries inaugurated a rush to enter Italian civil society fully and to expand their Italian cultural horizons. Much work remains to be done before this process is well understood. But some things safely may be said, especially that it was not a process of Jews seeking to abandon their Jewish culture. Rather, Italian Jews had much in common culturally with those German Jews who believed that "above all, in a study of Goethe one finds [and discovers] one's Jewish substance." Yet in believing this—convinced that they had achieved a true cultural symbiosis—these Italian Jews had also likened themselves to those German Jews who, as again Mosse comments, "chase[d] a noble illusion."[85]

For in Italy as in Germany, this striving for an acculturational symbiosis was found wanting—and, worse, out of step with the drive toward cultural, nationalistic, and religious particularism that took place in Italy in the 1920s. Some Italian Christians began querying whether Jewish acculturation was sufficient, whether, in fact, full Jewish absorption into Italian society was possible.[86] From here, of course, the road was open, directly or indirectly, to the racial anti-Semitism of Italian Fascist circles. The recent historiography that ascribes all anti-Jewish excesses in Fascist Italy to the Nazis alone, I would add, has ignored a great many cultural-historical events.[87] Paradoxically, this historiography's exponents seem to have extended to contemporary Italy that overly optimistic approach to Renaissance Jewish life which paints a simplified portrait of *convivenza*.[88] Rather, the complex modes of selective and conservative Jewish acculturation during the Renaissance and the *un*sympathetic reaction that this behavior evoked had not come to a halt, even in the fullness of the twentieth century.

This leads to a closing thought, a suggestion for comparative research. In the modes of coping, and the responses thereto, of an acculturated minority enticed by but not wholly submissive to a majority culture, a majority culture that would balk at the prospect of moderating its essence even one iota, there are features—features, not identities—that remain constant over the *longue durée*. And this is so, irrespective of the national or chronological clothing in which that coping is dressed, and irrespective also of specific majority and minority identities.[89]

3 / Social Reconciliation, from Within and Without

IN 1843, an English visitor to the Roman Ghetto wrote that the Jews there were "governed by Judges of their own."[1] This was not strictly true. Jews had no formally appointed Jewish judges, exercised no primary jurisdiction, and could not—nor had they ever been able to—require Jews to use exclusively Jewish tribunals in order to resolve internal disputes.[2] Roman Jews were also under no illusions, knowing well that they would be sharply censured should they enact a statute threatening to excommunicate Jews who turned to Christian tribunals—which is precisely what happened in Venice, whose Jewish Community did enact such a statute in the 1630s. During the debate on this statute in the Venetian Senate it was said for the first time that the Jews constituted "a small republic of their own," a phrase that would be developed about two hundred years later into the ominous "a state within a state."[3] Yet this charge, just like the claim of our nineteenth-century traveler concerning Rome, was not baseless. By cultivating an effective system of voluntary arbitration—an instrumentality long known in Jewish law but brought to perfection in the sixteenth century, thanks largely to innovations wrought by Jewish notaries, perhaps the real novelty of this time—the Jews of Rome found a way to resolve communal and interpersonal disputes despite their lack of

99

more coercive judicial means.⁴ In doing so, they had come upon a prime tool for coping and survival, one so efficient that the pope's Roman Vicar, the official in charge of all spiritual matters and violations in the city, tried to exploit the system of Jewish arbitration to his own advantage.

Arbitration, however, to whose details I will return, was only one of various modes of coping that the Jews employed. Moreover, coping through means like arbitration depended on selective absorption and conservative acculturation. Some words about Jewish social conservatism are thus in order.

Roman Jews were generally reluctant to change, adopt, and adapt. They had not followed the lead of Christian legislators in Tuscany and elsewhere, from about the later fourteenth century, who had decided to restrict severely women's rights to inherit and bequeath.⁵ This reluctance surfaces again in the operations of Jewish social confraternities, and was pervasive in intellectual realms, particularly Jewish mysticism, such as Lurianic Kabbalah. It has been suggested that through resort to what has been called Lurianic Kabbalah's mythical inversive potential, which exegetically allowed saying, thinking, and imagining the unabashedly new in the guise of the venerably old, the Jews paradoxically propelled themselves toward modernity.⁶ Yet true kabbalistic speculation was practiced by a highly select elite. Its product is no measure of how the moderately educated majority of the Jews thought, for their mystical knowledge went only so far as to reinforce traditional Jewish messianic hopes. The modernity in question looked essentially inward, and did not illuminate the high road traveled by most Jews toward encounters with later, particularly assimilationist, challenges.

The writing of history, too, made little progress. The desire of Joseph HaCohen, in his mid-sixteenth century work the ʿEmeq ha-bakha (*The Vale of Tears*), to write a sophisticated Jewish political history entwined with that of the nation's receded before a preference to recount tales of bloody woe. Other histories limited themselves to reciting chains of scholarly tradition, describing the transmission of learning from one generation to the next. The hurdle was not esoterism, separatism, or a resurgence of a rabbinic authoritarianism intent on preventing larger groups from reading suspect books now that printing might facilitate their distribution.[7] What had to be overcome was a Jewish world that could modify itself—modernize, if you will—no faster intellectually than it found it expedient to undertake social revision, which it did with caution.

This is not to say that the Jews had a retrograde society. In fact, Jewish resistance to indiscriminate adaptation paradoxically conferred what may seem today a modernistic quality upon sixteenth-century Jewish society, a quality visible in Jewish (as opposed to Christian) women's wide-ranging economic pursuits—even though these pursuits no doubt reflect the tenacity of medieval Jewish women's economic practices. No less modernistic was the degree of individual privilege within the family unit. Eventually, however, this social modernism failed to develop and, like intellectual advances, it began to march in place. Any real drive toward modernization was vanquished by the need to preserve what has been named "social memory": the consciousness of group identity perpetuated through repetitive social and intellectual practices and patterns.[8] Modification and modernization could be justified only as the embodiment of tradition rightly understood, the new created by reformulating the old. Yet such a process was, and is, necessarily self-limiting. It operates within a predefined set of ideas and cultural structures, the bounds of whose flexibility, like a radius jutting out from the center, define the size and circumference of the circle itself—in this case, the circle of permissible and admissible social programs, actions, and, most of all, novelty. Conservatism within this circle of permissibility provides, positively, a wall and a refuge against threatening external change. Negatively, it allows no change at all. In Rome it favored the continuity of institutions whose preservation was deemed vital for Jewish self-interest. Where this cultural and structural conservatism was most visible in Jewish Rome (the question of the status of women aside) was with respect to institutions of communal control.

One might say that a hallmark of early modernity was the achievement of truly formalized governmental institutions, whether in monarchies, duchies, or city-states, or through the effective application of discipline from the top down within the Church. These were institutions that created a new concept of right social order: hierarchical institutions run by a fully professional bureaucracy.[9] Jewish resistance to these forms, and to such formalization, was enormous. Jews never achieved a true definition of political office; what today is generally taken for applied Jewish political thinking in the Middle Ages and later are really discussions about the prerogatives of distinguished scholars as opposed to the powers competing laymen were claiming.[10] Similarly, Jewish debates about matters so crucial to Christian theorists as majority rule rarely considered majorities within the context of true representative bodies possessing *plena potestas*, the full power to bind constituencies, one of Christian political thought's major advances. When the notion of *plena potestas* was debated, it was quickly shunted aside. This happened in the case of the twelfth-century Jacob Tam, in French Champagne, and it would seem to have happened again in the case of the *Capitoli* of Daniel da Pisa, whose reference in the preamble to legislative sovereignty was never echoed in practice. But then again, any tendency—Jewish or Christian—toward institutional clarity in Rome was submerged by the confusion inherent in that city's multiplicity of judicial, administrative, and governmental bodies, no matter how formalized these bodies theoretically were.[11] Thus, although Roman Jewry was aware that without appropriate mechanisms the Community would be placed at the mercy of papal and Cameral policies, especially fiscal ones, as would its ability to provide essential services such as ritual slaughtering, a ritual bath, and halachic burial, nonetheless it paid little attention to the nature and development of its institutions per se. Institutional consciousness, let alone clear institutional definition, never properly matured.

The absence of a sense of office, and consequently officialdom, is well exemplified by Roman Jewry's failure to achieve a civic rabbinate—a formally appointed communal rabbi or a full-time rabbinic board—though the Communal Council did bestow the title "servant of the Community" upon rabbis who performed such tasks as overseeing the kashrut of meat and supervising the oaths people took to pay taxes. Throughout Italy, communal rabbis appear in only the smaller and, unlike Rome, constituently homogeneous communities, where the rabbi was frequently perceived as a communal servant, not as a leader. To be sure, rabbis were treated with respect and deference. Yet this respect was limited. The claim of some Italian rabbis to be called to the Torah ahead of *kohanim*—purported descendants of the ancient Jewish priestly tribe and whose precedence time-honored ritual prescribes—was not made good. How much the more, then, did rabbis never attain the sacrality accorded to priests at this sixteenth-century moment of enhanced priestly sacrality. The basis for rabbinic authority remained—as it always had among European Jews—individual charisma and prestige. It was the aura of grandeur surrounding Judah Mintz of Padua that ensured the observance, without appeal and for generations afterward, of ordinances he unilaterally issued in 1506.[12]

Even excommunication, the *niddui*, which by convention only rabbis could pronounce, must be understood as an administrative device, geared more to coercing proper behavior than to separating a renegade from the community—the paraphernalia of *potestas* or even *auctoritas*, one might say, not a sacramental instrument with sacral effects. So, too, at the bed of the dying, the rabbi may have heard a (sometimes perfunctory) confession—whether the rabbi, who was also the notary recording the confession, was functioning as the former rather than the latter is moot—but he never achieved any of the sacrality of a priest dispensing the last rites.[13] In the event, it would be hard to ascribe sacrality to heads of biological families, which, unlike celibate Catholic priests, rabbis *always* were. Sacrality would also be hard to ascribe to persons who, as was often the case, were forced to earn a living by engaging in such profane pursuits as lending money. Throughout the rabbinate's history, few if any were able to support themselves from the rabbinate itself; rabbinic sacrality as we sometimes think of it is a product of Eastern Europe in the nineteenth century rather than Western Europe in the sixteenth.[14]

None of this may be interpreted as a victory of lay over spiritual leadership after protracted struggle. Lay control at Rome was a fact of life. Hence, Roman Jewish authorities employed rabbinic "servants of the Community" to oversee certain rituals, but in most areas the laity acted directly, overseeing, for instance, the taxation whose regular collection was essential to maintain peace with the Apostolic Chamber. This is not to say that the body of three Jewish *fattori*, as confirmed by the formal Communal Constitution—the *Capitoli*, prepared by one Daniel da Pisa and ratified by the pope in 1524—ever emerged as an exclusive ruling institution.[15] Nor did da Pisa's mandated Communal Council of Sixty exercise definitive power. We may recall that in the case of the "knotted" Shem Tov Soporto the resolution was entrusted to a designated panel of "rabbis, rabbinical judges, and arbiters"; that is, nobody was quite sure where the seat of Jewish communal authority lay, not to mention the font of power. The *Capitoli* broach this subject, but no more than that.[16]

Contributing to this ambiguity was the continued existence of Jewish confraternities as separate entities. They were neither conterminous with the formal Community, nor, as Christian confraternities were increasingly becoming, veritable extensions of a hierarchical ecclesiastical regime. These Jewish confraternities, especially the Gemilut Hasadim, the good works burial confraternity, functioned much as confraternities *had* functioned in the medieval (Christian) city, but no longer did: as neighborhood organizations, united around common interests such as service and piety, complementary to other civic bodies, but not subsumed by them. Jewish confraternities also did not replicate the Catholic confraternal trend to be directly overseen by priests. Normally, Jewish confraternities operated without benefit of clergy, in this case the rabbis, who were needed only to clarify legal points, and who were employed, literally, at confraternal pleasure.[17]

Moreover, rabbis lagged well behind the Catholic clergy in attempting to sacralize hitherto mundane activities, confraternal or otherwise.[18] Nor did they begin such efforts before the seventeenth century; and even then we find the Jewish laity as arbiter of which sacral practices to accept. The members of one confraternity did not shirk even to modify a rabbinic initiative. Reshaping rabbinical and, in fact, Communal instructions to moderate, if not eliminate, the merrymaking characteristic of vigils commonly held on the eve of a boy's circumcision, they proposed offering the recently introduced stimulant, coffee, to those who had come to pray, ensuring their wakefulness. To those who had come only to socialize, coffee would be denied. Others seemed to have ignored these instructions entirely. In 1727, the most influential rabbi of the entire Roman Ghetto period, Tranquillo Corcos, was still bewailing the "vain and ridiculous activities" in which people engaged on circumcision eve.[19]

Despite claims to the contrary, therefore, it is doubtful that Jewish sacrality at this time ever managed to establish itself as a realm fully distinct from the profane. In Jewish practice, sacred and profane in varying proportions were permanently intermingled.[20] Indeed, in some ways, the principal statement made by even Jewish devotional confraternities was a social one. Through the introduction of coffee in their gatherings, with caffeine's well-known effects, these confraternities managed to shift the hour of often mystical and spiritually unfettered devotions from morning to night. Night, the time of enforced enclosure in the Ghetto, was being turned into a time of liberation. Thus enclosure in the Ghetto became a liberating space.[21]

The boundaries between sacred and profane were forever being crossed and innovations sometimes introduced, but there was no decisive tilt away from the status quo or, for that matter, toward new institutional formalization. This reserve is specially evident in the domain of sexuality. Christian manuals of comportment composed by priest-confessors aimed at sanctifying the profane through restraint, distance, and mostly abstinence.[22] By contrast, irrespective of the asceticism, even mysticism, that was entering prescriptive Jewish literature at this time concerning sexual behavior, this literature never advocated limiting sexuality to lessen sin; as in the past, sexuality itself remained a "gateway to sanctification."[23] One wonders whether the bawdy sexual innuendoes about "removing lids" and "taking the honey pot" voiced by women no less, in the acts drawn by the *rabbinical* notary recording testimony in the case of Shem Tov Soporto, do not reflect this uniquely Jewish sexual viewpoint.

To be sure, the legitimate arena for sexual expression remained the family. Just as in all other spheres of life, here, too, the family retained its primacy, and as a seat of rituality in particular. The turn to devotional confraternal activity as a focus for Jewish piety only supplemented the family's ritual role. This was a lesson that was rudely learned on an even broader scale by the members of a youth confraternity in Piedmontese

Asti. Their efforts to usurp the family's overall function led directly to the confraternity's disbandment.[24]

Throughout Jewish society, therefore, modifications left essences intact, as may be seen in the transformation that occurred during the sixteenth century in the nature of Rome's synagogues. These synagogues, we have noted, were once dependencies of a geographically defined Jewish community, but had now come to resemble confraternities, attempting to function like affiliates, rather than as the communal agencies that they really were. In addition, their fluid and voluntary memberships often did *not* reflect the ethnic identities that specific synagogal names—to wit, the Scola Castigliana-Francese (The Castilian French Congregation)—at once suggest *and* negate. Also like confraternities, Roman synagogues began to enjoy autonomies, especially with respect to liturgies, governing councils, and physical quarters. This was so much so that, housed as they all eventually were in a single building, individual synagogues began to flex their muscles, and they became perpetually embroiled with one another in disputes over such issues as the placement of doors, windows, dividing walls, and even a ritual washbasin.[25] What is more, the papacy recognized the Roman synagogues as distinct *universitates*, corporations. But this somewhat murky, if technically legal, recognition did not mean— as has been ventured—that each synagogue had been detached from the whole and authorized to form new and fully independent communities. The popes had no intention, as may be seen from individual synagogal charters, of granting full, especially self-governing, corporate rights. The unified communal structure remained intact, both formally and in the eyes of the Jews themselves.[26]

We should speak then not of fragmentation but of decentralization. There was an absence of coalescence and a lack of political definition, whether in the synagogues or throughout the community as a whole: in the governing bodies, the confraternities, and even within the rabbinate itself. Likewise, the formal Community, sanctioned by the *Capitoli* (Statutes) of Daniel da Pisa of 1524, was not sufficiently empowered to dominate communal institutions collectively or even to stand in their stead.[27]

In the long run, however, this decentralization, and the willingness of Roman Jews to live with decentralization, was made to work in their favor. For with respect to true Jewish institutional empowerment, the popes at Rome, like the Venetians in the 1630s, were not willing to confer upon the Community full juridical or jurisdictional rights; and the popes would have quashed any Jewish pretensions to imitate contemporary papal initiatives leading toward a centralized regime.[28] But the popes did condone the venerable practice of temporary Jewish panels of voluntary arbitration. Nowhere in Italy, in fact, did Jews enjoy more formal power than this, even where (outside Rome) there were regularly constituted rabbinic tribunals. Moreover, not only did papal authorities condone Jewish arbitration panels, but paradoxically they encouraged them.[29] And arbitration, as it turned out, was a perfect medium for maintaining harmony between the essentially conservative, decentralized, and unformalized institutions that existed and competed with each other in sixteenth-century Jewish Rome.

As put by John Bossy, speaking of Christian society: arbitration was considered by all to be the proper setting for "neighbors" to set things aright, placing, as it did, social harmony above often cold and harsh formal justice.[30] Accordingly, the essence of arbitration, whether Jewish or Christian, was to provide justice without resorting to rigid official tribunals. Furthermore, as a traditional means of achieving social peace— and one with Jewish roots—arbitration sat well with the Jewish penchant for selective absorption and acculturation. To be sure, arbitration is a process with carefully defined procedures and a legal, even legalistic, backbone.[31] Nonetheless, it avoids the pejorative sense of judicial finality often produced by the decree of a formal tribunal—an emotion usually more divisive than healing. Nor were arbiters bound by the strict letter of the law.

With respect to Jews, arbitration's flexibility was an inducement to air disputes in a Jewish setting rather than litigate formally before outsiders in non-Jewish surroundings. The latter was seen as a blight which Jewish leaders had struggled unsuccessfully to wipe out over many centuries— including under medieval Islam, where Jewish autonomy was generally the norm.[32] Arbitration also allowed room for apparent novelties such as *meʿun*, "refusal" (to marry), to soften a potentially sharp response. In the case of Ricca d'Aversa, the halfhearted threat of her fiance Menahem da Pisa's family to protest her "refusal" appears to have been mostly a face-saving maneuver. Arbitrational flexibility thus mitigated the possible shock of novelty itself, corresponding to the modalities we have seen of selective acculturation and change.

But arbitration's attractiveness was not absolute. Sixteenth-century Roman Jewish litigants sometimes tried to pit Jewish and non-Jewish tribunals one against the other. This was, of course, often a matter of legal manipulation. People turned, or proposed to turn, to the court they believed would serve them best. Yet even proposing outside adjudication was a threat to self-regulation, though moderated by the perception that ultimately, even under pressure—and such there often was—one did best by choosing Jewish arbitration. Still, nothing could erase fully the underlying causes of this indecision: the fluidity of the bonds linking Jews as individuals to Jewish communal institutions and the difficulty Roman Jews felt in distinguishing public from private spheres and their proper place in relation to both. This, as we have implied, was a problem that Roman Jews and Christians alike confronted in dealing with the city's multiple, sometimes layered, and often overly formalized judicial and administrative bodies. I might go so far as to suggest that Romans in general and sixteenth-century Roman Jews in particular lived in a state of being permanently liminal, never quite sure when they were leaving one realm, whether public or private, and entering the other. In the absence of clarity, Jews had to navigate along most unclear borders.[33]

Jews, indeed, found themselves in need of structures similar to those of the *vicinato*, the neighborhood, and the networks of patronage and *vicini*, or friends, that had once mediated between individuals and the institutions of government and power in Renaissance towns. Hence Rome's Jews kept alive the concept of the *shekhunah* (Hebrew for neighborhood) in their tiny Ghetto despite the contemporary weakening of the concept of *vicinato* among Christians.[34] At the same time, Rome's Jews were cultivating an even more effective means of compensating for the liminality of the public and private, as well as linking the individual with the prob-

lematically defined and decentralized institutions of the Jewish community. This means was the Jewish notary. The notary, the so-called *Sofer
Meta*, together with his registers, which include the texts of arbitration, at
once symbolized the Jewish public realm, to the extent that it existed, and
was the instrument of its activation.[35]

There is no way of knowing precisely when the first Jewish notary began drawing acts. But based on the work of earlier notaries from the 1530s,
it is clear that a quantum leap toward perfecting the Jewish notarial art
was taken by Isaac Piattelli, the principal author of the acts. Piattelli, it
should be stressed, developed his techniques during the 1540s and 1550s,
in other words before the Ghetto's foundation, not in response to it.
Moreover, despite Piattelli's training in rabbinical culture and Jewish law,
his perception of social organization seems to have been primarily by way
of the notarial act and its sophisticated application. Through these acts,
it has been observed, the Jewish notary became the essential communal
institution; in fact, the notary might be likened to the glue cementing the
Jewish public and private spheres in Rome, by dint of which he also promoted the viability of both.[36]

We might elaborate to suggest that the notary virtually created an
"alternative" Jewish community—overlapping the official Community,
the Comunità—because *without* his acts the Jews would have had no
instrumentality to formalize or give juridical validity to anything they
adjudicated internally. Indeed, these acts acquired juridical validity de
facto—not, of course, de iure—because appended to them was a clause
indicating that they had been drawn with the Vicar's (tacit, if not overt)
approval.[37] Besides, as Jewish notaries—Isaac Piattelli in particular—
certainly knew, the *ius commune* (Roman common law) tradition in effect
at Rome considered legally binding the result of all voluntary arbitration.

Yet everything Isaac Piattelli was doing should also be seen under the
rubric of conservative acculturation. For although the notarial art among
Christians was centuries old, Jews were perfecting their notarial skills at a
moment of some uncertainty for Christian notaries, at least in Catholic
lands, where priests rather than traditionally the notary were beginning
to preside over ceremonies such as marriage. By contrast, rabbis who

presided at weddings functioned much like notaries (as they always had): their task was to ensure the observance of forms; they did not even sanctify the wedding ring(s), as did the priest.[38] Likewise, just when priests were becoming spiritual directors of confraternities, it was Piattelli, again as notary (or more strictly as an amanuensis), who kept the minute books for the Gemilut Hasadim burial confraternity, the most influential Roman Jewish confraternity.

The notary was also the registrar of communal acts, such as the appointment of a committee of five rabbis, which the papacy mandated following its burning of the Talmud in 1554 to oversee the censorship of Hebrew books.[39] Yet the notary's most important task was to draw up and record acts pertaining to arbitration, including testimony. In strictly juridical litigation (as opposed to arbitration based on equity, or what the Jewish texts call *qarov la-din*, approximate law), a notary would have taken down such testimony using set forms and terminology, following instructions given him as an officer of the court. The Jewish notary, in the absence of precedent and, even more, the absence of a formal court, had to invent the language, formulae, and even the basic notarial format in which to couch what he heard. In other words, the Jewish notary created tools—whether for disputing parties or for the body of Roman Jewry and its institutional expressions—allowing the memory of Jewish disagreement and settlement formally to be preserved.[40]

What is more, the perfection of a notarial art made the appearance of truly professional advocates inevitable—upon whom Jewish law had previously looked with disfavor at best, and whose services Jews had little needed. Regrettably, there are no notarial records before the 1530s in corroboration, but we may speculate that the perfection of both professions, the notary and the advocate, went hand in hand. Which is also to suggest that the Jews were able to bring arbitration to a sophisticated level only when they had the means to endow it with the same or similar formal conventions and offices—notaries and advocates—that Christian arbitration had known for generations.[41]

This is not to say that Jewish or even Christian arbitration absolutely required a notary. Arbiters and arbitration without notaries like the Piattellis had existed within Judaism for centuries. They were discussed in rabbinic texts. And Jewish arbitration is also sanctioned by Justinian's sixth-century *Code of Roman Law*, as well as various medieval Latin legal texts. Christians, too, are known to have arbitrated informally. But how sophisticated such informal arbitration was is another matter.

It is just this sophistication conferred by notaries that so stands out in Jewish Rome, and it had communal ramifications. The contents of the Jewish notarial registers and the notarial ritual they disclose, including the various modes of turning to the notary and of manipulating the notarial function to partisan advantage, embody a Roman Jewish civic ritual. And it was this ritual that aided Rome's Jews in more fully managing their own affairs at a time when, through methods such as legislation concerning judicial venues and heavy increases in taxation, the papacy was about to make an assault on Jewish self-management.[42] This assault failed, however, in part because of the sophistication that Jewish procedures of arbitration had attained. Thanks largely to the development of a Jewish notarial art, therefore, arbitration had become a truly potent weapon of Jewish social reconciliation and unity.

Arbitration might take place over the small things in life, if only to smooth ruffled feathers. Why else would people arbitrate about a dagger taken from the wall of a store as a prank? One could arbitrate, or at least stipulate and depose before the notary, about anything, such as the rent one paid a father-in-law for a family visit at Passover or the dwelling one provided for aged parents.[43] Relatedly, people brought testimony to counter future suspicion that something untoward, rather than an accidental fall, had punctured a young girl's hymen (or had caused the blood that was taken as such a puncture to appear on her dress). One is tempted to see here a cover-up for incest, violence, and abuse, but one would also have to make the difficult assumption that the collusion came systematically from the top down and, moreover, in about seventy instances.[44]

Two litigants once debated the state of a horse's health before and after its sale, when it was used—for one last time—to journey to Rome, and it died on the way. Disputes over housing were heard time and again, especially in the months after the Ghetto was decreed, sometimes with the stipulation that the resolution was conditional on such and such a building's being encompassed by the Ghetto walls; it took four months to decide exactly where these walls would be built. Arbitration even took place about overdue rent: in particular, whether the *Scola*, the synagogue, of the Tedeschi, the Ashkenazi Jews, which had been closed by the Vicar in 1557 after prohibited books were found there and confiscated, should pay back-rent to its landlord, the Italian Scola Nova, for the nine months during which the Tedeschi was closed.[45]

There was notably little arbitration, about thirty examples in all, concerning "family peace"—*Shalom bayyit*, as it is called in Hebrew—meaning anything from restoring good relations between husband and wife to halting wife beating or the public berating of a husband by his spouse. Synagogues (all housed in the same building, remember) disputed each other about who was responsible for repairs or who should pay to move a staircase blocking another synagogue's windows. People argued over inheritances, monies they claimed were owed them either by individuals or the community, and over how to divide a major fine. In the case of Joshua Abbina, the entire community, its leadership and confraternal bodies, argued with the family over where Abbina was to be buried. This episode, retold of course by the notary, says much about Jewish civic ritual, communal power, and the way both of them worked. It also unites the various strands of our discussion.[46]

In July 1556, the late and much respected Abbina was about to be buried *outside* the choicest area of the Jewish cemetery. The notary's frustratingly brief account of this episode is limited to a single succinct act. Burial at that time was not in a new site, but in a previously used grave from which the bones were removed or in which they had completely disintegrated. The notary's account is corroborated indirectly by our knowledge of the repeated use of crypts in churches, not to mention by the visible testimony of the Jewish cemetery still extant in Prague. Otherwise, the details of interment—as opposed to funeral processions—were rarely mentioned.[47] At the moment of Abbina's death no choice grave was empty, resulting in a hue and cry from Abbina's widow and his relatives. The latter even managed to convince members of the Gemilut Hasadim confraternity to abandon their digging tools, which these relatives wanted to use to exhume and rebury the body interred only moments before. In the meantime, two people, likely confraternity members, tried to calm the distraught widow, Simhah Abbina, but in fact managed to insult her. "What does it matter where your husband is buried," they said, "as long as the soul goes to a pure place." And, in any case, Joshua Abbina would be buried in a "good place," this last a capricious Ashkenazi (at least) euphemism for a cemetery—any cemetery at all.[48] However, it was the *fattori*, the three elected lay communal heads, not the confraternity, which had made the original decision about where Abbina was to be laid to rest. The confraternity was ancillary to the Community, voluntary, and generally autonomous; but the *fattori*, distinguished persons who formally headed the Community, could not simply be ignored.

Accordingly, it fell to the lot of the notary, Isaac Piattelli, not only to take down all the testimony but—we may infer—to serve as referee, mediating between all three parties: the *fattori*, representing the Comunità; the bewildered—it seems—members of the Gemilut Hasadim; and the Abbina family. Piattelli himself was often named as an arbiter in such disputes. Yet what facilitated, indeed necessitated, this mediation was the regnant ambiguity concerning the exercise of Roman Jewish civic power and the modalities through which this power—to the extent that it existed—could be put into effect. The whole affair had degenerated into what looks like a brawl, as well as a rebellion against the *fattori*; the proposed exhumation was also as easy to mount as it was for Mrs. Abbina to yell and scream in front of the Gemilut Hasadim confraternity.

Yet what was Piattelli mediating? A dispute between family and community? We cannot know of a certainty, because no other document concerning the affair has survived. Had the *fattori* insisted that the Abbina accept their decision, or were the Abbina still hoping for a "better" burial? What might have bothered the Comunità most was the hubbub itself. Such raucous behavior was far from the norm at respectable Christian funerals. We may begin with the insults, so distinct from the decorum and rhetorical orations that characterized, or were supposed to characterize, Christian funerals after the late fourteenth century and into the fifteenth.[49] The funeral of the charismatic, 98-year-old grand Rabbi Judah Mintz of Padua in 1509 seems to have imitated this Christian model, including a pecking order of speakers, large waxen torches, and a most unobtrusive presence of women relatives, no longer allowed to wail publicly. The stately Christian funeral oration and subsequent decorous entombment, especially at funerals of the elite, had specifically come to take the place of women's keening, which had once included professional women mourners.[50]

This was all quite the opposite of the Abbina funeral. Here was a Roman Jewish notable whose funeral ceremony included pushing and shoving, vociferous women's participation, and clearly no torches ablaze. But most Jews, if the Abbina episode is indicative, seem to have known—or cared—little about funereal pomp; and the *carnavalesque* Giudiate, mocking the Roman Jewish funeral in particular, reinforces this suspicion, as do even more the complaints of the seventeenth-century Jehudah (Judah) Aryeh di Modena and his cousin Aron Berechiah concerning the Jewish funeral's customary "unseemliness." Perhaps, too, the need to dodge the stones Christian bullies sometimes threw at Jewish funeral corteges left no time, strength, or will for staid formalities.[51]

Perhaps. But the Jewish funeral offers an example of Jews moderating their ways to adopt Christian patterns selectively. Thus, Jews might agree with Christians that to some extent death ought to be ritualized, such as by having moribund men die dressed in an unfringed version of the traditional shawl (*tallit*) worn during prayer. Yet when this same person was encouraged to confess, also an innovation, the confession was made before a rabbi who was equally, if not principally, a notary. Moreover, wills prepared at death's door by Roman rabbinic notaries (whether for men or women) were only occasionally said to be accompanied by a confession. The various statutes of the Gemilut Hasadim, in addition, concentrate solely on the obligations of burial, not on accompanying acts of prayer or piety.[52]

In the case of Abbina, the behavior of his family thus represents an older tradition of mourning and interment according to what its individual members felt best. The *fattori*, may I suggest, were tending toward the institution of at least a modicum of decorum. They may also have been reacting against the possibility—a constant anxiety at this time among Christians—that organized rowdiness, expressed here as the ability of a family to decide where its members would be buried in a communally owned plot, would destroy any semblance of communal ritual consensus. Yet these Jewish *fattori* had no way, and perhaps no will, to exploit the funeral and to use it as a means of inculcating among constituents the essence of a common cultural heritage—for example, the ideal of the soul's salvation and its centrality, whose preservation has been called the raison d'être of the theorizing underlying Renaissance Christian funeral rites. Christian funeral pomp was also a way of showing due respect to public officials, as well as a means—it has been argued—of establishing gender boundaries.[53]

Lacking rationalizations like these, let alone power, Jews had no choice but to let the notary, or more precisely the notarial register, establish the boundaries of propriety, to serve as the central forum for safeguarding traditional social peace. It was here that conflicts were resolved and public and private interests brought together, aired, and recorded. So, too, the notary and his register provided the cement whose binding power gave a semblance of unity to the loosely articulated Roman Jewish Community. We should not be surprised, therefore, that more than once litigating parties appeared before a Jewish notary to draw up a *compromesso* initiating arbitration only *after* they had flouted communal instrumentalities and then failed to settle their dispute in the Vicar's court.[54]

It is also no wonder that the ability of the notary and the notarial art to substitute for otherwise flaccid or absent communal institutions was appreciated by more than the Jews. Jewish instrumentalities of control, such as rabbinic excommunication, had traditionally been authorized by papal officials when they found the ban useful, for example, to force the payment of taxes destined for papal coffers or to ensure that testimony be given.[55] The same pragmatic reasoning now led the Vicar and sometimes other Christian officials to sustain—and on occasion directly intervene—in Jewish arbitrational proceedings. They did this most frequently in cases concerning housing, outlandishly presenting themselves as champions, as it were, of the ordinance ascribed to the twelfth-century Rabbi Jacob Tam (or sometimes the eleventh-century Rabbi Gershom) issued to prevent Jewish evictions and unfair rents. The Vicar was seeking to make himself the supervisor of internal Jewish affairs, a goal various church-men had pursued since the mid-thirteenth century.[56]

But what the Vicar might really find himself supervising was Jewish autonomous control, especially when cases initiated in the Vicar's court were later transferred to Jewish arbiters. One Mazliah, who was originally instructed *by the Vicar* to occupy the house of Moise di Sabato, eventu-ally turned to Jewish arbitration, saying that he preferred "to act in the way of 'kosher' Jews."[57] On another occasion, the Vicar instructed two rabbis to judge whether the *fattore* Haim Anav had violated Jacob Tam's ordinance. This had been a particularly sticky case, in which the thrice repeated refusal of Raffaele di Sezze to do as the Conservatore, the civic head of Rome, had asked him resulted in Sezze's torture with the cord, hoisting him into the air by the arms, which were tied behind his back. The Conservatore had entreated Sezze not to occupy a *taberna* close by the home of Anav, and emotions were running high. However, the rab-bis Isaac Piattelli and Abramo Scazzocchio took charge not because the Vicar had ordered them to do so, but—at least formally—because the disputing parties, Haim Anav and Raffaele di Sezze, agreed to accept Jew-ish arbitration. And perhaps it is no accident that precisely here the ar-biters most unusually decided to judge according to strict halachic legal precedent, which they also cited. One suspects that Piattelli and Scazzoc-chio were indirectly stating the ideal, contrasting the authority of the Vicar iconographically to the rule of Jewish law.[58] By supporting Jewish arbitration, it thus appears the Vicar could sometimes defeat his own best interests—but not always.

For the issue was not one-sided. Jews had to beware, especially when competing Christian authorities in Rome tried to exploit Jewish arbi-tration to partisan advantage. In 1552, the papal Governor (as opposed to the Vicar) agreed to release Isach di Segni—arrested on undisclosed charges—from prison, provided that Isach convert to Christianity and divorce his wife. The details are murky, and we must not jump to conclusions; we do not know whether Isach converted. But he did order a *ghet*, a bill of divorce, written and delivered to his wife.[59] Papal officialdom was a formidable lot. No wonder that among the confraternities of Roman Jewry we find those devoted to succoring and freeing prisoners—especially Jews imprisoned for debt, who were subject in jail to heavy conversionary pressures—just as the Jewish Community raised funds to assist such people and other vulnerable poor to flee Rome after Paul IV issued *Cum nimis absurdum*.[60]

For the most part, adroit Jewish manipulation, especially by the notaries, reduced the Vicar's involvement in Jewish arbitration sometimes to technicalities and obstructed his wished-for supervision of Jewish religious affairs. Selectively exploiting Christian cultural elements, Jewish notaries first assimilated the *compromesso*, the formal (Christian) instrument drawn up to initiate arbitration, into older Jewish arbitrational procedure. Then they concluded each *compromesso* with a clause declaring it "valid as though drawn by an authentic Christian public notary in Cameral form," a clause surely sanctioned by the Vicar himself, who no doubt believed—wrongly, in most cases—that it gave him substantial control over proceedings.[61] The clause served mostly to give Jewish arbitration teeth. It also made already flexibly equitable Jewish arbitration more attractive, because ipso facto—and inscribed into an act of *compromesso* no less—it narrowed the gap separating Jewish from Christian forms of litigation. And so it effectively reduced, if it did not actually eliminate, what some may have seen as the procedural advantages of turning to a Christian court.[62]

In any case, the potential effects of Vicarial interference were attenuated by the strikingly loose concept of corporations applied in Rome, which allowed the Vicar to interfere at will—as he did—in the arbitrational proceedings of even Rome's true corporations, guilds of craftsmen and their like, which putatively enjoyed some form of real original jurisdiction. How much the more, then, might his interference in the arbitrational proceedings of Jewish bodies be construed as neither exceptional nor diminishing their luster? The Jews were certainly under no illusions about the corporate status of these bodies, lacking as they were in formal jurisdictional powers and regardless of the indiscriminate papal usage, whatever its legal propriety, to call Jewish institutions, whether synagogues or the central Comunità, by the name of *universitas*, or corporation.[63]

It was thus left to the initiative of Rome's Jewish notaries with respect to arbitration to provide the city's Jews with a means of achieving stability in their daily lives. But perhaps even more, through the structures spawned by the exercise of the notarial art—the forms and techniques of arbitration they practiced—Roman Jews were enabled to envision and perhaps even verbalize a sense that they inhabited a sacred space. This was a space at least conceptually their own, theirs to manage, and whose functional determinants were not the product of papal edicts or even the Ghetto itself, but of their own ability to settle internal disputes. In other words, through the dramatic rituals and rhythms of arbitration, which the absence of rigid hierarchical internal controls and institutions had done so much to prompt, Rome's Jews had acquired the ability to reinvigorate that sine qua non of communal life—social harmony.

It was, indeed, specifically this end that the Piattellis must have had in mind when they introduced into their acts phrases to indicate that the parties before them were publicizing their doings or making them public. It was also toward this end that the notaries declared that their acts were drawn as though by "true, or authentic Christian public notaries," irrespective of any real judicial authority or verisimilitude of form that the use of this title conveyed. For what the Piattellis meant by these phrases was ratification and the granting of a recognized status—a public and official standing. This was much as one spoke in contemporary non-Jewish society of matters such as publicly administered punishments or the public auto-da-fé of inquisitions. But this was also the publicity, the public standing, of the public sphere—the public realm, to the extent that it existed—which, as we have said, was in danger of eluding the Roman Jewish grasp.

This latter was a point that the Jews who turned to the Piattellis understood well. Recognizing both the necessary and evanescent nature of Jewish publicity, they supported their arguments over and again by emphasizing, for example, that a contract had been made public or that an insult, by husband, wife, or business colleague, had been made in front of all. The many Hebrew words and expressions used to express the idea— such as "to reveal," "to bring to light," "to bring before the *kahal*," or simply "to publish"—vary as do the nature of the complaints and the importance to the complainer of publicity's effects. Publicity's achievement, therefore, was a measure of the Jewish success in cultivating social harmony, not to mention success in cultivating the institutions of arbitration and the notary that were so instrumental in realizing this goal.[64]

But just because of its official or quasi-official nature, what was made public was also potentially dangerous. Excessive or wrongly expressed publicity, or power, might attract unwanted outside attention, especially that of the Vicar or other Roman officials. And to judge from the low frequency with which emotion is recorded in the notarial acts, publicly expressed emotions were deemed fraught with danger, capable of upsetting delicate structural balances. Haim Anav's rebuff by Raffaele di Sezze angered Anav so much that he turned to a civic authority, the Conservatore, instead of to Jewish arbiters. And when Raffaele di Sezze refused the Conservatore, the latter was angered to the point of ordering Sezze tortured, provoking in turn interference from both the Auditore (the judge of the papal Governor) and the Vicar.[65] Unfettered emotional publicity thus had brought all three competing Roman Christian jurisdictions—the municipality, the papal Governor, and the papal Vicar—into play, boding only ill for the Jews caught in between. No wonder that when Jewish control was somehow restored—had the Vicar misjudged his great advantage?—the terms of peacemaking were especially severe. Symbolic of enduring covenants, Haim Anav agreed to have Sezze circumcise (most likely by delegating the real operation to the formal communal *mohel*) any son born to Anav in the future.[66] It was indeed significant, not merely a restatement of ideals, that to settle this so potentially destabilizing case the arbiters resorted to strictly interpreted halachah rather than to arbitration's normal rules of equity. It also became indispensable to take steps minimizing the repetition of scenarios like this one and to ensure, instead, Jewish arbitration's firm public status and, to the extent possible, the universality of its resort.

Such steps are reflected in the regularity with which expressions of emotion were codified in notarial texts, indicating an apparent intention to limit unguarded use of these expressions. This codification also suggests a consciousness that use of a term or concept revealing, or implying, emotion was an intentional signifier. Graduated emotional terminology supplied a measure of the degree to which a particular situation was feared to be socially destabilizing. Real emotion appears freely only when it is extraneous, or at least does not threaten the continuance of arbitration. There was great happiness when a man of wealth joined the Gemilut Hasadim, and joy that an engagement had been finalized or a marriage consummated—independent, in this case, of the false claim, as all knew, that the bride was not a virgin. A man, now dead, is said to have been *inamorato* of a woman, for whom he left his wife—but the suit was over the paternity of his now mature son, who was seeking to inherit some property. There was also a father's compassion for his daughter, beaten by her husband—surely related to the fact that his own mother had been beaten, yet expressed to strengthen the argument in favor of returning her dowry, not as a purely emotional appeal.[67]

But such instances of undisguised affect were rare: *inamorato* appears but once, "compassion" twice, and the sentiment that the poor or old not be made to "suffer," three times, in the entire notarial record.[68] Thus emotion, at least formally, was restrained for the most part from impinging on real justiciable issues. The anger that raised havoc in the housing dispute between Haim Anav and Raffaele di Sezze and was a source of anxiety in two or three other similar litigations barely emerges, for example, in the lengthy and complex dispute between Obadiah ben Joab and Casher Ashkenazi over an eviction. And this was one in which the Vicar was intermittently involved, but which was finally being decided by Jewish arbiters. It was this dispute that reflected the norm.[69] Indeed, in the over 6,000 documents I have culled, including 860 whose subject is litigation, strong emotion such as anger or that signified by public violence or insult appears in fewer than forty cases and then only when it is unavoidable, integral to the issues litigated, or at their heart. Emotions directly concerning the dead, such as bereavement, loss, and pain, are absent; but perhaps such emotions should not be expected—wholly out of place in the pragmatic context of notarial acts.

It would, of course, be absurd to say that Roman Jews repressed their true emotions. Rather, both petitioners and notaries alike seem to have been observing a convention generally to refrain from expressing emotion publicly. In notarial texts particularly, emotion was exposed only in precisely encoded juridical formats; one might hint at, but never openly reveal, the depths of underlying feeling. Accordingly, to be "content" meant invariably and unexceptionally to accept stipulations and avoid conflict; to "honor," to give a person his or her due; to "make peace," formally to end a quarrel; to "take an oath," to put one's honor at stake and so allay anxieties; and to be "faithful," as well as to be credited with "love," to be loyal, although the Italian *amorevole* seems to convey a measure of true affect. The appearance of these terms is also skimpy: content (willing, accepting), 43 times; honor, 20; make peace, 26; oaths, 98 (including 24 over taxes and a large number simply to repay a loan or to stop gambling); faithfulness and love, together, 29 times. In all there are 216 instances, in addition to 45 more expressing emotions ranging from anger, fear, hate, and compassion, to pleasure and, three times, suffering: barely 261 traces of emotion, in other words, scattered through nearly 6,000 texts.

What people were feeling, they normally refrained from saying, apparently convinced that unrestrained emotional expression signified excessive or wrongful publicity. And this, in turn, threatened to blur the borders of consensus, and subsequently confuse role-playing, remove masks, and eventually erase the scripts and dramas on which the potential for social reconciliation through arbitration rested. The very bases of Jewish daily ritual, that which has been called "the appropriate verbal [and nonverbal] contexts for sustaining action or ceremonial,"[70] would be placed under heavy attack. Uncontrolled *public* expression of emotion—the eruption of feeling from the private into the public sphere, as opposed to its normally smooth passage and transition—was thus attributed with the power to threaten the continued management of at least some aspects of Jewish individual and communal fate. This threat was thus to be warded off, first, as encapsulated in the pithy *non dabará*, Judaeo-Romanesco for "do not speak out," whether emotionally or, in fact, in any way, and, second, by resorting to a most traditional means of collective defense.

On various occasions, the acts use Italian terms such as *scumunica* [*sic*] or *publicare una scumunica* [*sic*], or, in Hebrew, *le-hakhriz humr'a*. The meaning of all three is identical, but that meaning was not, as one might think, based on today's common usage—a ban or an excommunication in the sense of separating an individual from the flock. It was rather the meaning attributed to the term by the tenth-century Ashkenazi Rabbi Gershom, called Light of the Exile. For Rabbi Gershom is said to have decreed that all the members of a Community must "enter into a *herem*" in which "should anyone have information about [matters such as] lost objects, then they must report the matter, *le-hakhriz* [making it public], instead of appealing to a court." The literal meaning here is "a sacred space," similar to the Islamic *haram* and following the word's usage in the Book of Joshua. Thus *herem* in Rabbi Gershom's usage was a loaded term. Its best meaning perhaps is "a sovereign (= sacred) sphere created through a communal pact of public obligation." And it was in this sense, as Roman Jews absolutely knew (just as they explicitly affirmed their continuing resort to the *herem* about evictions attributed to Rabbi Jacob Tam), that the term appears in the notarial texts mentioned above: for instance, *le-hakhriz* a *humra*, a *herem*, a *scomunica* [*sic*], that anyone who had information about the property of one Raffaele Yair or the clothing of Ventura di Cori must report it; on the basis of which, arbitration might be successfully concluded.[71] Anxieties, that is, were to be channeled by creating a communal, consensual, and *virtually* sovereign forum for ventilation and reconciliation.

The *herem* or *scomunica*, in other words, provided an outlet to redirect emotion's potentially unguarded expression. No wonder that Abramo Scazzocchio had the disputing members of the Scola Castigliana-Francese and the Scola Tempio enter into a *herem* stipulating that they would withdraw the accusations they had rashly made against each other in the Vicar's court and accept arbitration instead.[72] And no wonder that a *herem* or a *scomunica* was announced on no fewer than 58 occasions over the years. For what the *herem* effectively did was to reify Jewish publicity, providing it with institutional tangibility and creating mutual trust; and, mostly, it kept the Vicar at a safe distance. But the *herem* also guaranteed publicity's correlate: the sense of intrinsically Jewish (sacred) space under Jewish control.[73] In addition, the *herem*—paradoxically, some might comment—offered a judicial alternative to rabbinical decision, which in Italy throughout the sixteenth century, if not afterward, was marked by incessant, virulent, and lengthy feuds.[74] And thanks much to its consensual nature, the *herem* helped maintain that balance between community and individual which insisted on such as defending the honor of Ricca Soporto or upholding the self-respect of Simhah Abbina. In a minor key, after all, this was government by mutual obligation—which we might go so far as to call a fledgling "social contract."

Yet if this was true, then to jeopardize the *herem* was, consciously or at least capriciously, to endanger the continuity of Jewish publicity. It would undermine the foundations of even that minimal concept and exercise of sovereignty that Jews had managed to develop, not to mention their self-consciousness of communal existence. The faint lines separating the public sphere from the private, publicity from privacy, in Jewish Rome constantly remind us how fragile that sovereignty was. Accordingly, it was imperative to safeguard the *herem*, which is also to say that it was imperative to keep publicly expressed emotion in check. Otherwise, communal harmony, Jewish social reconciliation—Jewish publicity itself—would whither not only in fact but in theory.

To say these things not only emphasizes how fragile, inchoate, and vulnerable were Jewish institutions of sovereignty. It also points to a fatal systemic flaw. However beneficial, even appropriate, the *herem* may have been at first, the resort to it means that Jewish self-regulation could be achieved only by perpetuating venerable and to some extent outmoded means—venerable and outmoded, in this instance, with respect to Christian, not Jewish institutions. For were not the mechanisms of Jewish social reconciliation essentially those once so well situated in the Christian confraternity—a judicial forum whose place, at least in Italy, was now being challenged by the formalized Catholic reform concept of "discipline," or, simply put, by clerical control? The goal was to eliminate the kind of competition confraternal adjudication of disputes posed, replacing that control even with that of the papal Inquisition itself and its priestly confessors. Jewish self-regulation had thus become dependent on preserving means and venues which, however venerable, in Christian society had been seriously questioned.

This dependency was no small matter. For one, it may help to explain why the transition so common at this time in Christian confraternities, from a social and public basis to one of personal and interiorized piety, never fully took place in Jewish confraternities. The latters' very statutes often prescribed the confraternity as the seat of all intramural arbitration.[75] The Jewish insistence on preserving now-challenged forums of social reconciliation no doubt also complicated the difficulties endemic to the Jewish quest for internal jurisdiction. Whether at Rome or elsewhere, this insistence generated suspicion, projecting a negative image of discordant and hence inappropriate Jewish communal behavior. However, the most damaging effect of preserving what was suspect and venerable in Rome was what it portended regarding unforeseen challenges.

The issue was not so much that in about 1640 the Vicar dealt a frontal blow to the Roman Jewish system of self-regulation and arbitration, when—for reasons still unclear—he halted the activity of the Jewish notaries, replacing them with Christian ones. Had the Vicar finally understood the necessity of dominating this vital institution, as well as why he had not dominated it in the past?[76] The Jewish *notaio publico autentico*, with all this office's multiple signification, was now no more. To be sure, a good part of the resulting slack in arbitration may have been taken up by such groups as members of the various synagogues or the Gemilut Hasadim, as the statutes of both prescribed, or through the agency of the more recent *sukkat shalom* confraternity devoted exclusively to fostering a spirit of arbitration. To some extent, as the visitor of 1843 said, the Jews continued to be "governed by Judges of their own."[77] The perceptions, the drama, and, to some small degree, the reality of publicity, self-regulation, and Jewish space had not completely evaporated. But they were constantly eroding. And the ingrained Jewish penchant for conservatism, as it had to contend directly with the obviously limited means for innovation at the Jews' disposal under Ghetto conditions, was unable to compensate. However much internal governance would continue to exist, therefore, its common conception, perception, and consensual basis was destined to suffer. In practice, community-wide social reconciliation had become, and would increasingly continue to be, an ever greater and thornier challenge.

The case of internal governance was also indicative of the whole. For a similar inability to change course from within and respond innovatively to external challenge, to the extent this was possible, touched the entire breadth of Roman Jewish life and culture, which was growing ever more static, rigid, and resistant to new winds blowing from the outside. The time lag in acculturation that initially was salutary, allowing constructive and beneficial change to seep in slowly, had become stifling. We need only glance at what seems to have been the normal school curriculum for adolescents, which required them to learn the rudiments of the weekly Torah portion along with some commentaries, to confirm this impression of limitation. It is confirmed once again by looking at the small intellectual achievements of the one noted rabbi of the period, the early eighteenth-century Tranquillo Corcos.[78] This decline was entrenched by problems of a more practical nature. Constant threats, like that of being dragged off to the House of Catechumens, which was the experience of Anna del Monte, or of being proselytized while jailed for civil and criminal offenses, or of being stifled demographically within the Ghetto confines, were compounded in the seventeenth century by the psychological effects of devastating plague and in the eighteenth century by a renewed papal determination to enforce — in fact, to expand — existing canonical edicts. There was also the enormous debt of the Jews of Rome to the Apostolic Chamber, the papal treasury, which placed a heavier-than-could-be-borne weight on the shoulders of the formal Community. The definitive closure of Jewish loan banks in 1682 effectively impoverished the few remaining well-to-do.[79] The only thing left to say is that if Jewish tools of acculturation had at first, in the earlier sixteenth century, allowed Roman Jews to manipulate the Ghetto space advantageously, by the seventeenth and eighteenth centuries the contracting perimeters of Ghetto space were manipulating the Jews. Culturally—and, perhaps even more, acculturationally—they were falling ever more definitely behind.

The final word, however, is best spoken by our British traveler of 1843: "Of the 3,600 Jews of Rome comprising 800 families, 1,900 are paupers, 1,000 support themselves by their industry, and the rest are in easy circumstances. The paupers are generally employed in gathering old rags, the industrious are dealers in old clothes, and those in easy circumstances are merchants. Few learn the useful or fine arts or cultivate literature, the highest class among them being contented with that portion of knowledge that fits them for mercantile pursuits." [80] What precisely our traveler meant by "easy circumstances" one may debate. Wealthy by any standard, these Jewish merchants certainly were not, and their cultural level was unquestionably pitiful. The socioeconomic profile of the Jewish Ghetto community did not match that of the city as a whole, with the distinctly rich a class set apart. Even crude measurements of Jewish individual wealth reveal a constant and precipitous decline, especially during the eighteenth century, with no more than three or four Jewish families capable of being called wealthy and even the upper stratum having little more in its purse than the poor. Nor had the situation begun to ameliorate even *after* the brief Napoleonic pause and breath of air between 1797 and 1799, the moment when our British traveler paid his call.[81] One indeed suspects that had not the long-range effect of the Napoleonic invasion been to number the Roman Ghetto's days (as it did the days of the Papal State itself), the Jews of Rome, perhaps even the "comfortable" merchants, would have withered into irreversible poverty accompanied by nearly absolute cultural arrest. Gregorovius's description of ghetto misery, with which we began our tour of Jewish Rome, dates, after all, to the 1850s.[82]

AFTERWORD

ROMAN JEWISH CULTURE thus eventually succumbed to stasis. However, stasis means neither cultural rejection nor abandonment; nor should the two be confused. Wide as it was, the cultural gap between Italian culture in general and the particular Italian culture of Rome's Jews never became so great that it prevented the Jews' amalgamation into Italian society following emancipation and the fall of the Ghetto in 1870. Admittedly, the diversity of Jewish culture evoked questions—especially in the early twentieth century—about how thorough Jewish amalgamation and integration would be, questions similar to those raised contemporaneously in France and Germany. And the pernicious consequences of these questions north of the Alps had their repercussions in the racial laws under Italian fascism during the late 1930s, and then in the deportations that began in October 1943, during the German occupation of Rome.[1]

This is far from the American Jewish experience. It has been said that in America the ghetto of immigrant Jews at the turn of the twentieth century was entered into only to be abandoned.[2] There were those who opposed this process, and especially its ramifications. Signs declaring "restricted clientele" were still visible on some hotels in the immediate post–World War II years. Yet even during the height of American

127

anti-Semitism, in the 1930s—a far cry from the European version, of course—virtually nobody, Jew or Gentile, doubted that for American Jewry the ghetto was temporary, a one-way street leading out. In the Roman Ghetto, the process was reversed. One either converted, with all its social—not only religious—implications, or one remained irreversibly in. To be sure, through subtlety, through tradition, and especially through selective acculturation, but largely by making of their *ghet* a place of (admittedly fictitious, if not theatrical) "liberation"—their "sacred space," which they imagined to be much under their direct control—the Jews collectively and individually somehow managed to survive. But ultimately their energies were devoted to doing precious little else. And their ghetto experience lasted three hundred years. The American ghetto lasted barely fifty. The imprint of Roman ghetto life would be difficult to erase.

Remnants of this imprint are found in Roman Jewry even today. Nobody speaks Yiddish; but then in Rome no one ever did. Nor does anybody speak a Judaeo-Romanesco dialect, although a few words remain, even in reasonably common parlance. For the most part and not unsurprisingly, these are words with Italianized Hebrew roots that denominate the "other," rituality, or food: *ngesaui* (Esaus), *nangareli* (uncircumcised), *ciachtare* (pronounced "shahtare"; in Hebrew, *lishehot*, to slaughter ritually), *mangode di purimi* (in Hebrew, *ma'ot shel purim*, gifts of money for the Purim festival), and *orrechie di haman* (in Hebrew, ʿaznei haman, Haman's ears, and *hamentaschen*, the three-cornered Purim pastry).[3] Toward the end of the nineteenth century there was a flight from the Ghetto's area—all of whose buildings (save the Five Synagogues, which burned to the ground, accidentally, in 1894) were torn down as health hazards. There was a sharp drop, too, in formal membership in the Comunità. But by the 1920s this trend reversed itself, which is indicative of certain more subtle constants.[4] Thus many of Rome's current Jews—who still bear the traditional family names already in use in the sixteenth century—retain modes of comportment similar to those of their parents and grandparents. They foster the same kind of multigenerational circles of friendship as did these earlier generations. Children and grandchildren of friends move together in tight-knit social circles, networking circles that on occasion are more binding and supportive than the family circle would ever hope—or want—to be. These circles sometimes continue even among members, and their children, who have migrated abroad. To call such circles by the Renaissance term *vicinati*, neighborhoods, would not be to err. Did not the Roman Jewish notaries translate the term literally into the Hebrew *shekhunah*?

Externally, therefore, one may look, talk, or eat like a Roman (albeit, if he or she observes the Jewish dietary laws, the pasta, when served with meat, is also served *without* cheese). But inwardly, emotionally, and by mentality and memory, one's primary identity is Jewish. It is no accident that the minority in which this perspective is most ingrained—people who also spend a good deal of time in the area of the Ghetto (and who are by no means drawn from a single social, financial, or even educational stratum)—are called *Ghettaroli* by Rome's other Jews. That is, they are considered Ghetto people, who are set in patterns of conservatism and diffident about forming close relationships with non-Jews (and sometimes with Jews as well) outside.

Nonetheless, a word of caution. For in many spheres conservatism typifies Roman society as a whole, especially among the upwardly mobile, increasingly educated, lower middle classes. These are the same lower middle classes to which a large component of Roman Jewry still belongs: the Jewish small-merchants and shop owners, street vendors, and, most of all, the vendors of postcards outside the Pantheon and the Colosseum, and the hawkers of statuettes and rosaries from stalls outside Saint Peter's Square—a virtual Jewish monopoly.[5] And in observing precisely these Jews, side by side with their non-Jewish counterparts, we may ask whether our vision has not been turned upside down. For those multigenerational circles of friendship that may seem at first to be so distinctively Jewish are equally distinctive among Rome's lower-middle-class Christians. By preference, many of them move nearly exclusively within such circles, and they, too, are diffident about forming close relationships outside. Who then—Rome's lower-middle-class Jews or its lower-middle-class Christians—copied social manners from whom? And on this level, albeit not on others, just what was the direction of acculturation?

By contrast, the majority of Rome's Jews—a majority perhaps smaller than in other cities such as Turin, where they have become Italian artists, intellectuals, professionals, and politicians—have followed the American pattern. For them, apart from its nostalgia, the Ghetto symbolizes a place that was necessary to abandon. This perception incorporates all the precariousness of "leaving the nest," including intermarriage and the (ever decreasing) denial of being a Jew at all, or, at the very least, the problem of giving one's Jewish identity concrete expression. Nonetheless, in Rome, even for many of these highly amalgamated Jews, but especially for that large number who retain their formal communal membership and pay the communally levied (and state-enforced) tax, there remains a piece of the Ghetto that is very much alive. It is known as *piazza*, that spot of mostly foot traffic and site of the Jewish bakery, which strictly speaking lies just outside the borders of the original Ghetto enclosure. But if you say to almost any Roman Jew, "I will meet you in *piazza*," even though Rome has hundreds of such squares, there is only one place, one particular *piazza*, where most definitely you will be met.

This, of course, is the ultimate Roman Jewish drama, fittingly played on the virtual stage of *piazza* and capped by ritualized, time-bending pilgrimages to the bakery located at "stage left." This stage—we should not expect otherwise—is also an exclusive one. Outsiders, non-Jews, are permitted to strut on it for but a fleeting hour, as was the case in the summer of 1997 when Rome's mayor, warmly welcomed, appeared on the lawn below the Tempio Maggiore—the main synagogue occupying about one-third of the Ghetto's original area—said his words, and was just as warmly, but swiftly, escorted back to his Campidoglio office, five hundred yards away. And, as though to complete both staging and setting, the mayor spoke with his back turned to the Portico d'Ottavia, this ancient structure, located a few feet beyond the line of the sometime Ghetto wall, which Rome's current Jews have mythologized into the symbol of Ghetto times.[6] Even today the site of the Ghetto is a reserved Jewish space. Even for the most Roman, the most acculturated, and the most amalgamated of Rome's Jews, the selective absorption of Roman culture—that balance between being at once a Roman and a Jew which engendered Jewish stability in the sixteenth century—is still in operation.

Yet, if this balance has operated so well and for so long in Rome, what about elsewhere? How typical are Roman Jewry's structures, rituals, and dramatic rhythms of other Italian Jewish communities? Had it been composed earlier, for example, a rabbinic (legal) opinion of the northern Menaham Azariah da Fano concerning marital choice could have been cited as direct, positive precedent by Aron Scazzocchio when Aron represented Ricca d'Aversa at Rome.[7] By contrast, the Jews who settled in Livorno after the 1590s were all Sephardim, many with special ex-converso life styles, and these Jews rigidly retained their own patterns in all social and religious concerns, almost autocratically barring the inroads of other, especially Ashkenazi, practices.[8] One suspects that the Sephardim of Ferrara, and also Venice, adopted similar, if less authoritarian, postures. Florence raises a more complex question. For there, as we have seen, Christian women were heavily restricted.[9] Were Florentine Jewish women equally deprived? Or, by virtue of conservative modes of acculturation, were their privileges never curtailed, especially with respect to inheritance, which would have likened their status, paradoxically, to that *regained* by Christian women in Siena—Florence's nearby neighbor—only in the seventeenth century?[10] Moreover, before the founding of the Ghetto in 1569, Florence's Jews numbered about 100. Afterward, as Jews moved to Florence from surrounding towns and villages, the number swelled to 500, and a formal community was founded, with Jewish men holding public communal office for the first time. Did these Jewish men, as it has been argued, then try to impose on Florentine Jewish women accepted Christian patterns of restriction? Or did they follow the more balanced pattern so visible in Rome, or the lopsided pattern of Turin, investing the bulk of patrimonies in young women's dowries, a source of jealousy, competition, and sometimes conversion on the part of Turin's Jewish men, especially in the eighteenth century? And how would all three possible patterns have fared at the time of emancipation, and afterward?[11] This last question has yet to be seriously broached.

Jews, however, have not been alone in addressing acculturation. The modes of coping that minority cultures, subcultures, and microcultures exploit on their way to acculturation—as well as their effects—we have suggested have much in common. This suggestion, I believe, is reinforced by the words of Henry Louis Gates, Jr., describing the meeting of African American culture with American culture in general. "The thing about black culture," Gates says, "has always been that it was fundamentally dependent on the dominant culture, but it turned it inside out. It mimics it. It signifies upon it. It ironizes it. It riffs on it. . . . It was a relationship that was hostile, but it was also the opposite, complicitous, in the way that matter can't exist without anti-matter, in the way that black people by pushing the limit, living on the fringe, define what happens in the rest of society."[12] A preexisting African American minority culture—bounded by a physically shrinking ghetto, yet an ongoing social and emotional one—thus has drawn selectively and tentatively from the outside to preserve and reshape itself, but also to leave its imprint on majority culture at the same time. How different is this from the Jewish experience in Rome? Indeed, how different is this from the experience of contemporary American Jews?

For American Jews, this is truly a post-ghetto era. The stamp of the ghetto has all but disappeared, except for bits of nostalgia. Nonetheless, Gates's words echo in the reasoning of Arnold Eisen as, within the thicket of modernity, logic, and reason, he seeks to delineate the necessary components of a viable American Jewish community, struggling—like the African American one—for cultural perseverance in a perpetually turgid cultural sea.[13] Such a community, Eisen argues, exists, yet its parameters include not only the nouminal aspects of sacrality, but the ritual of daily, private, public, and even political Jewish life, embracing as well the question of the Diaspora Jew in relation to the Jews, the Land, and the State of Israel. Community thus becomes a conglomerate of the venerable modulated by thoughts and actions of the present: Jewish objectivity derived through consensus out of the subjective; hence, the public, the private, the sacred, and the profane interwoven with the frequently ill-defined traditional to build structure where otherwise it might not exist. Needless to say, this structure is constantly endangered by the challenge of the American cultural mainstream and by its own recoil from the daunting imprint minority cultures may make on majority ones.

As though beginning with a common script, retouched to meet individual circumstance, American blacks and American Jews, like the Jews of Rome before them, have thus borrowed, adopted, resisted, flirted, and pursued meaningful drama and dramatic convention to create and perpetuate a cultural community.[14] And this they have done against the backdrop of unrelenting calls to renounce much, if not all, that is their own. That minor historical moment, as I referred to it at the start of my journey, suddenly strikes directly and closely to home.

NOTES

INTRODUCTION

1. On this subject, see below, toward the end of this Introduction. For the remark of Amos Funkenstein, see his "The Dialectics of Assimilation," *Jewish Social Studies* 1/2 (1995): 1–15. See also David N. Myers, "'Distant Relatives Happening onto the Same Inn': The Meeting of East and West as Literary Theme and Cultural Ideal," *Jewish Social Studies* 1/2 (1995): 75–100, especially his discussion of "hybrid cultures."

2. Charles Beard, "That Noble Dream," *American Historical Review* 46 (1935): 74–87.

3. The standard works on the Jews of Rome remain H. Vogelstein and P. Rieger, *Geschichte der Juden in Rom*, 2 vols. (Berlin, 1895); A. Milano, *Il Ghetto di Roma* (Rome, 1964); and also Abraham Berliner, *Storia degli Ebrei di Roma* (Milan, 1992; trans. of German original, Frankfurt am Main, 1893). Some of their conclusions have been updated by K. Stow, *Catholic Thought and Papal Jewry Policy* (New York, 1977), esp. 291–98, for the text and trans-lation of *Cum nimis absurdum*. See also, K. Stow, *Taxation Community and State: The Jews and the Fiscal Foundations of the Early Modern Papal State* (Stuttgart, 1982); A. Esposito, "Gli Ebrei a Roma nella seconda metà del '400 attraverso i protocolli del notaio Giovanni Angelo Amati," in AA.VV. [Various Authors], *Aspetti e problemi della presenza ebraica nell'Italia centro-settentrionale (secoli XIV e XV.)* (Rome, 1983), 29–126; A. Toaff, *Il Ghetto di*

Roma nel Cinquecento (Rome, 1984); and, most recently, see *Oltre il 1492*, ed. A. Foa, M. Silvera, and K. Stow (= *La Rassegna Mensile di Israel* 58 [1992]) and the rich literature cited in the articles and notes. On Rome in general from the later fifteenth through the early seventeenth centuries, see, among others, John D'Amico, *Renaissance Humanism in Papal Rome* (Baltimore, 1983), Frederick McGinness, *Right Thinking and Sacred Oratory in Counter-Reformation Rome* (Princeton, 1995), Charles L. Stinger, *The Renaissance in Rome* (Bloomington, 1985), John O'Malley, *Rome of the Renaissance* (London, 1981), and Laurie Nussdorfer, *Civic Politics in the Rome of Urban VIII* (Princeton, 1992).

4. For a complete listing of the material in this *fondo*, see K. Stow and S. Debenedetti Stow, "Donne ebree a Roma nell'età del ghetto," *Rassegna Mensile di Israel* 52 (1986): 107–16. Two thousand of these acts are registered, summarized, and amplified with citations in K. Stow, *The Jews in Rome* (Leiden, 1995 and 1997); when noted, these acts will appear with a simple running number from 1 to 2005, with the attached prefix RJ (Roman Jews), e.g., RJ444. Other acts, not included in those two volumes, will be cited using the following code: *Notai ebrei*, 2,1,58r (the numbers standing for, in order, fascicle, book, folio). Additional archival material concerning Italian Jews similarly presented may be found in Shlomo Simonsohn, *The Jews in the Duchy of Milan*, 4 vols. (Jerusalem, 1982); Renata Segre, *The Jews in Piedmont*, 3 vols. (Jerusalem, 1986); and Ariel Toaff, *The Jews in Umbria*, 3 vols. (Jerusalem and Leiden, 1993–94).

5. On the notion of notarial art, the *ars dictaminis*, see Martin Camargo, *Ars dictaminis, ars dictandi* (Turnhout, 1991). Benjamin Gampel, in his *The Last Jews on Iberian Soil, Navarese Jewry 1479/1498* (Berkeley, 1989), gives the impression that there were real notaries in Navarre, although he does not pursue this (for his study, tangential) issue. One suspects that the institution may have existed in Verona and Padua, where there were communal record books. However, there is a vast distinction between note taking and the structuring of a true notarial act, as was happening in Rome. In Verona, the record books distinguish sharply between what is called the "civic notary" and the "communal notary." The specified task of the latter is to write *ketubot*, wedding contracts, that of the former to register contracts as a true notary. And this notary is a Christian, Ser Andrea DeBonis; Yacov Boksenboim, ed., *Minute Books of the Jewish Community of Verona, 1600–1630* (Tel

Aviv, 1990), texts nos. 102, 160, for example. Riccardo Calimani, *Storia del Ghetto di Venezia* (Milan, 1985), 250, describes rich notarial records in Venice, perhaps similar to those of the Roman collection, but in Italian, and drawn by a non-Jewish notary, outside the ghetto. Roman Jews, too, used non-Jewish notaries to register rentals and the contents of dowries. References to these notaries, by name, often appear in the Hebrew acts themselves; see note 7, below. On the notarial art in general in Rome and its importance, see the forthcoming work by Laurie Nussdorfer, *Brokers of Public Trust: Notaries in Baroque Rome.*

6. See the introduction to these subjects in K. Stow, "La Storiographia del ghetto romano: Problemi metodologici," in *La Storia degli ebrei nell'Italia medievale: tra filologia e metodologia*, ed. M. G. Muzzarelli and Giacomo Todeschini (Bologna, 1991), 43–57, which also includes copious archival references for the specific items mentioned here. See, too, K. Stow, "Ethnic Rivalry or Melting Pot: The "Edot" in the Roman Ghetto," *Judaism* 163 (1992): 286–96.

7. Acts of a different nature, those concerning rentals, lending, imprisonment, and other issues involving Jews and Christians, are housed in vast collections of the Archivio di Stato, Roma, Camerale I. Thousands of such acts were drawn up by such Christian notaries as Evangelista and Ceccarelli, both of whom are mentioned in the Hebrew acts. The most well known *fondo* for Jewish materials, the Camerale II, Ebrei, largely contains printed texts and copies, many of which have been discussed by Vogelstein and Rieger—who, incidentally, were the first to make good use of the *Notai ebrei*—and, of course, by Milano in *Il Ghetto*. On Christian notaries at Rome drawing acts for Jews, see Carmelo Trasselli, "Un ufficio notarile per gli Ebrei di Roma," *Archivio della R. Deputazione Romana di Storia Patria* 60 (1938):231–44.

8. *Notai ebrei*, 8,3,125r–v.

9. *Les Toscans et leurs familles* (Paris, 1978) and the English abridged version of 1985.

10. RJ1049, 1094 (*Notai ebrei*, 7,1,165,190v).

11. Concerning the shape, dimensions, and numbers of Roman Jewry, the texts of the *Notai ebrei* allow reasonable approximations, especially of such matters as birthrates and population size. Likewise, the notaries may not have drawn up all Jewish prenuptial agreements, but the percentage of

prenuptial agreements the notaries prepared remained roughly stable over time, providing information about the average fluctuation of dowries, number of children in a family, and thus family size, and also the marital rate for given years and the rates and modalities of out-marriage. Roman Jewry was essentially homogeneous, an "urban middle class." Thus dowries averaged about 100 scudi (a salary of about three years for a skilled laborer), apparently similar to the dowries given Roman Christian girls of roughly the same social and economic level as the Jews; see also Esposito "Gli Ebrei," 80. Of 65 Jewish dowries constituted and reported in prenuptial agreements made between 1580 and 1582, only two fell below 100 scudi and only another two were higher than 200 scudi. The one exception was the daughters of bankers, whose dowries ranged from 250 to 400 scudi, but this gap was hardly the enormous one separating the dowries of most Christian girls from those given, or at least promised, the daughters of very rich Christians; see Stow, "La Storiografia," 48 – 49. This same sample of 65 prenuptial agreements provides important information regarding the number of children. Adopting a practice that since has been discarded, Roman Jews resolved the problem of *halizah* through an obligatory oath taken individually by the groom's brothers—or through the agency of their father should one of them be a minor or in a distant location—binding themselves unconditionally to accept *halizah* should the need arise. (*Halizah* is the ceremony freeing a childless widow from the need to marry her late husband's brother, the so-called Levirate, without which the woman remains an ʿ*agunah*, literally anchored, and therefore technically unmarriageable.) Brothers, however, meant *all* the brothers in a family, since the halachah (Jewish law) makes all male children over the age of three months liable for *halizah*. In the 65 texts in our sample, 19 lack the oath, in 24 one brother swears, in 17 two brothers, and in 5 three brothers. This translates into as many as 19 families with only one male offspring, the groom ("as many as" because one can never be sure whether the oath was accidentally omitted, even though the Jewish notarial art at Rome was well systematized by 1580); the other 46 families have one male more than the number of oath-takers (again, the groom). The total thus is 138 sons. There is no way, of course, to estimate the number of daughters accurately, except by using a sex ratio of one/one; on this problem, see E. A. Wrigley, "Fertility Strategy for the Individual and the Group," in C. Tilly, ed., *Historical Studies of Changing Fertility* (Princeton, 1978), 135–54. This is surely high. But it does provide a probable maximum of 276 children, or 4.3 per family (for the 65 families surveyed). Hence, the Jewish family was small; it was highly nuclear, possessing few characteristics typical of complex familial structures; and the same state held during the Middle Ages, certainly in Ashkenaz, where, again, the family was singularly nuclear. See K. Stow, "The Jewish Family in the Rhineland: Form and Function," *American Historical Review* 92 (1987): 1085–1110. Moreover, our figures here may be even more than maximal. Eugenio Sonnino, studying population in seventeenth-century Rome as a whole, has cited the extraordinary, if constant, sex ratio favoring males, which he emphatically attributes to factors other than a heavy clerical presence. He argues against any kind of linearity in Rome's population growth; that is, there is no reason to assume a steady growth rate, however low, in the Roman Jewish population. Although not speaking specifically of Jews here, Sonnino is well aware of their demography. See Eugenio Sonnino and Rosa Traina, "The Population in Baroque Rome," in P. van Kessel and E. Schulte, eds., *Rome-Amsterdam: Two Growing Cities in Seventeenth Century Europe* (Amsterdam, 1997), esp. 58–70. My own thoughts are that the population size remained essentially unchanged, fluctuating in the hundreds, never more.

12. For Passapaire, *Notai ebrei*, 14,1,105r. See also Beatrice Gottlieb, *The Family in the Western World from the Black Death to the Industrial Age* (New York, 1993), 28, where she shows contracts between the generations reflecting a certain wariness in intergenerational intrafamilial behavior. However, these contracts were not, as they were with Passapaire, for the short term, but they regulated what might amount in practice to an older couple's (the parents') pension, hardly a light matter.

13. The regulation on taxation appears in *Notai ebrei*, 18,1,8r–11r, a collection of statutes rather than acts. One may corroborate here by noting that of 245 declarations received in 1692 by the Roman Jewish Comunità to serve as a basis for estimating taxes (admittedly somewhat beyond our specific period), 116 were made by individual family heads, 56 by fathers and sons together, 15 by brothers, and 53 by people with the same family name, but not necessarily related; Archivio della Comunità Israelitica, Roma, IE1, *Libro dei giuramenti per la tassa sul capitale*, 1692.

14. See Tacitus, *Histories*, trans. K. Wellesley (Harmondsworth, 1972),

book 5, par. 5; and on Cicero, Hans Lewy, *'Olamot Nifgashim* (Jerusalem, 1960).

15. Some of the Jews captured and enslaved were surely redeemed, just as a society for redemption was eventually founded at Rome. Inscriptions in the Roman catacombs record twelve synagogues and their officials. About coordination of activities nothing is known.

16. This did not stop Gregory from censuring bishops in southern France who were forcibly converting Jews, a censure requested, moreover, by Jewish merchants traveling between Rome and the cities of Marseilles and Arles; these particular letters are easily consulted in J. R. Marcus, trans., *The Jew in the Medieval World* (New York, 1965), 111–14. At the same time Gregory also enforced laws making conversion to Judaism illegal; nor might Jews prevent conversions to Christianity.

17. For this reconstruction of the Pierleoni, see K. Stow, "Jewish Approaches to the Papacy and the Papal Doctrine of Jewish Protection, 1050–1150" (in Hebrew), *Studies in the History of the Jewish People and the Land of Israel* 5 (1981): 75–90, summarized in English in K. Stow, *Alienated Minority: The Jews of Medieval Latin Europe* (Cambridge, Mass., 1992, 1994), 39–40.

18. On these matters, see K. Stow, *The '1007 Anonymous' and Papal Sovereignty: Jewish Perceptions of the Papacy and Papal Policy in the High Middle Ages* (Cincinnati, 1984), esp. 26–33. The matter was taken up again in some detail at the World Conference on Jewish Studies, June 1993, and in the notes to K. Stow, "The Avignonese Papacy, or After the Expulsion," in Jeremy Cohen, ed., *From Witness to Witchcraft: Jews and Judaism in Medieval Christian Thought* (Weisbaden, 1996), 292–97. Yitzhak Baer's article, "Ha-megamah ha-datit-ha-hevratit shel Sefer Hasidim," *Studies in the History of the Jewish People* (Jerusalem, 1985), 178, shows conclusively that the 1007 and *Sicut iudaeis* have identical clauses. Thus it is impossible to predate the 1007 to before 1119, which is the earliest possible appearance of *Sicut iudaeis*, without suggesting that it is based on the 1007. Moreover, the real issue with the 1007 is its perceptions of events, not the events themselves, whose precise unfolding we will never know on the basis of invariably idealized medieval chronicles; see e.g., Aaron Gurevitch, *Medieval Popular Culture*, trans. J. Bak and P. Hollingsworth (New York and Cambridge, 1990). See most recently, the remarks of Norman Golb, *The Jews in Medieval Nor-*

mandy (Cambridge, 1998), 3–15, esp. 3, and my review of Golb in *The Medieval Review* (electronic), July 1999.

19. On the movement of Jewish scholarship from Italy into France along these routes, see K. Stow, "By Land or by Sea: The Passage of the Kalonymides to the Rhineland in the Tenth Century," in *Cross Cultural Convergences in the Crusader Period*, ed. M. Goodich, S. Menasche, and S. Schein (New York, 1995).

20. See Robert Bonfil, "Myth, Rhetoric, History? A Study in the Chronicle of *Ahimaʿaz*" (in Hebrew), in M. Ben-Sasson, R. Bonfil, and J. Hacker, eds., *Culture and Society in Medieval Jewry* (Jerusalem, 1989).

21. See note 11, above.

22. Milano, *Il Ghetto*, 40; Vogelstein and Rieger, *Geschichte*, 1:256–57, citing passages from the text published in Abraham Berliner's *Kobez al Yad* 4:27–31.

23. See Joshua Starr, "The Mass Conversion of Jews in Southern Italy, 1290–1293," *Speculum* 21 (1946): 203–11; and the reappraisal by J. Cohen, *The Friars and the Jews* (Ithaca, 1982), 85–88.

24. See the text in Solomon Grayzel, *The Church and the Jews in the Thirteenth Century*, Vol. 2, 1254–1314, ed. K. Stow (New York, 1989), 147–48, no. 45.

25. The term is mine, but see the description of the stoning in A. Toaff, *Il Vino e la carne* (Bologna, 1989), 67–68, 224–25; and also Esposito, "Gli Ebrei," 96, this time on ritual violence in fifteenth-century Rome. On this phenomenon in Spain, see David Nirenberg, *Communities of Violence: Persecution of Minorities in the Middle Ages* (Princeton, 1996).

26. Milano, *Il Ghetto*, 37–38, 65–66.

27. Esposito, "Gli Ebrei," 95; Vogelstein and Rieger, *Geschichte*, 1:492; and see esp. Shlomo Simonsohn, *The Apostolic See and the Jews, Documents: 1464–1521* (Toronto, 1988–91), nos. 490, 670, 1055, and 1139.

28. On various fines for not wearing the badge, see Esposito, "Gli Ebrei," 56.

29. See the texts cited from Simonsohn in note 27, above.

30. The last of Immanuel's adventures, *Tofet ve-Eden* (loosely, *Inferno and Paradise*), resembles parts of Dante's *Divine Comedy*, employing rhymed prose and containing touches of the so-called *dolce stil nuovo* of Tuscan poetry upon which the works of Dante are built; see Dan Pagis, "Baroque

Trends in Italian Hebrew Poetry," *Italia Judaica, Gli Ebrei in Italia tra Rina-scimento ed Età Barocca, Atti del II Convegno Internazionale, Genova 10–15 giugno 1984* (Rome, 1986), 63–77. The *Shibbolei ha-leqet*, mentioned below, was first published in Venice, 1546.

31. Simonsohn, *Apostolic See*, 719, but esp. 739, and his *History*, vol. 7 of *Apostolic See*, 74–75, for this interpretation; on which see K. Stow, "Simon-sohn's *Apostolic See and the Jews*," in *Jewish Quarterly Review* 85 (1995): 410–11; see also Esposito, "Gli Ebrei," 47–48, affirming that Jews were regulated "normalmente [by] il diritto comune."

32. See the arabesque wording of the papal letter authorizing but not obligating sermons, *Vineam sorec*, in Grayzel, *The Church and the Jews in the Thirteenth Century*, 2:142–45, where the unique penalty clause leaves no question that forced sermons were illicit; see also the discussion, p. 141.

33. On the Roman Monte di pietà, see K. Stow, "The Good of the Church, The Good of the State: The Popes and Jewish Money," in Diana Wood, ed., *Christianity and Judaism* [= *Studies in Church History* 29 (Oxford, 1992)], 248. See, relatedly, Simone Luzzatto, *Discorso*, ed. A. Z. Ascoli; Hebrew trans., *Maʿamar ʿal Yehudei Veneziah*, by Riccardo Bacchi and Moshe Shulvass (Jerusalem, 1951), "Eighth Investigation," 97, which says that "throughout the world, the Jews are but one element of that blood—that is, the money—which nourishes the body politic." This is surely a direct response to those Franciscans who said that money was indeed the blood, but that Jewish activity was like a gangrenous clot in that blood. Luzzatto's emphasis is that Jews do not control the blood flow, but strengthen it. It should be added that Luzzatto's use of body politic is metaphoric, to be sure, but he is quite literalistic, too. Thus Jews are like limbs; they are not the head. I emphasize this to avoid what may seem to contradict what is said elsewhere in this study about the Jews lacking a true political, theoretical sense of the concept of body politic. If anything, Luzzatto's realism and graphic description of this body suggest he does not at all have in mind the *gestalt*, the overall theoretical, in fact, spiritualized Christian concept, which, among other important things, depends on the body politic personifying on earth the ultimately non-Jewish divine body of Christ.

34. Revealing the ambivalence, Sixtus IV did not repeat Innocent IV's thirteenth-century precedent declaring blood libels to be generically unfounded, but rather cited Innocent III's issuance of *Sicut iudaeis*, as found in

Grayzel, *The Church and the Jews in the Thirteenth Century*, vol. 1 (Philadelphia, 1933; reprint, New York, 1966), and vol. 2, no. 5, whose special codicil repeats in the text of Martin IV (Grayzel, vol. 2, no. 45). Ronnie Hsia, *Trent 1475* (New Haven, 1992), 127, mistakes the reference of Sixtus for the bull of Innocent IV, which concerns the libel at Valreas in 1247; recently followed by David Berger, "From Crusades to Blood Libels to Expulsions: Some New Approaches to Medieval Antisemitism," Second Annual Lecture of the Victor J. Selmanowitz Chair of Jewish History, Touro College, March 16, 1997, 10–11. However, the bull of Sixtus IV, as published by Simonsohn, *Apostolic See*, no. 999, says clearly Innocent III, and indicates *in concilio generali editum*. This is some kind of confusion by the chancery for "edited in the Decretals." Most important, the context of the bull cited by Sixtus IV matches Innocent III's *Sicut iudaeis* perfectly.

35. I thank Susan Einbinder for this reference to the Siddur of 1447, Hebrew Union College, in Cincinnati, Ohio, Klau Collection, ms. 396.

36. See Stow, *Taxation*, passim, on the *vigesima*; also the many texts on this tax published by Simonsohn in volume 6 of *Apostolic See*. See also Esposito, "Gli Ebrei," 61–65, on the Agone and Testaccio tax, as well as J. C. Maire Vigueur, "Les Juifs à Rome dans la seconde moitié du XIVe siècle: informations tirés d'un fonds notarié," in AA.VV., *Aspetti e problemi*, 24, 25.

37. Maire Vigueur, "Les Juifs," 28; Esposito, "Gli Ebrei," 90–91.

38. Esposito, "Gli Ebrei," 40, and esp. 91; Maire Vigueur, "Les Juifs," 28; see also RJ1007, 1313.

39. See Esposito, 80–81, for examples of leaseholds from the early sixteenth century; Maire Vigueur, "Les Juifs," 22–23.

40. See the list of Jewish professions in Esposito, "Gli Ebrei," 72; on the growth of Rome's general population, see J. Delumeau, *Vita economica e sociale di Roma nel cinquecento* (Florence, 1979), 60.

41. See *Notai ebrei*, 11,3,59r–v, and 11,4,62r–v, 69r; see the discussion of Roman Jewish economic status as a whole as modest in Ariel Toaff, "La vita materiale," in C. Vivanti, ed., *Gli ebrei in Italia, Storia d'Italia, Annali 11* (Turin, 1996), 1:239–61.

42. Maire Vigueur, "Les Juifs," 23; Esposito, "Gli Ebrei," 68–71.

42. Maire Vigueur, "Les Juifs," 23; Esposito, "Gli Ebrei," 68–71.

43. RJ80, 355, 403, 405, 486, 525.

44. Archivio di Stato, Roma, Camerale I, Diversa Cameralia, contains hundreds of such licenses, issued for a first time and with subsequent renewals; e.g., *busta* 410, folios 52v–53v.

45. See K. Stow, "The Papacy and the Jews: Catholic Reformation and Beyond," *Jewish History* 6 (1991): 268. Note that even Paul IV when establishing the Ghetto did not wholly prohibit lending (he otherwise did restrict the Jews economically by forbidding them to continue dealing in foodstuffs); rather, he cut the rate of permitted interest from 24 to 18 percent. Thirty years later, Sixtus V promoted Jewish lending to the poor by issuing hundreds of licenses to open or reopen banks in dozens of places (from which Jews had formally been expelled in 1569 by Pius V) in Lazio and elsewhere. These banks, and those in Rome, continued to operate until 1682, when they were closed, not because lending violated the canons, but because of the (then regnant) mercantilist argument that Jewish lending no longer benefited the state; see Stow, "The Good," 250. Even in the most difficult of moments, therefore, Jewish fortunes were linked to the political fortunes of the Papal State—in which, at least until 1682, the Jews were considered in one way or another to play a contributory role. The Jews, in other words, like so much else in the Papal State, were judged by a dual scale of sacred and profane values. The State pursued sacrality—its head was the chief official of (Catholic) Christendom; the State had political ends, like any other sovereign political body; and the two were always in conflict. Usually, it was the secular ends, cloaked albeit in a religious mantle, that gained the upper hand; on which, see Paolo Prodi, *Il Sovranno Pontifice* (Bologna, 1982), passim.

46. See the thorough discussion of this problem in Robert Bonfil, *Rabbis and Jewish Communities in Renaissance Italy* (Oxford, 1990), 209–30, with certain reservations by Stow, *Taxation*, 37–38. The issue is where de iure and de facto differed and how Jews, on the one hand, and the Vicar, on the other, manipulated this gap to their advantage.

47. Esposito, "Gli Ebrei," 41: and Francisco Delicado, *La Lozana Andaluza*, ed. Claude Allaigre (Madrid, 1985), 244; see also Milano, *Il Ghetto*, 210. And see note 49, here, and chap. 2, note 39, below.

48. *Notai ebrei*, 2,5,11r. See also the discussion of these synagogues in chapter 2. There are at least six prayerbooks for women with Italian trans-

lation in the library of the Hebrew Union College in Cincinnati, Klau Collection, ms. 243, 245, 247, 248, 264, 290, for which references I again thank Susan Einbinder.

49. See the classic study of E. Ashtor, "Palermitan Jewry in the Fifteenth Century," *Hebrew Union College Annual* 50 (1979): 242–43; and now Shlomo Simonsohn, *The Jews in Sicily*, vol. 1 (Leiden, 1997), although this volume reaches only 1300 and subsequent volumes now in press will arrive at the fifteenth century until the 1492 expulsion.

50. Stefano Infessura, *Diario della Città di Roma*, ed. O. Tommasini (Rome, 1890), 288.

51. Anna Foa discusses this in great depth in "Un vescovo marrano: il processo a Pedro de Aranda," *Quaderni Storici* 99 (1998): 536–52; and see also Milano, *Il Ghetto*, 56. Cf. Renata Segre, "Sephardic Settlements in Sixteenth Century Italy: A Historical and Geographical Survey," in Alisa Meyuhas Ginio, ed., *Jews, Christians, and Muslims in the Mediterranean World after 1492* (= *Mediterranean Historical Review*), 1992, although note that Segre's identification of Salomone Caviglia Marrano as a marrano is incorrect, since the name appears in the *Notai ebrei* a number of times after the Ghetto was established, RJ1824, 1891, always with this nickname. Caviglia's presence in pre-Tridentine Rome is no indication of papal acceptance of marranos. See also, on immigration into Italy, Segre's *The Jews in Piedmont*.

52. See Milano, *Il Ghetto*, 63, and B. D. Cooperman, "Venetian Policy Towards Levantine Jews in Its Broader Italian Context," in G. Cozzi, ed., *Gli Ebrei e Venezia* (Milan, 1987), 72–74.

53. On the Ancona episode, see S. W. Baron, *A Social and Religious History of the Jews* (Philadelphia, 1952–), 14:39; Cecil Roth, *The House of Nasi: Dona Gracia* (Philadelphia, 1948), 134–75; A. Toaff, "Nuova Luce sui Marrani di Ancona, 1556," *Studi Sull'Ebraismo Italiano* (Rome, 1974), 261–80; and esp. I. Sonne, *Mi-Pavolo ha-Rev'i 'ad Pius ha-Hamishi* (Jerusalem, 1954), 19–100.

54. See how Infessura, *Diario*, 288, and Ibn Verga, cited in note 55 below, are used by Ariel Toaff, "Ebrei spagnoli e marrani nell'Italia del Cinquecento: una presenza contestata," in A. Foa, M. Silvera, and K. Stow, eds., *Oltre il 1492* (= *La Rassegna Mensile di Israel* 58 [1992]): 47–60. To view these stories and the overall problematic of Sephardi immigration to Rome in an essentially modern "ethnic" perspective is to remove them from their con-

textual perspective. The use of the term *natio* would be far better. Indeed, the term was still used in Italy in the eighteenth century when referring to regional Italian origin, that is, whether from Tuscany, the Veneto, or Rome (Lazio); see, e.g., Renata Ago, *Carriere e clientele nella Roma barocca* (Rome-Bari, 1990), 22–28.

55. Shelomo ibn Verga, *Sefer Shebet Yehudah*, ed. Y. F. Baer and A. Shohat (Jerusalem, 1947), 123–24. The context has to do with the overall problems of Spanish Jewish refugees, and the specific background is grave hunger throughout Italy, which created pressures on all sides to refuse entry to these Jews.

56. This report was most recently evaluated positively by A. Toaff, "The Jewish Communities of Catalonia, Aragon and Castile in 16th Century Rome," in A. Toaff and S. Schwarzfuchs, eds., *The Mediterranean and the Jews: Banking, Finance and International Trade (XVI–XVIII Centuries)* (Ramat-Gan, 1989), 249–70. But see the objection of Robert Bonfil, *Gli ebrei in Italia nell'epoca del Rinascimento* (Florence, 1991), 55 (= Robert Bonfil, *Jewish Life in Renaissance Italy*, Berkeley, 1994, 83–84).

57. On the Jewish population and the census of 1527, see G. Gnoli, "Descriptio urbis, censimento della popolazione di Roma avanti il sacco borbonico," *Archivio della R. Deputazione Romana di Storia Patria* 17 (1905): 365–520. See the survey of Alan C. Harris, "La demografia del ghetto in Italia, 1516–1797 circa," *Rassegna Mensile di Israel* (Rome, 1967); and Roberto Bachi, "The Demographic Development of Italian Jewry from the Seventeenth Century," *Jewish Journal of Sociology* 4/2 (1962): 172–91, which is a condensed version of the unpublished "L'evoluzione demografica degli ebrei italiani dal 1600 al 1937" (Florence, 1939). As said, the increase in the Jewish population was probably not a serious factor in evolving attitudes, since the overall ratio of Jews and Christians in Rome likely remained stable, at least visibly so. One might, to be sure, object that the Jewish population seemed to be increasing at a rate far greater than that of the general population, since it had apparently more than doubled by midcentury. Further, since its rate of increase slowed to a maximum of 20 percent during the subsequent half-century, this would be a clear indication that the physical and economic constraints of the Ghetto were responsible for this reduced rate. (See Stow, "The Consciousness of Closure," in David B. Ruderman, ed., *Essential Papers on Jewish Culture in Renaissance and Baroque Italy* [New York, 1992].)

In which case, the Ghetto was somehow a response to an "excessive" Jewish population, an attempt to control its growth. The probability of concern about Jewish population growth might also be sought in the expansion in Jewish sites of residence in Rome, as noted in detail in note 74, chap. 1, below. However, in 1555, Paul IV protested *only* that Jews were dwelling in *domos in nobilioribus civitatum*, not about their numbers. And, more important, famine, flood, and plague, which took their toll in Rome in the 1590s, certainly affected Jews no less than Christians, so that we should be especially wary of the raw numbers, particularly the seeming decrease to 20 percent (which, in any case, must reflect immigration, since no population grows this rapidly through increased fecundity). The problem of drawing results from premodern censuses is discussed brilliantly in David Herlihy and Christiane Klapisch-Zuber, *Tuscans and Their Families: A Study of the Florentine Catasto of 1427* (New Haven, 1985), chaps. 3 and 5. On plague, but especially famine in Rome toward the end of the sixteenth century, see Peter Burke, "Southern Italy in the 1590s: Hard Times or Crisis?" 179, and N. S. Davidson, "Northern Italy in the 1590s," 157–60, both in *The European Crisis of the 1590s: Essays in Comparative History*, ed. Peter Clark (London, 1985).

58. See Bonfil, *Jewish Life*, 179–80; and see chapter 3, below, again on the question of borrowings from Italian institutions.

59. M. A. Shulvass, *The Jews in the World of the Renaissance*, trans. E. Kose (Leiden, 1973), 62. See, too, A. Milano, "I 'Capitoli di Daniel da Pisa' e la comunità di Roma," *La Rassegna Mensile d'Israel* 10 (1935–36): 409–26 (the text). But see the reflections on the concept of sovereignty in the *Capitoli* and the actual political management of the community in chapter 3, below.

60. For texts of such ordinances, see L. Finkelstein, *Jewish Self-Government in the Middle Ages* (New York, 1964), 196, 250.

61. RJ282,670; however, see the contrasting views about there being more than one community in Anna Esposito, "Le 'comunità' ebraiche di Roma prima del Sacco (1527): problemi di identificazione," *Henoch* 12 (1990): 178–85.

62. Ibid., 178–80.

63. But see the discussion in Milano, *Il Ghetto*, 175–80; and, even more, Toaff, *Ghetto di Roma*, 12–15, and Toaff, "Ebrei spagnoli," 47–60; and Esposito, "La 'comunità'" 165. The unsure footing of the Congrega of sixty is

shown by the enormous infrequency of its meetings, usually to sanction measures of taxation; see fascicle 18 of the *Notai ebrei* of the mid-1570s.

64. One should add that in 1571, following an influx of Italian Jews into Rome on the heels of expulsions, in 1569, from the smaller centers of the Papal State, the Congrega was restructured. No longer divided 30/30, as da Pisa had dictated in 1524, the Congrega was now to be composed of 35 *Italiani* and 25 *ultramontani*. Comprising more than 75 percent of the local Jewish population, an even division of legislative power no longer corresponded to reality. Yet, all the while, since 1524, the restricted Council of Twenty (one-third of the sixty members of the Congrega), which had run the community's day-to-day affairs, had been composed of twelve *Italiani* and eight *ultramontani*, just as there were two *fattori Italiani* and one *ultramontano*; see Milano, "Capitoli," 426; *capitolo*, 36. True political parity the *ultramontani* had never attained. By 1571, moreover, one's identity as an *Italiano* might be the fruit of marriage, or choice, far more than of birth; see immediately below.

65. Toaff, *Ghetto di Roma*, 64–72. For the lists, see Milano, *Il Ghetto*, 223–24; and Stow, "Ethnic Rivalry," no. 21, for further specific textual references. For various intersynagogal difficulties and litigation, see Stow, "Prossimità o distanza: etnicità, sefarditi e assenza di conflitti etnici nella Roma del sedicesimo secolo," in A. Foa, M. Silvera, and K. Stow, eds., *Oltre il 1492*, (= *La Rassegna Mensile di Israel* 58 [1992]): 61–74; as well as Toaff, "Jewish Communities," 250–51, Vogelstein and Rieger, *Geschichte*, and Milano, *Il Ghetto*, 217–20.

66. On which, see Shimon Schwarzfuchs, "Controversie nella Comunità di Roma agli inizi del secolo XVI," *Scritti in Memoria di Enzo Sereni* (Jerusalem, 1970), 95–100 (Italian section), 133–44 (Hebrew). On a related issue, that of a separate liturgy, see J. B. Sermoneta, "The Liturgy of Sicilian Jews," (Hebrew) in Haim Beinart, ed., *Jews in Italy* (Jerusalem, 1988), 24–108. The Sicilian Jews had their own synagogue but almost aggressively married with non-Sicilian Jews, reflecting again on the many ambivalences—and the need for historiographical reserve on such matters as alleged ethnic dispute—in sixteenth-century Jewish Rome.

67. *Notai ebrei*, 12,1,113r,117r.

68. The match of 1557, moreover, was between the Corcos and the Trigo, two families noted for money and learning; *Notai ebrei*, 12,1,74v,

hence a match parallel to that in 1538 between the Piattelli and the Piccio, RJ268. These conclusions are based primarily on contrasting contracts of engagement and the like with the synagogal membership lists noted above; see Stow, "Ethnic Rivalry," 291–96, and contrast the earlier situation in Sicily itself, in H. Bresc, "La famille dans la societé sicilienne médiévale," in *La famiglia e la vita quotidiana* (Rome, 1986), 187–93. What comparison showed was that for the whole of Rome's Jews, of 229 marriages observed for the period 1536 to 1633, 56 (24.5 percent) were "out-marriages." Between 1536 and 1545, such out-marriages between different Jewish groups reached a rate of 22.2 percent, and by 1596 the rate had climbed to 33.3 percent. Italian men, the largest single marrying and out-marrying group, and hence the one yielding the most reliable statistics (perhaps, given the ethnic construction of the Roman community—over 70 percent Italian—the most revealing ones, since this high a percentage favors heavy in-marriage), were already out-marrying at a rate of 16.6 percent in 1536, and 21.4 in 1596. The percentage of out-marriages of Sephardi men is even higher; yet the small absolute number of these marriages (found in the *Notai ebrei*) prohibits drawing any conclusions. The parallels between these percentages and those in effect in the State of Israel since 1948 is striking; see U. O. Schmelz, S. Della Pergola, and U. Avner, *Ethnic Differences Among Israeli Jews: A New Look* (Jerusalem, 1991), 37–41, 46–49. To better appreciate Jewish social parity with regard to the complete lack of formal differences of rank, compare the conclusions about *popolo* and magnates in Christiane Klapisch-Zuber, "Kinship and Politics in Fourteenth Century Florence," in David Kertzer and Julius Kirschner, eds., *The Family in Italy, from Antiquity to the Present* (New Haven, 1991), 208–27.

69. On this kind of "social rhetoric," see Nancy Struever, *The Language of History in the Renaissance* (Princeton, 1970), 140; on clothing and social status, see *Notai ebrei*, 3,2,69v–70v (22 Oct. 1582). On sustaining the ceremonial action, see Dennis Brissett and Charles Edgley, eds., *Life as Theater: A Dramaturgical Source Book* (New York, 1990), 119; and see the use of the term "ritual" as attributed to Kenneth Burke by Charles Edgley and Ronny Turner, "Death as Theater," 285–99; as well as the appendix by Burke himself, 411–19.

70. On repetitiveness as essential to Jewish ritual, see Jonathan Z. Smith,

To Take Place (Chicago, 1987); on Christian ritual, see the exposition of Edward Muir, *Ritual in Early Modern Europe* (Cambridge, 1997), esp. 55–80. See also chapter 1, below, and the discussion of ritual there.

71. See the discussion by David Biale in "Confessions of an Historian of Jewish Culture," *Jewish Social Studies* 1/1 (1994): 40–52.

72. Victor Turner, *From Ritual to Theater: The Human Seriousness of Play* (New York, 1982), 121, goes beyond illusion and writes: "The soul of theater . . . is . . . fantasized reality even while it realizes fantasy." Of course, all illusion includes an element of fantasy, but with respect to the Ghetto, this might be too strong a term. The Jews were pretending certain things to themselves, especially, as we shall see, that they were in control of many of their affairs. But they had no fantasies that they were truly in control. Nor did they ever believe, or want to believe, that there were no cultural or behavioral differences between them and Rome's Christians.

73. To wit, Richard Schechner, "From Ritual to Theater and Back," *Essays on Performance Theory* (New York, 1977), 79, as cited by Turner, *From Ritual to Theater*, 112: "Theater comes into existence when a separation occurs between audience and performers." This position is also taken by many of the articles in the collection *Life as Theater*. However, I am arguing for a different kind of stage, one on which Jews performed often for themselves, on an everyday basis, not solely in times of crisis or social anxiety, which would be the case in Turner's concept of "social drama." In this connection, see Peter Berger, "Sociological Perspectives—Society as Drama," in Brissett and Edgley, *Life as Theater*, 55, saying: "society as a whole has the character of a play," but noting that Berger's interpretation of Huizinga's *Homo Ludens* is not precise, since Huizinga was referring only to what he called "the game factor *in* society," whereas Berger means that "society at large has . . . an artificial character," 55; and also see 57, "society exists as a network of social roles . . . ," and 60, "Society gives us names to shield us from nothingness," and "we can say that deception and self-deception are at the very heart of social reality." In this case, differentiating between actor and audience would be difficult. I add that I am not thinking in terms of Clifford Geertz's "Theater State," as in his *Negara* (Princeton, 1980), on which, recently, see Aletta Biersack, "Local Knowledge, Local History, Geertz and Beyond," in Lynn Hunt, ed., *The New Cultural History* (Berkeley, 1989).

I believe I am also going beyond Peter Burke, whose discussion of social drama follows the lines set out by Turner; Peter Burke, *The Historical Anthropology of Early Modern Italy* (Cambridge, 1987), 11–16.

74. On Scazzocchio see Stow, "Abramo ben Aron Scazzocchio: Another Kind of Rabbi" (forthcoming: Proceedings of a conference held at Bar Ilan University, December 1993).

75. Eli Lederhendler, *Jewish Responses to Modernity: New Voices in America and Eastern Europe* (New York, 1994), 51. And on illusion, see the texts of Peter Berger cited in note 73 above.

76. Esther Cohen in a personal communication, points out that ritual was pervasive in all medieval urban life, and see, notably, the work of Richard Trexler, *Public Life in Renaissance Florence* (New York, 1980).

77. The one real chronicle of events at the time of the Ghetto's inception is by one Benjamin ben Elnatan; Isaiah Sonne, *Mi-Pavolo ha-Reviʿi ʿad Pius ha-Hamishi* (Jerusalem, 1954). His discussion specifically of Rome, however, is limited almost wholly to matters concerning the jail of the Inquisition where he was a prisoner. For a discussion of the parallels between historical writing and modes of behavior, see K. Stow, "The New Fashioned from the Old: Parallels in Public and Learned Memory and Practice in Sixteenth Century Jewish Rome," in B. D. Cooperman and Barbara Garvin, eds., *Memory and Identity: The Jews of Italy* (College Park, Maryland, 2000).

78. See the discussion of boundary-maintaining mechanisms in Victor Turner, *Dramas, Fields, and Metaphors: Symbolic Action in Human Society* (Ithaca, 1974), 269; also for the concept of social arena, see Peter Marsh, "Identity, an Ethnogenic Perspective," in R. C. Trexler, ed., *Persons in Groups* (Binghamton, 1985); and Milton Gordon, *Assimilation in American Life* (New York, 1964), for the idea of sociological walls. An interesting parallel is the medieval statesman Ibn Khaldun's concept of *communitas*, or *asabiya*; see E. I. J. Rosenthal, *Political Thought in Medieval Islam* (Cambridge, 1968), 84–112, esp. 87, albeit the concept applies to common social forces as much, if not more, than to an arena in which these forces are played out, although the arena in question is as mental in its structure as it is concrete. By contrast, one may also see the ghetto, from the outside in, as a stage, but one on which the Jews are actors, if not marionettelike, placed there to "perform" for Christians, in the sense of being placed there in order somehow to retain the theologically necessary Jewish presence, which

was no longer tenable while Jews lived freely, as they had done for centuries, in the wider Roman society; this idea will be explored elsewhere.

79. Brissett and Edgley, *Life as Theater*, 163.

80. This social theater should be distinguished from what Stephen Greenblatt would call dissimulation, cited by John Martin in "Inventing Sincerity, Refashioning Prudence: The Discovery of the Individual in Renaissance Europe," *American Historical Review* 102 (1997): 1309–42; nor is this Martin's own concept of "sincerity." What I am arguing is that the theatrical became the norm, with Jews not distinguishing between role-playing and what might be called cautiously unguarded behavior.

81. For this point in more detail, see chapter 2.

82. See Robert Bonfil, "Changes in the Cultural Patterns of a Jewish Society in Crisis: Italian Jewry at the Close of the Sixteenth Century," *Jewish History* 3/2 (1988): 11–30. In fact, the move to Italian was a protracted one, which depended to some extent on the nature of the document. Pompeo del Borgo, perhaps as an apprentice of Isaac Piattelli, was writing Italian documents before even 1566, ASC, Sezione I, vol. 877. These were simple rentals, contracts of obligation, and preliminary agreements to arbitrate, not the testimony itself. By contrast, he was drawing acts, on his own, in Hebrew through 1600, when the bulk of his work was already in Italian (Sez. I, vols. 879, 883). The language used was thus a matter of the notary's habit and choice. Notably, testimony in cases of arbitration was recorded as often as possible in Hebrew, at least through about 1600.

83. See Stow, "The Consciousness of Closure."

84. On this concept, see Milano, *Il Ghetto*, 529, 540, and also Cecil Roth, "La festa per l'istituzione del Ghetto a Verona," *Rassegna Mensile di Israel* 3 (1928): 33–39.

85. See the further discussion of this point in chapter 1. Specifically on rogations, see Muir, *Ritual*, 66–67 and 282, and note 1 in Chapter 1, below.

86. Turner, *Dramas, Fields, and Metaphors*, 269.

87. See Simona Feci, "The Death of a Miller: A Trial *contra hebreos* in Baroque Rome," *Jewish History* 7/2 (1993): 15–20. On the rock-tossing, see Archivio di Stato, Roma, *Relazioni dei Sbirri*, no. 104 20-1-1611; *Costituti, busta* 676, 21.1.1611; I thank Robert Davis for graciously sharing this text with me. In fact, there were often scuffles between Jews and Christians, on which see *Notai ebrei*, 18,1,3v (25 Sept. 1573). The story of the two felons is

treated in full in Simona Foà, ed., *La Giustizia degl'ebrei* (Rome, 1987), and in context, in Simona Foà, ed., *Le "Chroniche" della Famiglia Citone*, trans. A. A. Piattelli (Rome, 1988). On the importance and concept of space in Rome, see Laurie Nussdorfer, "The Politics of Space in Early Modern Rome," *Memoires of the American Academy in Rome* 42 (1999): 161–86.

88. This would parallel the point of Emile J. Pin and Jamie Turndorf, "Staging One's Ideal Self," in Brissett and Edgley, *Life as Theater*, 163–81, esp. 177: that "performers risk failure, if they stage performances that are too distant from their actual life experiences."

89. On the notion of social memory, see particularly Paul Connorton, *How Societies Remember* (Cambridge, 1989).

1 / The Jew in a Traumatized Society

1. Further on rogations *and their meaning*, see Martine Boiteux, "Espace urbain, pratiques rituelles, parcours symboliques: Rome dans la second moitié du XVIième sieècle," in F. Hinard and M. Royo, eds., *Rome: L'Espace urbain et ses représentations* (Tours, 1993). And on sanctified urban spaces with relation to the ghetto, see Elizabeth Crouzet-Pavan, "Venice between Jerusalem, Byzantium, and Divine Retribution: The Origins of the Ghetto," *Mediterranean Historical Review* 6 (1991): 164.

2. For a clear discussion of the state and bodily metaphors, with implications about retaining the body politic's soundness, see Guido Ruggiero, "Constructing Civic Morality, Deconstructing the Body: Civic Rituals of Punishment in Renaissance Venice," in J. Chiffoleau, Lauro Martines, and A. Paravicini Bagliani, eds., *Riti e rituali nelle Società Medievali* (Spoleto, 1994).

3. A thorough discussion of the rhetoric and preaching of contemporaries about sixteenth-century Rome is in Frederick McGinnis, *Right Thinking and Sacred Oratory in Counter-Reformation Rome* (Princeton, 1995). And see John O'Malley, *Rome of the Renaissance* (London, 1981), on the hopes and expectations, including millenarian ones, of the Church Triumphant in the sixteenth century.

4. Fears of pollution by Judaism first appear in Paul's Epistles to the Corinthians and Galatians, where they are either likened to the yeast that can sour an entire lump of dough or the Temple altar of the "carnal Jews" as

opposed to the spiritual one of the Christians; Galatians 4:20–5:9, and 1 Corinthians 10:16–22. On Paul's radical view of Judaism that made such interpretations possible, see most recently Daniel Boyarin, *A Radical Jew: Paul and the Politics of Identity* (Berkeley, 1994). These themes are continued in the works of John Chrysostom, on whom see especially Wayne Meeks and Robert Wilkin, *Jews and Christians in Antioch in the First Four Centuries of the Common Era* (Missoula, Mont., 1978), and Agobard of Lyon, on whom, see Bernard Blumenkranz, "Deux compilations canoniques de Florus de Lyon et l'action antijuive d'Agobard," *Revue Historique de Droit Français et Étranger* 33 (1955): 227–54, 560–82; Mgr. Bressolles, *Saint Agobard, Évêque de Lyon, 760–840* (Paris, 1949); and Akiva Gilboa, ed. and trans., *Agobardi Lugdunensis Archiepiscopi, Epistolae Contra Iudaeos* (Latin text with Hebrew trans.) (Jerusalem, 1964).

5. On the foundations of the Venetian Ghetto, the best discussions are by Benjamin Ravid, "Republica nifredet mikol shilton 'aher," in A. Greenbaum and A. Irvy, eds., *Thought and Action* (Tel Aviv, 1983), 27–53; idem, "From Geographical Realia to Historiographical Symbol: The Odyssey of the Word Ghetto," in Ruderman, ed., *Essential Papers*, 373–85; and idem, "The Religious, Economic, and Social Background and Context of the Establishment of the Ghetti of Venice," in G. Cozzi, ed., *Gli Ebrei e Venezia*, (Milan, 1987); and also Robert Bonfil, *Jewish Life in Renaissance Italy*, 39–41.

6. Ruggiero, "Constructing Civic Morality," 184.

7. The fullest description of Jewish life in Rome remains Hans Lewy, *'Olamot Nifgashim* (Jerusalem, 1960). And see, most recently, Leonard V. Rutgers, *The Jews in Late Ancient Rome: Evidence of Cultural Interaction in the Roman Diaspora* (Leiden, 1995).

8. These events are recorded in the so-called *Avvisi*, anonymous recordings of events, copied and gathered in Biblioteca Apostolica Vaticana, Codex Urb. Lat. 1038, f. 140r; 1039, 104r–v, 108v, 112v, 120r–v, and various other volumes there.

9. On the moment of the awakening of this consciousness, see K. Stow, "The Consciousness of Closure: Roman Jewry and Its 'Ghet,'" in Ruderman, ed., *Essential Papers*. On circumstances at the inception of the Ghetto, see Stow, *Catholic Thought*; on those at the Ghetto's end, see Stefano Caviglia, *L'identità salvata* (Bari, 1995). See also Milano's *Il Ghetto*, Vogelstein and Rieger's *Geschichte*, and Berliner, *Storia degli Ebrei di Roma*. These works

cite from the Piattelli notarial texts, and they investigate family life and other similar issues that normally historians at the end of the nineteenth century avoided, as does Bluestein, *Storia degli ebrei in Roma* (Rome, 1920). Nobody has systematically exploited these texts. Recent investigations of Rome during the Ghetto period concentrate on political issues. See Mario Rosa, "Tra tolleranza e repressione: Roma e gli ebrei nel '700, *Italia Judaica III* (Rome, 1989); Marina Caffiero, "Le insidie de' perfidi Giudei,' Antiebraismo e riconquista Cattolica alla fine del settecento," *Rivista Storica Italiana* 105 (1993): 555–81; and idem, "Tra Chiesa e Stato: Gli ebrei in Italia nell'età dei Lumi e della Rivoluzione," in Corrado Vivanti, ed., *Gli ebrei in Italia, Storia d'Italia, Annali 11* (Turin, 1996), 1091–1132.

10. On inundations and their calamitous effects, see Peter Burke, "Southern Italy in the 1590s: Hard Times or Crisis?" 179, and N. S. Davidson, "Northern Italy in the 1590s," 157–60, both in Peter Clark, ed., *The European Crisis of the 1590s: Essays in Comparative History* (London, 1985). The population of the Ghetto has never been fixed of a certainty, but 4,000 would be an acceptable average; see Milano, *Il Ghetto*, 97–98; and see note 57 in the Introduction.

11. Ferdinand Gregorovious, *Der Ghetto und die Juden in Rom* (repr., Berlin, 1935; trans., *The Ghetto and the Jews of Rome* [New York, 1948]). One might also profitably consult Bluestein, *Storia*, and Nello Pavoncello, *I Toponimi del vecchio Ghetto di Roma* (Rome, 1978), as well as Ettore Natali, *Il Ghetto di Roma* (Rome, 1887). For excellent maps of the ghetto, including a reconstruction of the "ground floor" of the ghetto buildings, see Carla Benocci and Enrico Guidoni, *Il Ghetto* (Rome, 1993), 36–37.

12. RJ1735. See Pavoncello, *I Toponimi*, and Jean Delumeau, *Vie économique et sociale de Rome dans la seconde moitié du XVIe siècle*, 2 vols. (Rome, 1959); Italian abridgment, *Vita economica e sociale di Roma nel cinquecento* (Florence, 1979), 1:478, describing the work constructing the Ghetto perimeter.

13. On immigrants and migrant workers, see Ivana Ait, "Mercanti 'stranieri' a Roma nel secolo XV nei registri della 'dogana di terra,'" *Studi Romani* 35 (1987): 25–30. On customs of the time, see Maria Luisa Lombardo, *La Dogana Minuta a Roma nel primo quattrocento* (Viterbo, 1983), 134–38; concerning foodstuffs imported into Rome, identical to so-called Jewish food, see G. Franco Romagnoli, "Rome's Jewish Quarter: A Rich Culinary

Heritage," *Gourmet Magazine*, August 1995, 52–55, 90–94. The illustrations in Therese and Mendel Metzger, *Jewish Life in the Middle Ages: Illuminated Hebrew Manuscripts of the Thirteenth to Sixteenth Centuries* (New York, 1982), show that Jews and others dressed alike. Language will be discussed below.

14. On Christian Kabbalah, see most recently Moshe Idel, "Particularism and Universalism in Kabbalah, 1480–1650," in Ruderman, ed., *Essential Papers*, 345–71; and idem, "Major Currents in Italian Kabbalah Between 1560–1660," in *Italia Judaica II*, 243–62. See also the classic studies of Chaim Wirszubski, *Three Studies in Christian Kabbala* (Jerusalem, 1975), and *A Christian Kabbalist Reads the Law* (in Hebrew) (Jerusalem, 1977). Jewish attraction to magic is seen well in Ruderman's study of Abraham Yagel, *Kabbalah, Magic, and Science: The Cultural Universe of a Sixteenth Century Jewish Physician* (Cambridge, Mass., 1988), esp. 102–20. On Jewish humanism, see Hava Tirosh Rothschild, "In Defense of Jewish Humanism," *Jewish History* 3/2 (1988): 31–58, and various essays of David Ruderman, among which, "The Italian Renaissance and Jewish Thought," in A. Rabil, ed., *Renaissance Humanism: Foundations and Forms* (Philadelphia, 1988), 1:382–432, and "The Impact of Science on Jewish Culture and Society in Venice," in *Gli Ebrei e Venezia*, 417–48 (repr. in *Essential Papers*, 519–53). See also the essays in David Ruderman, ed., *Preachers of the Italian Ghetto*, (Los Angeles, 1992). On the case of the Jewish book of divination desired by Christian clergy see Archivio di Stato, Roma, Tribunale del Governatore, Criminali, Costituti, vol. 38, fols. 11–13.

15. For example, two of the sons of Rabbi Abramo Scazzocchio were known for this practice—as well as reproved; RJ988. Gambling in particular occasioned rabbinical censure; on which, see Robert Bonfil, "Toward a Social and Spiritual Portrait of the Jews of the Veneto in the Early Sixteenth Century" (in Hebrew), *Zion* 41 (1976): 77. Other occasions where Jews and Christians rubbed elbows intimately: when they litigated before Jewish courts—with the sanction of the Vicar, RJ566; in partnership, RJ1028–29; or even when Christian arbiters were selected by Jews, RJ822, 1007—practices which either ceased sometime after the Ghetto was established or were manipulated, hopefully to his advantage, by the Vicar. See chapter 3.

16. See Romagnoli, "Rome's Jewish Quarter." The most popular of these Jewish foods today is *carciofi alla giudia*, deep-fried artichokes cut so they open like the flowers they are; completely edible, with no leaves to dis-

card, these artichokes are a work of gastronomic splendor or disaster—depending on the chef's skill. On the consumption of non-Jewish, nonkosher wine, see Yacov Boksenboim, ed., *The Letters of Rabbi Leon Modena* (Tel Aviv, 1984), 134–38. Modena protests the opposition to this long-standing Italian practice; contrary to common perceptions, indigenous Italian Jews are neither Sephardim nor Ashkenazim, but Italian, with their own rites and liturgies. In fact, the Ashkenazi rite derives largely from the Italian one, whereas a Sephardic input is felt in Italian ritual after the thirteenth century; see Stow, *Alienated Minority*, chapter 3, passim, and the literature cited there.

17. RJ867, for a scandal over the sale of a sick, thus nonkosher, animal. See RJ9,1498,1927 on prices, and 995 for price gouging.

18. This subject has been pursued by Anna Foa, "The Marranos' Kitchen," in Proceedings of the II Conference on Mediterranean Jewry, Bar Ilan University, December 1993 (forthcoming).

19. On women and observance in the home through the contemporary period, see Paula E. Hyman, *Gender and Assimilation in Modern Jewish History: The Roles and Representation of Women* (Seattle, 1995), 29–40, and Marion Kaplan, "Priestess or Hausfrau: Women and Tradition in the German-Jewish Family," in S. Cohen and P. Hyman, eds., *The Jewish Family* (New York, 1986), esp. 68–72. On Jewish women today regulating sexuality through determining the end of their menstrual period, see Rahel Wasserfall, "Menstruation and Identity: The Meaning of Niddah for Moroccan Women Immigrants to Israel," in Howard Eilberg-Schwartz, ed., *People of the Body: Jews and Judaism from an Embodied Perspective* (Albany, 1992), 309–29.

20. Muir, *Ritual in Early Modern Europe*, passim, where family and ritual are by default mutually exclusive categories; and see Dyan Elliott, *Spiritual Marriage: Sexual Abstinence in Medieval Wedlock* (Princeton, 1993). An excellent basic description of the medieval Christian family and the antitheses of spiritual versus biological families is David Herlihy, *Medieval Households* (Cambridge, Mass., 1985), and idem, "The Making of the Medieval Family: Symmetry, Structure, and Sentiment," *Journal of Family History* 8 (1983): 116–30. See also the literature cited in K. Stow, "The Jewish Family in the Rhineland." On changes occurring in the fifteenth century, especially to the image of the Holy Family, in art as well as in prose, see Christiane Klapisch-Zuber, "Zacharias, or the Ousted Father: Nuptial Rites in Tuscany

between Giotto and the Council of Trent," in *Women, Family, and Ritual in Renaissance Italy*, trans. Lydia Cochrane (Chicago, 1985).

21. On the director of souls, see Natalie Davis, *Women on the Margins* (Cambridge, Mass., 1995), 67–71; also Adriano Prosperi, *Tribunali della conscienza: Inquisitori, confessori, missionari* (Turin, 1996), passim.

22. See the lucid presentation in Samuel K. Cohn, Jr., "Last Wills: Family, Women, and the Black Death in Central Italy," *Women in the Streets: Essays on Sex and Power in Renaissance Italy* (Baltimore, 1996). See, too, the works cited in note 26, chapter 2, below, esp. Thomas Kuehn, who discusses the gap between law and practice, even as the courts often privileged propriety over hard law.

23. The Christian ritual cycle is discussed in Muir, *Ritual*, 55–80, esp. 59 for a synoptic graph.

24. The initial and principal proponent of Jewish-Christian mixing at the start of the Renaissance was Cecil Roth, *The Jews in the Renaissance* (Philadelphia, 1959). These themes were last discussed in full at the sixth conference of the Associazione Italiana per la Studia di Giudaismo in 1986; see esp. Robert Bonfil, "Società cristana e società ebraica nell'Italia medievale e rinascimentale: riflessioni sul significato e sui limiti di una convergenza," in M. Luzzati, M. Olivari, and A. Veronese, eds., *Ebrei e Cristiani nell'Italia Medievale e Moderna: Conversioni, Scambi, Contrasti* (Rome, 1988). One may also see the discussions of M. G. Muzzarelli, *Ebrei e Città d'Italia in Età di transizione: Il Caso di Cesena dal XIV al XVI secolo* (Bologna, 1983); idem, "Ebrei, Bologna e sovrano-pontifice: la fine di una relazione tra verifiche, restrizioni e ripensamenti," in M. G. Muzzarelli, ed., *Verso l'epilogo di una convivenza: gli ebrei a Bologna nel xvi secolo* (Florence, 1996), 19–54; and Anna Esposito, "Gli Ebrei a Roma nella seconda metà del '400 attraverso i protocolli del notaio Giovanni Angelo Amati," in AA.VV., *Aspetti e problemi della presenza ebraica nell'Italia centro-settentrionale (secoli XIV e XV)* (Rome, 1983), 29–126.

25. To be wary of these antinomies has been argued cogently by David Sorkin, "The Impact of Emancipation on Germany Jewry: A Reconsideration," in Jonathan Frankel and Steven Zipperstein, eds., *Assimilation and Community* (Cambridge, 1992); see also George L. Mosse, *German Jews Beyond Judaism* (Bloomington, 1985).

26. A somewhat different slant is offered by Robert Bonfil, *Jewish Life*,

283: "They [Jewish cemeteries] were the expression of a mentality formed as a mirror image of the Other, even though at times in open opposition to it, a mentality that though separate, shared the same mind-set and was therefore intent on reproducing in miniature the same social world, of which the cemetery too was an integral part." This outlook, however, would view subculture as derivative, which is not necessarily true. See also the observations on Bonfil's argument by David Ruderman, "Cecil Roth, Historian of Italian Jewry: A Reassessment," in David N. Myers and David B. Ruderman, eds., *The Jewish Past Revisited: Reflections on Modern Jewish Historians* (New Haven, 1998), 40, who proposes "negociation" as a more proper term, in line with Funkenstein's "dialectics."

27. On Catholic space, see Martine Boiteux, "Espace urbain," cited in note 1, above.

28. The idea of Jerusalem's wall as a sacred perimeter was originally proposed but never put into published form by the late Gerson D. Cohen. See its elaboration in K. Stow, "Sanctity and the Construction of Space: The Roman Ghetto," in S. Boesch and L. Scaraffia, eds., *Luoghi sacri e spazi della santità* (Turin, 1990); and revised in M. Mor, ed., *Jewish Assimilation, Acculturation and Accommodation* (Lanham, 1992).

29. On varying Protestant and Catholic concepts of space and its sacrality, see Natalie Zemon Davis, "The Sacred and the Body Social in 16th Century Lyon," *Past and Present* 90 (1981): 40–70.

30. Stow, "Sanctity and the Construction of Space," in Mor, *Jewish Assimilation*, 60: the members of this synagogue, the Scola Nova, also described themselves as "the flock that is holy."

31. The classic study of Jewish and Christian liturgy, with that of Christianity being originally derivative, remains Eric Werner, *The Sacred Bridge* (New York, 1959).

32. Archivio di Stato, Modena, Fondo dell'Inquisizione, *busta* 26:6, 26 April 1604, *Contra Davide de Nurscia*; I thank Katherine Aron Beller for this reference.

33. The episode is reported and recorded by Giustino Sorani, "Appunti storici," *Il Vessillo Israelitico* 56 (1908): 171–73; see also 235–37.

34. On the rules concerning a waiting period prior to baptism, see Amnon Linder, *The Jews in the Legal Sources of the Early Middle Ages* (Jerusalem and Detroit, 1997), e.g., 653; for a contemporary sixteenth-century reprise,

Marquardus de Susannis, *De Iudaeis et Aliis Infidelibus* (Venice, 1558), part III, chaps. 2 and 3. The notion of waiting three days is also present in charters Jews received in the Rhineland in the eleventh century; see Ivan Marcus, "Kiddush haShem in Ashkenaz and the Story of Rabbi Amnon of Mainz," in Gafni and Ravitzky, *Kiddush haShem and the Suffering of the Soul* (Jerusalem, 1992), 142–45.

35. Paul, Epistle to the Romans 9–11, and also the references in note 4, above; and Augustine, especially in his *Adversus Judaeos*, in *Fathers of the Church* (Washington, D.C., 1965), 27:391–416.

36. Such a conversion was called "indirect force." This was considered licit since Innocent III's letter *Maiores* (Solomon Grayzel, *The Church and the Jews in the Thirteenth Century*, vol. 1 (New York, 1966 repr.), no. 12, 100–103. Indirect force stood opposed to "absolute force." Victims of the former were forced to remain Christians; those of the latter were not. But even here the issue was complex, and in 1538 doubts that had existed throughout the Middle Ages were finally put to rest; see K. Stow, "Church, Conversion, and Tradition: The Problem of Jewish Conversion in Sixteenth Century Italy," *Dimensioni e problemi della ricerca storica* 2 (1996): 28; and for the important text of 1538, Pier Paolo Pariseo, *Consilia* (Venice, 1570), 4: no. 2, fols. 5–10, esp. 6. See on these matters in general, the introduction of Y. H. Yerushalmi to A. Herculano, *History of the Origin and Establishment of the Inquisition in Portugal* (New York, 1972), esp. p. 23, and the texts cited there. In particular, see the text of January 20, 1482: "quamplures alii, justo timore perterriti, in fugam se convertentes, hinc inde dispersi sint, plurimique ex eis se Christianos et veros Catholicos esse profitentes, ut ab oppressionibus huiusmodi releventur, ad sedem prefatam, oppressorum ubique tutissimum refugium, confugerint, et interpositas a variis et diversis eis per dictos inquisitores illatis . . ."

37. This extraordinary story was published as a small booklet and then in a longer work about the Citone family: Simona Foà, ed., *La Giustizia degl'ebrei* (Rome, 1987), and idem, *Le "Chroniche" della Famiglia Citone*, trans. A. A. Piattelli (Rome, 1988). The story is also the subject of a penetrating film seeking to understand the motivations of the confessors—fearsome in their dedication—but strongly revealing the humanity of the Jewish protagonists as well (*Il Confortorio*, produced and directed by Paolo Benvenuti, 1993).

38. This theme is treated especially by Lyndal Roper, "'Going to Church and Street': Weddings in Reformation Augsburg," *Past and Present* 106 (1985): 67; and Robert Kingdon, *Adultery and Divorce in Calvin's Geneva* (Cambridge, Mass., 1995). Both discuss the ending of the perception of marriage as symbolizing the unity of faith or the Church and its being placed under lay tutelage, including in matters touching divorce, now finally possible; see below. But it would be erroneous to say that because Catholic marriage—until the end of the fifteenth century in some cases—was often effected by notarial registration of the *verbum de presenti*, it was once a civil institution that became sacralized during the Catholic Reform era. What sixteenth-century Catholics accepted was a formal and necessary role of priests in marriage ceremonies; see Guido Ruggiero, *The Boundaries of Eros: Sex Crime and Sexuality in Renaissance Venice* (Oxford, 1985), 27–28; John Bossy, *Christianity in the West: 1400–1700* (Oxford, 1985), 22–26; and Klapisch-Zuber, "Zacharias," 187–89, 194–95. On the sacrament of marriage in all its aspects, see James Brundage, *Law, Sex, and Christian Society in Medieval Europe* (Chicago, 1987).

39. Again see John Bossy, *Christianity*, but in particular one should consult Adriano Prosperi, "L'inquisitore come confessore," in Paolo Prodi and Adriano Prosperi, eds., *Disciplina dell'anima, disciplina del corpo e disciplina della società tra medioevo ed età moderna* (Bologna, 1994), 187–224; and more widely, Prosperi's *Tribunali*, whose central theme is that inquisitors eventually took on the role of being principally confessors, but this means that private life took on a highly disciplined aspect, or at least this was the intended result. Specifically and relatedly on the subject of discipline, see Aurelio Musi, "Lo 'scalco spirituale': un manuale Napoletano di disciplina del corpo (sec. xvii)," in Prodi and Prosperi, *Disciplina*. But on the dangers of seeing "disciplining," as it is called, as fully representing the results of Catholic Reform activity, see the caveats of William Hudson, "Religion and Society in Early Modern Italy," *American Historical Review* 101 (1996): 783–804.

40. A. D'Alvray, and M. Tausche, "Marriage Sermons in *Ad Status* Collections of the Central Middle Ages," *Archives d'histoire doctrinale et littéraire du Moyen Âge* 47 (1980): 71–119, 100. Such claims about exaggerated Jewish sexuality go back to John Chrysostom and also Agobard of Lyon; see note 4 above. The latter accuses Jews of unspecified acts with young Christian women.

41. The picture of Jewish mothers as truly cruel appears in the *Glossa Ordinaria*, the standard Christian biblical gloss, originating in the earlier Middle Ages; see Willis Johnson, "Before the Blood Libel: Jews in Christian Exegesis After the Massacres of 1096" (M. Phil., Cambridge, 1994), 20–26. One sees it again, from a different aspect, in Christian tales of Jewish parents who killed their children rather than accept their conversion in the period of the First Crusade and slightly afterward; on this see Mary Minty, "Kiddush HaShem in German Christian Eyes in the Middle Ages" (in Hebrew), *Zion* 59 (1994): 233–44. Attitudes did not change by the period of the Ghetto; see the opinion of Victor von Carben as cited by Yisrael Yaacov Yuval, "Vengeance and Damnation, Blood and Defamation: From Jewish Martyrdom to Blood Libel Accusations" (in Hebrew), *Zion* 58 (1993): 88.

42. The clearest Jewish source is the *Sha'are qedushah* in the latter twelfth century Abraham ben David of Posquierres, *Sefer Ba'alei ha-Nefesh*, ed. J. Kafah (Jerusalem, 1964). This work discusses sexuality openly and emphasizes the need for mutuality between spouses, and it remains at the heart of nearly all halachic writings since then on the subject of marital relations. Of course, many of these accretions reflect differing attitudes, such as the greater asceticism at just the period of the Ghetto as seen in the works of Yeshaiah Hurwitz, *Shenai luhot ha-berit* (Furth, 1764), 102b; and, especially, Eliezar Azqari, *Sefer Haredem* (Venice, 1601), part 3, chap. 2; or in the quasi-magical accretions in works distributed in contemporary Israel by the ultra-orthodox.

43. The case of Salamone di Marino of Verona is Archivio di Stato, Roma, Camerale I, *busta* 421, f. 105, August 12, 1598. On Christian second marriage, see Kingdon, *Adultery and Divorce*, 8 and 41.

44. Bruni is cited by Herlihy and Klapisch-Zuber, *Toscans*, 231. This subject is treated in depth in the opening pages of Peter Brown, *The Body and Society: Men, Women, and Sexual Renunciation in Early Christianity* (New York, 1988), 6–10, 94. For satire on presumed centrality of the family in what Ruggiero calls "civic society," see Guido Ruggiero, *Binding Passions: Tales of Magic, Marriage, and Power at the End of the Renaissance* (Oxford, 1993), 24–26.

45. Nowhere is this clearer than in the events surrounding Shem Tov Soporto's false charge impugning his bride's virginity; on which, see chapter 2, below. Corporate unity was, of course, a prime goal of Catholic reform,

achieved through such as the Council of Trent or Sixtus V's organization of the Congregations; see the general outlines of institutional reform in the recent work of Ronnie Hsia, *The World of Catholic Renewal, 1540–1740* (New York, 1998). The Inquisition in its various manifestations also pressed for the unity of discipline, all, of course, under the rule of the papal sovereign in the Papal State; see Paolo Prodi, *Il Sovranno Pontefice* (Bologna, 1982). On "discipline," see note 39 above. What this signifies is that Jewish life, whether in its private or its organizational form, stood essentially at odds with the Catholic social vision, again a reason for specially "disciplining" the Jews through social segregation.

46. Brian Pullan, *Rich and Poor in Renaissance Venice* (Cambridge, Mass., 1971), 232. On confraternities a great deal has been written, especially about their transformation from social, if not neighborhood institutions devoted to maintaining domestic tranquility, into bodies with a primarily religious purpose. See most recently Ronald F. E. Weissman, "From Brotherhood to Congregation: Confraternal Ritual between Renaissance and Catholic Reformation," in J. Chiffoleau, Lauro Martines, and A. Paravicini Bagliani, eds., *Riti e rituali nelle Società Medievali*, and previously Weissman's *Ritual Brotherhood in Renaissance Florence* (New York, 1982), 58–105. Among the legion of other recent studies on Christian confraternities in the urban setting and in relation to the clergy, especially mendicants, see Nicholas Terpstra, *Lay Confraternities and Civic Religion in Renaissance Bologna* (Cambridge, 1995); Christopher Black, *Italian Confraternities in the Sixteenth Century* (Cambridge, 1989); and esp. Roberto Rusconi, "Confraternite, compagnie e devozioni," *Storia di Italia, Annali 9: La Chiesa e il potere politico dal Medioevo all'età contemporanea*, ed. G. Chittolini and G. Miccoli (Turin, 1986), 473–76, where he argues that in rural sectors in particular, the lay confraternity is never purely that, but more (p. 473) heavily infiltrated by religious orders. Consult also Charles de la Roncière, "Les confréries en Toscane aux XIV et XV siècles d'aprés les travaux récents," 50–64, esp. 61–62 on confraternities as a mode of escape or, alternately, safe refuge, for aristocrats from Medici pressures, and also Giulia Barone, "Il movimento francescano e la nascita delle confraternite romane," 71–80, and Paola Pavan, "La confraternità del Salvatore nella società romana del Tre-Quattrocento," 81–91, also Anna Esposito, "Le 'confraternite' del Gonfalone (secoli XIV–

XV)," 91–136—all in Luigi Fiorani, ed., *Le confraternite romane: esperienza religiosa, società, committenza artistica* [= *Ricerche per la storia religiosa di Roma* 5 (1984)]. Finally, Paola Pavan, "Permanenze di schemi e modelli del passato in una società in mutamento," 304–15, in Massimo Miglio, Francesca Niutta, Diego Quaglioni, and Concetta Ranieri, eds., *Un Pontificato ed una città: Sixto IV (1471–1484)* (Città del Vaticano, 1984); and Lester Little, "Una confraternità di giovani in un paese bergamasco, 1474," *Società, Instituzioni, Spiritualità: studi in onore di Cinzio Violante* (Spoleto, 1994).

47. On this figure, see Ariel Toaff, *Ghetto di Roma*, 12–15, and esp. 31–32. On confraternities and Jewish youth, see the essay of Elliott Horowitz cited in note 24, chap. 3, below.

48. On education, see the references in RJ196 (1537) and *Notai ebrei* 6,2,42v–43r (1590), and 6,2,141r (1592), texts dealing directly with apprenticeship, not education itself.

49. Ruggiero, *Passions*, 24–26, for Aretino. The question of ritualized mockery remains to be studied in full. Discussions of the Giudiate, plays that mocked weddings and funerals, are to be seen in Lynn Gunzberg, *Strangers at Home: Jews in the Italian Literary Imagination* (Berkeley, 1992). See also Paolo Toschi, *Le origine del teatro italiano* (Turin, 1955), and G. Giannini, *La Poesia popolare a stampa nel secolo XIX*, 2 vols. (Udine, 1938) 1:61–65, describing the farce of the marriage of Barruccabà with Gnora Luna. See also the text of a (late) version of the play, *Diana infedele di Baruccabà*, in the Vatican Library, BAV, Racc. Gen. Miscell IV, 94, int. 2, a collection of pamphlets. In the play of Gnora Luna, a Jewish girl is forced on an octogenarian and Jews appear as wholly perverse in both sexuality and all other aspects of marital life. See further the references in Milano, *Il Ghetto*, 327.

50. This term was introduced by Thomas V. Cohen, "The Case of the Mysterious Coil of Rope: Street Life and Jewish Persona in Rome in the Middle of the Sixteenth Century," *Sixteenth Century Journal* 19 (1988): 209–22, esp. 209 and 214.

51. Bernardino's arguments appear in *Le prediche Volgare*, ed. Ciro Cannarozzi (Florence, 1958), sermons nos. 19–21; and see Stow, *Alienated Minority*, 208. For this recent reconstruction of the Jewish male image, see Daniel Boyarin, "The Married Monk: Babylonian *Aggada* as Evidence of Changes in Babylonian Halacha," in Yael Azmon, ed., *A View into the Lives*

of Women in Jewish Societies (in Hebrew) (Jerusalem, 1995), and more fully in *Unheroic Conduct: The Rise of Heterosexuality and the Invention of the Jewish Male* (Berkeley, 1997), 33–80, esp. 68–71.

52. Thomas Aquinas indeed made it clear that what the Jews witness, testify to, if anything, is the existence of evil as opposed to good, the existence of the absence of faith and its presence, with their respective punishments and rewards (*Summa Theologica*, II–II, 10–12). Augustine's citation of Ps. 59: 12 was strictly a prooftext. It appears in papal letters, for example, well into the early modern period, but of itself it possessed no binding theological character. It really referred to an entire body of principles well developed in Augustine's day. Any doubts on the actual function, or even the legitimacy of the presence of Jews in Christian society, did not affect this verse's construed citation. Policies toward Jews rested foremost—theologically, at least—on Paul's dicta in the Epistle to the Romans, in which the Jews' presence becomes a given in Christian society. Legally, this position was rooted in Roman Law, as seen in the Theodosian and Justinianic Codes, then elaborated by Gregory the Great in particular, ultimately to be expressed in tens of canons. See Gratian's *Decretum* and the *Liber Extra*, *Decretals* of Gregory IX; E. Friedberg, *Corpus iuris canonici* (Graz, 1959, reprint). It is thus incorrect, in my estimation, to speak historically about an Augustinian doctrine that lost ground some time about the twelfth century. There was, rather, a broadly based policy of inclusion. The challenge came from Paul, especially in the passages in Corinthians and Galatians cited in note 4 above, and the commentaries on these passages. Paul meant Christian Judaizing, but commentators soon read Paul as meaning the corruption induced by Jews themselves, as is attested by so much early medieval legislation; see Linder, *Jews in Legal Sources*, passim, esp. 562–680, and see my review of Linder in the *Jewish Quarterly Review* 89 (1999): 432–37, on this point. For a different view of Augustine, see Jeremy Cohen, *Living Letters of the Law: Ideas of the Jews in Medieval Christianity* (Berkeley, 1999).

53. See Stow, *Alienated Minority*, 281–308, and the literature cited there.

54. See the full discussion in K. Stow, "Expulsion Italian Style: The Case of Lucio Ferraris," *Jewish History* 3/1 (1988): 51–64. And on the consilia of Oldradus, see Norman Zacour, *Jews and Saracens in the Consilia of Oldradus da Ponte* (Toronto, 1990). See, on expulsions, Stow, "The Avignonese Papacy, or After the Expulsion," in Jeremy Cohen, ed., *From Witness to Witch-*

craft: Jews and Judaism in Medieval Christian Thought (Weisbaden, 1996), 292–97, and Stow, *Catholic Thought*, 34–35.

55. For the dictum of Bernardino da Feltre, see K. Stow, "The Good of the Church, The Good of the State: The Popes and Jewish Money," in Diana Wood, ed., *Christianity and Judaism* (= *Studies in Church History* 29) (Oxford, 1992). On blood libels at this time, see Ronnie Po-Chia Hsia, *The Myth of Ritual Murder* (New Haven, 1988); and idem, *Trent 1475* (New Haven, 1992). More fully on Trent, see Anna Esposito and Diego Quaglioni, *Processi contro gli ebrei di Trento, 1475–1478* (Padua 1990), 37–41; Quaglioni, ed. and trans., Battista De' Giudici, *Apologia Iudaeorum* (Rome, 1987); Quaglioni, "Propaganda Antiebraica e Polemiche di Curia," in Massimo Miglio, Francesca Niutta, Diego Quaglioni, and Concetta Ranieri, eds., *Un Pontificato ed una città: Sixto IV (1471–1484)* (Città del Vaticano, 1984), 262–65, esp. 264; also Quaglioni, "Fra tolleranza e persecuzione: Gli ebrei nella letteratura giuridica del tardo Medioevo." in C. Vivanti, ed., *Gli ebrei in Italia, Storia d'Italia, Annali 11* (Turin, 1996), esp. 661–65, on the Paduan school of law at this time. But see the evaluation of papal and legal attitudes with regard to the Trent libel in K. Stow, "Papal Mendicants or Mendicant Popes: Continuity and Change in Papal Policies toward the Jews at the End of the Fifteenth Century," in S. McMichael and L. Simon, eds., *The Friars and the Jews* (Leiden, 2000). On Maryan beliefs and the Jews, see especially Denise Despres, "Immaculate Flesh and the Social Body: Mary and the Jews," *Jewish History* 12/1 (1998): 45–66, on the function of the Virgin as the guarantor of social purity; and Robert Stacey, "From Ritual Crucifixion to Host Desecration: Jews and the Body of Christ," *Jewish History* 12/1 (1998): 9–25, on ecclesiastical manipulations linked to issues of blood libels.

56. The fundamental program of Catholic reform was presented in the *Libellus ad Leonem Decem*, written in 1513 by the ex-aristocrat monks, Quirini and Giustiniani. The enormous presence of conversion in this text is often ignored, especially on the need to convert the Jews; Paolo Giustiniani and Pietro Quirini, *Libellus ad Leonem Decem*, ed. J. B. Mittarelli and A. Costadoni, *Annales Camuldulenses*, vol. 9 (Venice, 1773). On problems with accepting converts, see Kenneth Stow, "Church, Conversion, and Tradition: The Problem of Jewish Conversion in Sixteenth Century Italy," *Dimensioni e problemi della ricerca storica* 2 (1996): 26–35.

57. The question of millenarianism is discussed at length in chapter 11

of Stow, *Catholic Thought*, esp. 274–75, Paul IV's letter to his sister. See also Adriano Prosperi, "New Heaven and New Earth: Prophecy and Propaganda at the Time of the Discovery and Conquest of the Americas," in Marjorie Reeves, ed., *Prophetic Rome in the High Renaissance Period* (Oxford, 1992), 279–309; and O'Malley, *Rome of the Renaissance*.

58. On Sigismondi di Foligno, see Anna Foa, "The New and the Old: The Spread of Syphilis (1494–1530)," in Edward Muir and Guido Ruggiero, eds., *Sex and Gender in Historical Perspective* (Baltimore, 1990), 36–37. On Trent, see note 55 above.

59. The name appears in Marquardus de Susannis, *De Iudaeis*, III, 2; and see especially Brian Pullan, "A Ship with Two Rudders: 'Righeto Marrano' and the Inquisition in Venice," *Historical Journal* 20/1 (1977): 25–58. The clearest introduction to Marranism remains the classic one of Yosef Yerushalmi in *From Spanish Court to Italian Ghetto* (New York, 1971). See, too, Anna Foa, "The Marranos' Kitchen," note 18 above, an analysis of Marrano eating habits with a precise indication of how incomplete Marrano rites de passage might be.

60. On these arguments, as well as the entire background to the problem, see Stow, "Church, Conversion, and Tradition." See also Herculano, *History of the . . . Inquisition in Portugal*; and the discussion of Marranos at Rome who sought reconciliation to Christianity rather than, as so often assumed, fleeing from it: Anna Foa, "Un vescovo marrano: il processo a Pedro de Aranda," *Quaderni Storici* 99 (1998): 533–52. Again, on this trial in the wider context of Marranos at Rome, see Anna Foa, "Converts and Conversos in Sixteenth Century Italy: Marranos in Rome," in B. Cooperman and B. Garvin, eds., *Memory and Identity: The Jews of Italy* (College Park, Md., 2000). See also the works and texts cited in note 36 above.

61. Paolo Prodi, *Il Sovranno Pontifice*, remains the best overall treatment.

62. Most recently, see Bernard Cooperman, "Venetian Policy Towards Levantine Jews," but see also Salo Baron, *Social and Religious History*, 143: 39–40, which discusses all the relevant charters and texts, from the earliest; and see also K. Stow, *Taxation Community and State: The Jews and the Fiscal Foundations of the Early Modern Papal State* (Stuttgart, 1982), docs. 35, 36, pages 103–5.

63. On Sixtus V and the Jews, see Stow, "The Consciousness of Closure," but also the fundamental discussion of revived Jewish banking by Ermano

Loevinson, "La Concession de banques de prêtes aux Juifs par les papes," *Revue des Études Juives* 92 (1932): 1–20; 93 (1933): 27–52; 157–78; 94 (1934): 57–72, 167–83; 95 (1935): 23–43; as well as the treatment by Bonfil of the growth of the Monti di Pietà in his *Jewish Life*, 34–36.

64. The text of the bull appears in Solomon Grayzel, *The Church and the Jews*, 1:92–94. It was then incorporated in the *Decretals* of Gregory IX as X.5,6,9, but frequently reissued for reinforcement nonetheless. See also the renewed statement of Jewish rights in texts 499 and 670, found in Simonsohn, *The Apostolic See*; these texts emphasize that Jews are *cives* in Rome.

65. The texts of the *Notai ebrei* leave no doubt that Jews owned what were called *cazagot* (= Heb., *hazaqot*), leaseholds. They seem never to have owned property outright. References indicating that Jews were forced to sell their homes in 1555 almost assuredly are about the sale of *cazagot*. See Stow, "Prossimità," 67–68, and RJ858, 876, 887, and 1431, among many others. Also on Jewish property holding, see Anna Esposito, "Gli Ebrei a Roma," and J. C. Maire Vigueur, "Les Juifs à Rome dans la seconde moitié du XIVe siècle."

66. Jewish professions are detailed in Esposito, "Gli Ebrei a Roma," as well as in Ariel Toaff, "Gli ebrei a Roma," in C. Vivanti, ed., *Gli Ebrei in Italia, Storia d'Italia, Annali 11* (Turin, 1997). Paul IV sought to oust Jews from the professions of purveyors, which he did with success. These prohibitions were reversed briefly by Pius IV, but then reinstated by his successor, Pius V.

67. Jean Delumeau, *Vie économique et sociale . . . du XVIe siècle*. 2 vols. (Rome, 1959), 491.

68. This episode is described by Angela Groppi, "Ebrei, donne, soldati e neofiti: l'esercizio del mestiere tra esclusioni e privilegi (Roma XVI–XVIII secolo)" (unpublished).

69. See the full text explaining the legal grounds for allowing Jews into Venice proper, translated in Bonfil, *Jewish Life*, 39–41, as well as the observations of Elizabeth Crouzet-Pavan, "Venice between Jerusalem, Byzantium, and Divine Retribution," 164; and Edward Muir, "The Virgin on the Street Corner: The Place of the Sacred in Italian Cities," *Religion and Culture in the Renaissance and Reformation* (Kirksville, Missouri, 1989), 28.

70. See K. Stow, "The Burning of the Talmud in 1553, in the Light of Sixteenth Century Catholic Attitudes Toward the Talmud," *Bibliothèque d'Humanisme et Renaissance* 34 (1972): 435–59. For a thorough review of all

issues concerning the Talmud during the Middle Ages and the Renaissance, see Fausto Parente, "La Chiesa e il Talmud," in Vivanti, ed., *Gli Ebrei in Italia*.

71. Loyola's conversionary activities here have recently been examined thoroughly within the context of Jesuit policies, especially those on the Spanish laws of purity of blood, by Anna Foa, "The Religious Orders and Conversion," in McMichael and Simon, eds., *The Friars and the Jews* (Leiden, 2000). And on the use of taxation as a conversionary means, see Stow, *Taxation*, passim.

72. This argument is presented more fully in Stow, *Alienated Minority*, 306–8. See also Stow, "Castigo e delitto nello Stato della Chiesa: gli ebrei nelle carceri romane dal 1572 al 1659," *Italia Judaica* II (Rome, 1986), 173–74, 191–92; and "The Papacy and the Jews Catholic Reformation and Beyond," *Jewish History* 6: (1991): 273–74.

73. This is suggested by Anna Foa, "Il gioco del proselitismo: politica delle conversioni e controllo della violenza nella Roma del Cinquecento," in M. Luzzati, M. Olivari, and A. Veronese, eds., *Ebrei e Cristiani nell'Italia Medievale e Moderna: Conversioni, Scambi, Contrasti* (Rome, 1988), 155–70, who also goes beyond the specific to suggest that it was becoming ever more difficult to contain Jews within Christian society on the basis of older medieval stances.

74. Jews had long lived outside the future Ghetto precincts. The census of 1527 (Gnoli, "Descriptio urbis") reports 1,169 Jews in the Rione S. Angelo (effectively the location of the Ghetto), but 5 in the Campo Marzio, 49 in Parione, 356 in Regula, all bordering S. Angelo, and with 145 in Ripa and 14 in Trastevere proper. Was there then a real change in Jewish demographic patterns, or was Paul IV incensed by a slow, outward spread? In fact, already in 1545, Paul III had sought to check this spread, prohibiting all Jews from living outside the Jewish quarter in the Piazza and Via Guidea—that is, effectively, the future Ghetto precinct; Simonsohn, *Apostolic See*, no. 2566, but see no. 2723 for an exemption. Exemptions like this and surely others, may have provoked the real or feigned nonchalance recorded by the text of 1555, cited in note 78, below. By 1555 the number of Jews in Rome had more than doubled since the 1527 census; it would grow even more by the end of the century, rise still more in the early seventeenth century, but would fall by up to 800 during the plague of 1656; see Milano, *Il Ghetto*, 92, and Eugenio Sonnino and Rosa Traina, "La pesta del 1656–57 a Roma: organizzazione

sanitaria e mortalità" in *La demografia storica delle città italiane*, S.I.D.E.S. (Bologna, 1972). See above, Introduction, note 57.

75. Shelomo ibn Verga, *Sefer Shebet Yehudah*, ed. Y. F. Baer and A. Shohat (Jerusalem, 1947), 164.

76. This was traditional Jewish opinion, too. See Finkelstein, *Jewish Self-Government*, 331, where in 1354, among other instances, Jews in Catalonia turned to the king and threatened they would petition the pope directly were he himself not to seek papal clarifications—clarifications which were made defending the Jewish position; K. Stow, "Ebrei e inquisitori, 1250 – 1350," in M. Luzzati, ed., *L'inquisizione e gli ebrei in Italia* (Bari, 1994), 3–18. See, too, the bulls cited in note 64 above.

77. This admittedly speculative reconstruction is summarized in Stow, *Alienated Minority*, 39–40, and given at some length, to show its congruence with both papal policy and normal patterns of urban patronage, in Stow, "Jewish Approaches to the Papacy."

78. RJ1723, a text concerning an assessment. The remark is tangential, and hence its real value.

79. This proviso appears in bulls no. 499 and 670 in Simonsohn, *Apostolic See*.

80. For the text of *Cum nimis absurdum*, see Stow, *Catholic Thought*, 291–98, for both the Latin and an English translation.

81. This extraordinary chronicle, valuable for seeing the operation of such as the inquisitional jails and the attitude of non-Jews in Rome to Paul IV, as well as Jewish positions, was published by Isaiah Sonne, *Mi-Pavolo ha-Reviʿi ʿad Pius ha-Hamishi* (Jerusalem, 1954), 11–100.

82. See Dagmar Herzog, "Carl Scholl, Gustav Struve, and the Problematics of Philosemitism in 1840s Germany: Radical Christian Dissent and the Reform Jewish Response," *Jewish History* 9/2 (1995): 53–72, and, specifically, Dagmar Herzog, *Intimacy and Exclusion: Religious Politics in Pre-Revolutionary Baden* (Princeton, 1996), 55, showing how preachers might be liberal about Jews until they encountered the overall Jewish refusal to convert and complete the process of assimilation—or what these preachers considered its conclusion.

2 / What Is in a Name? or, The Matrices of Acculturation

1. See the Introduction, above, on the subject of social theater and the literature cited there.

2. RJ1567, for Elia and Joab. On gambling, see Yacov Boksenboim, *The Letters of Rabbi Leon Modena* (Tel Aviv, 1984), no. 146; see also Mark R. Cohen, trans. and ed., *The Autobiography of a Seventeenth-Century Venetian Rabbi: Leon Modena's Life of Judah* (Princeton, 1988), 100, 103, 105, 129, and passim.

3. This again reflects on Amos Funkenstein's concept of the "dialectics of assimilation" while also taking a wider tack; see note 1 in the Introduction.

4. The text of Tutto Bene's adoption is *Notai ebrei*, 2,3,9rv, 2 January 1569; see also RJ271, a far less complete adoption, more the taking in of children with the presumption of their future marriage to children already in the household, although dependent on the children's eventual consent. On adoption in Italy, see Herlihy and Klapisch-Zuber, *Tuscans*, where adoption is referred to on a number of occasions, as distinct from foster children—*trovatelli*, *innocenti*, and the like. For France, in great detail, see Kristin E. Gager, *Blood Ties and Fictive Ties* (Princeton, 1996), esp. 44, 71, 75, 79, 83, 87, 136.

5. RJ1566, the case of Tatò. See Finkelstein, *Jewish Self-Government*, 171–204, and 171 in particular, for Rabbi Tam's ordinance, also attributed to Rabbi Gershom of Mainz (early eleventh century); and also Stow, *Alienated Minority*, 171. The Christian usage of Judaeo-Romanesco reported here is of a Christian defendant who reported what a wife (who had purchased some goods from him) said in *hebraico* to her husband; Archivio di Stato Roma, Tribunale del Governatore, Criminali, Costituti, 37, fol. 63.

6. RJ31, 82, 1199, 1624, and many more.

7. RJ1218; it is worth investigating similar phenomena elsewhere, such as the possible inclusions of Slavisms even in Polish Yiddish, to determine degrees of at least linguistic acculturation.

8. RJ1216. See the descriptions of marital procedures in Christiane Klapisch-Zuber, "Zacharias, or the Ousted Father: Nuptial Rites in Tuscany between Giotto and the Council of Trent," in her *Women, Family, and Ritual in Renaissance Italy* (Chicago, 1985).

9. The notary thus also facilitated Jewish social ritual and what I have

called social theater. On the prominence of ritual in late medieval and Renaissance cities and in their governance, see Richard Trexler, *Public Life in Renaissance Florence* (New York, 1980).

10. On possible prior notarial activity in Navarre, see again Benjamin Gampel, *The Last Jews on Iberian Soil, Navarese Jewry 1479/1498* (Berkeley, 1989); and also again on the notarial art in general, Camargo, *Ars dictaminis*. Scazzocchio appears in about 140 acts, but see in particular RJ1562, which is most representative.

11. Fano referred to one woman as *melumedet*, coached by her lawyer; Menahem Azariah da Fano, *Sefer she'elot ve-teshuvot* (Jerusalem, 1963), no. 81.

12. RJ1943, 1889, 1919, 1519, 1530, in that order.

13. He said this in a poem, implying balance, not assimilation, nor a hierarchy of Jewish versus secular values.

14. RJ525, 554; *Notai ebrei*, 1,1,74r. The word "caste" is used here much as Mary Douglas does in the article cited in note 16 below. This is an appropriate place to mention the brilliant study of Michele Luzzati, "Matrimoni e apostasia di Clemenza di Vitale da Pisa," in *La Casa del Ebreo* (Pisa, 1985), where Luzzati argues that the conversion of Clemenza da Pisa and the subsequent actions of her father and brothers point to the existence of an upper class in fifteenth-century Tuscany in which Jews and Christians, at least those of this upper class, could move freely and without religious distinction, and that the brothers of Clemenza accepted with no reservations her conversion and marriage to a Christian. I believe that what is illustrated here is far more the kind of picture I am painting. The apparently smooth negotiations over Clemenza's dowry are a matter of, first, accepting a fait accompli—conversion was something nobody could dispute and win—and, second, minimizing the damage by paying the dowry and drawing a sharp line of demarcation guaranteeing, through notarial record, that Clemenza had no further claims; that is, she could not further weaken her father's family. So, yes, there was free interplay, free enough to lead to what Luzzati pictures as a love match (I am not wholly convinced, if only for lack of precise indications), but that interplay was not supposed to go so far as to imitate actions more normal in the late twentieth century than in the late fifteenth. When it did, it was time to take definitive note, as the brothers did. Clemenza had not simply married out, she had changed "caste."

15. Maria Luisa Lombardo, *La Dogana Minuta a Roma nel primo quat-trocento* (Viterbo, 1983), 102.

16. Mary Douglas, "Deciphering a Meal," *Daedalus* 101 (1972): 61–82.

17. K. Stow, "A Tale of Uncertainties: Converts in the Roman Ghetto," in D. Carpi, M. Gil, and Y. Gorni, eds., *Shlomo Simonsohn Jubilee Volume* (Tel Aviv, 1993), text 1, p. 267.

18. Diego Quaglioni, ed. and trans., *Battista De' Giudici, "Apologia Iu-daeorum"* (Rome, 1987).

19. Lombardo, *La Dogana Minuta*, 134–38, on market laws; and 102, on Jewish spice merchants.

20. Cited in chap. 1, note 78, above.

21. Only after 1581 was there thorough empowerment of the Inquisition, the papal Inquisition, to deal with all manner of issues concerning the Jews. See *Antiqua improbitas*, in *Bullarium Diplomatum et Privilegiorum Taurensis Editio* (Turin, 1857–72), 8:378–81 (cited in Stow, *Catholic Thought*, 33). The full weight was felt at Bologna, on which see below, note 24, and later at Modena, now the subject of a dissertation in preparation by Katherine Aron Beller. At Modena, inquisitional behavior corresponded to what Prosperi, *Tribunali*, reports in general, that the Roman Inquisition became primarily an instrument of social discipline rather than one of terror—social discipline meaning heavy restriction for Jews, and stiff fines, but rarely imprisonment. Real difficulties were, as always, encountered by conversos, on whom see Brian Pullan, *The Jews of Europe and the Inquisition of Venice, 1550–1670* (Oxford, 1983), and Pier Cesari Ioly-Zorattini, *Processi del S. Uffizio di Venezia contro ebrei e giudaizzanti*, 14 vols. (Florence, 1980–97).

22. Isaiah Sonne, *Mi-Pavolo ha-Reviʿi*, 20–24.

23. For example, RJ1273, 1632.

24. See "Haqirot ʿal ʿinyanei ha-nozrim maʿet R. Yishmaʾel Haninah," ed. Aharon Jellinek, *Ha-Shahar* (1871), 17–23, and Abraham Berliner, *Kobez al Yad*, 4:27–31, for the Hebrew text; also David B. Ruderman, "An Apologetic Treatise from Sixteenth Century Bologna," *Hebrew Union College Annual* 50 (1979): 253–75. And see the translation of Mauro Perani, "Documenti sui processi dell'Inquisizione contro gli ebrei di Bologna e sulla loro tassazione alla vigilia della prima espulsione (1567–1568)," 245–85; Rosella Rinaldi, "La giustizia in città: indagini sulla comunità ebraica di Bologna tra '400 e '500," 55–99, esp. 89–94; and M. G. Muzzarelli, "Ebrei, Bologna e

sovrano-pontifice: la fine di una relazione tra verifiche, restrizioni e ripensamenti," 19–54—all three in M. G. Muzzarelli, ed., *Verso l'epilogo di una
convivenza: gli ebrei a Bologna nel xvi secolo* (Florence, 1996).

25. On marital procedures, see Klapisch-Zuber, "Zacharias" (note 8
above). See RJ1215 for the *teqiʿat kaf*, and A. Freimann, *Seder kiddushin ve-
nissuin ʿaharei hatimat ha-Talmud* (Jerusalem, 1964), 82, 86–87, on Jewish
marital behavior.

26. On these issues, see Stanley Chojnacki, "Marriage Legislation and
Patrician Society in Fifteenth-Century Venice," in B. Bachrach and D. Nicholas, eds., *Law, Custom, and the Social Fabric in Medieval Europe: Essays in
Honor of Bryce Lyon* (Kalamazoo, 1990); and Eleanor S. Riemer, "Women,
Dowries, and Capital Investment in Thirteenth-Century Siena," in Marion
A. Kaplan, ed., *The Marriage Bargain: Women and Dowries in European History* (= *Women and History* 10 (1985): 59–81), which describes the onset of
restrictions; and see also Thomas Kuehn, *Law, Family, and Women: Toward
a Legal Anthropology of Renaissance Italy* (Chicago, 1991), 238–57. But on exceptions and changes to restrictive legislation, as well as women's economic
prerogatives, see Chojnacki, "The Power of Love: Wives and Husbands
in Late Medieval Venice," in Mary Erler and Maryanne Kowaleski, eds.,
Women and Power in the Middle Ages (Athens, Ga., 1988), 134 and 136–38;
and esp. Samuel K. Cohn, Jr., "Women in the Streets, Women in the Courts
in Early Renaissance Florence," "Last Wills: Family, Women, and the Black
Death in Central Italy," and esp. "Women and the Counter-Reformation in
Siena: Authority and Property in the Family," *Women in the Streets: Essays
on Sex and Power in Renaissance Italy* (Baltimore, 1996), 73–74.

27. Ariel Toaff shows this absence of stratification in "La vita materiale," in Vivanti, ed., *Gli ebrei in Italia*, 239–61. On Roman dowries in the
sixteenth century, see K. Stow, "La Storiographia del ghetto romano: problemi metodologici," in M. G. Muzzarelli and Giacomo Todeschini, eds., *La
Storia degli ebrei nell'Italia medievale: tra filologia e metodologia* (Bologna,
1991), 43–57; also Tidhar Gilboa, "Dowries in the Roman Ghetto," Seminar
paper, University of Haifa, 1997, who calculated the low value of the average
Jewish dowry.

28. See RJ1012, in which a widow is said absolutely to inherit all, even
if she remarries. This situation among Roman Jews grew entrenched to the
point that in 1611, 56 years after the Ghetto's initiation, one wife, Gratia,

returning to her husband, Agnilo—an apparently bankrupt one, at that (eventually she left again, or to be more precise, she made her husband leave home)—made him swear that upon his death, all the properties he held would go to her, and that his sons from a former marriage could not appeal this stipulation; for what Agnilo had was really hers to begin with; *Notai ebrei*, 10,3,90v–91r (1611) and 5,3,155v (1617). Women were accorded great control over estates in Turin, where Jewish dowries grew to immense size, embracing sometimes nearly the entire patrimony; see Luciano Allegra, "A Model of Jewish Devolution," *Jewish History* 7/2 (1993): 29–58, and also Allegra, *Identica in bilico: Il Ghetto ebraico di Torino nel Settecento* (Turin, 1996). So taken for granted was it that widows would have a say about this disposition of estates that in 1613 one widow—in the absence of any testament by her late husband—was completely running affairs. We would not even know about this event were it not for one of her children, a neofito, who was claiming an immediate share; *Notai ebrei*, 3,20,76–84.

29. See especially Samuel K. Cohn, Jr., "Women and the Counter-Reformation in Siena," and Chojnacki, "Power of Love," 129. It is for this reason that it is at times carefully stipulated that a woman is appointed: "tutrice et pro tempore curatrice," until, that is, she remarries or settles the claim on her dowry. With respect to the return of the dowry itself, Anna Esposito informs me that Christian women in Roman documentation dating from the first decades of the sixteenth century and the end of the fifteenth often had trouble. Jewish women did not, although we should recall that there were different standards for Ashkenazi, Sephardi, and Italian communities at this time.

30. The law of 1580 is discussed by Simona Feci, "'Sed qua ipsa est mulier. . . .' Le risorse dell'identità giuridica femminile a Roma in età moderna," *Quaderni Storici* 98 (1998): 275–300. Innocent XI's statute of 1680 is examined by Renata Ago, "The Family in Rome, Structures and Relationships," in P. van Kessel and E. Schulte, eds., *Rome-Amsterdam: Two Growing Cities in Seventeenth Century Europe* (Amsterdam, 1997), 90–91. Ago argues that, in practice, women might be preferred over collateral males, although apparently not over a direct line when judges chose—despite its being technically irregular—to interpret the flat prohibitions in local statutes in the light of *ius commune*, Roman Law, which did accord women rights. The point remains, nonetheless, that a Roman Christian woman inheriting was

technically irregular, and thus problematic. Also ironic: as in the case of a certain Magdalena neofita, who, as a Jew, did not need a *mundualdus*, but after her conversion, did; *Notai ebrei*, 20,1,186, although the person who filled this post was her brother, also a neofito. On women's difficulties with contracts, see Feci, "Sed qua ipsa est mulier," esp. 292. The complex issue of the *mundualdus* is probed in Kuehn, *Law, Family, and Women*, 216–22.

31. For Jewish women contracting, litigating, and choosing arbiters as their own agents, see the litigation in RJ1743. The comments of Eliezer bar Natan are cited in Abraham Grossman, "The Bond Between Halachah and Economics Regarding the Status of Jewish Women in Early Ashkenaz," in Menahem Ben-Sasson, ed., *Religion and Economy, Connections and Inter-actions* (in Hebrew) (Jerusalem, 1995), 158.

32. For Leon Modena's grandfather, see Cohen, ed., *Autobiography*, 78. Dolcebella appears in *Notai ebrei*, 1,1,67r. The story of one Consola Ambron, told by Angiolina Arru, "'Donare non è perdere'; I vantaggi della reciprocità a Roma tra Settecento e Ottocento," *Quaderni Storici* 98 (1998): 361–63, although from the eighteenth century, shows that Jews slowly, very slowly, were really conforming to the law of 1580, however, in a way that was advantageous, hence, again, an acculturational manipulation, typifying, too, the kind of delayed acculturation to be discussed toward the end of this chapter.

33. On the matter of Geneva and the novelty of remarriage following divorce, see Robert M. Kingdon, *Adultery and Divorce in Calvin's Geneva* (Cambridge, Mass., 1995), passim. For Christian women, see Cohn, "Last Wills," 44, and Joanne M. Ferraro, "The Power to Decide: Battered Wives in Early Modern Venice," *Renaissance Quarterly* 48 (1995): 492–512, esp. 495. On Jewish women leaving on their own volition and then refusing to return to their husbands, see the case of Berechiah and Fiore, *Notai ebrei*, 9,1,124 (July 1579); and also the case of Gratia and Agnilo, cited in note 28 above.

34. On the Talmudic expression and its commentaries underlying the idea of refusal (*me'un*), see Babylonian Talmud, and the discussion of Kiddushin, 41a, Menahem Ha-Meiri, *Beit ha-Behirah*, ed. Abraham Sofer (Jerusalem, 1963), cited also in Freimann, *Seder kiddushin*, 86; but also the *Responsum of Azriel Diena*, no. 134, ed. Y. Boksenboim (Tel Aviv, 1977), and the text of Menahem Azariah da Fano, no. 81, cited in note 11 above. See K. Stow, "Marriages Are Made in Heaven: Marriage and the Individual in the

Roman Jewish Ghetto," *Renaissance Quarterly* 48 (1995): 445–91. On the
ubiquitousness of Jewish marriage, see Simone Luzzato, *Discorso sopra gli
ebrei di Venezia*, fourth argument, and its Hebrew trans., *Ma'amar 'al Yehudei Venezia*, ed. A. Z. Ascoli and Riccardo Bachi (Jerusalem, 1951), 90,
that "it is forbidden to remain without a wife." For the dramatic element
in pleading, much like the halachic drama of Ricca, see Natalie Z. Davis,
*Fiction in the Archives: Pardon Tales and Their Tellers in Sixteenth-Century
France* (Stanford, 1987; repr. Cambridge, 1988). On the general issue of matrimony and choice of spouses in Catholic and Protestant societies, see Luisa
Accati, "Matrimony and Chastity, Symbolic Change and Social Control
N.E. Italy 1550–1750," *International Journal of Moral and Social Studies* 5
(1990): 23–24; Sara Mendelsohn, "The Weightiest Business: Marriage in an
Upper-Gentry Family in Seventeenth Century England," *Past and Present* 85
(1979): 126–35. John Bossy, *Christianity in the West*, 22–26; Lyndal Roper,
"'Going to Church and Street': Weddings," 62–101; Klapisch-Zuber,
"Zacharias"; and Steven Ozment, *When Fathers Ruled: Family Life in Refor-
mation Europe* (Cambridge, Mass., 1983). On the introduction of notions
of choice, but specifically in the lower middle class, besides Ralph A. Houl-
brooke, *The English Family, 1450–1700* (London, 1984), 77, see David Cressy,
*Birth, Marriage, and Death: Ritual Religion, and the Life Cycle in Tudor and
Stuart England* (Oxford, 1997), 252, 536, n. 50.

   35. Chojnacki, "The Power of Love," 133, and also idem, "'The Most
Serious Duty': Motherhood, Gender, and Patrician Culture in Renaissance
Venice," in M. Migiel and J. Schiesari, eds., *Refiguring Woman: Perspectives
on Gender and the Italian Renaissance* (Ithaca, 1991). For further studies on
contemporary Christian women, see Merry E. Weisner, *Women and Gender
in Early Modern Europe* (Cambridge, 1993); and idem, "Family, Household,
and Community," in T. Brady, Jr., H. Oberman, and J. D. Tracy, eds., *Handbook of European History, 1400–1600* (Leiden, 1994), 65, on affection and
companionability as linked to Protestantism or to Catholic ideas of free
consent. Also Sandra Cavallo and Simona Cerutti, "Onore femminile
e controllo sociale della riproduzione in Piemonte tra Sei e Settecento,"
Quaderni Storici 15 (1980): 347–83. Most recently on Italian families, with
new insight into family formation, see Anthony Molho, *Marriage Alliance
in Late Medieval Florence* (Cambridge, Mass., 1994). In general, see Beatrice
Gottlieb, *The Family in the Western World from the Black Death to the Indus-*

trial Age (New York, 1993). It should be added that the age at marriage for Florentine women reported by Herlihy and Klapisch-Zuber in *Tuscans*, 87, is somewhat higher than as per Chojnacki, cited here; although he, too, is really saying that marriage might have occurred at thirteen, not that it actually did.

36. *Notai ebrei*, 4,2,105r–106r (22 January 1619) concerns a butchery owned by women. And see on working Jewish women, Emanuel Etkes, "Family and Study of Torah in Lithuanian Talmudist Circles in the Nineteenth Century" (in Hebrew), *Zion* 51 (1986): 87–106; Hyman, *Gender and Assimilation*, 50–92. For non-Jewish women, see N. Z. Davis, "Women in the Crafts in Sixteenth-Century Lyon," but even more Kathryn L. Reyerson, "Women in Business in Medieval Montpellier," both in B. Hanawalt, ed., *Women and Work in Preindustrial Europe* (Bloomington, 1986), 167–97, 117–44. On Christian women eased out of the workplace, see David Herlihy, "Women's Work in the Towns of Traditional Europe," in Simona Cavaciocchi, ed., *La donna nell'economia Secc. XIII–XVIII: Atti della "Ventunesima Settimana di Studi"* (Florence, 1990), 103–30, and the response of Angela Groppi, "Il lavoro delle donne: un questionario da arricchire," in Cavaciocchi, 143–54. See also on restrictions on women in economic activity or their controlled status, Joan Kelly-Gadol, "Did Women Have a Renaissance," in Claudia Koonz and Renata Bridenthal, eds., *Becoming Visible* (Boston, 1977); also Barbara A. Hanawalt, "Peasant Women's Contribution to the Home Economy in Late Medieval England," in Hanawalt, ed., *Women and Work*, 3–19.

37. For a useful English synthesis on halachah and women, see Rachel Biale, *Women and Jewish Law* (New York, 1984); and for textual citations arranged by halachic topic, see Eliakim Elinson, *ʾIsh ve-ʾIshto*, vol. 3 of *Ha-ʾIshah ve-ha-mitzvot* (Jerusalem, 1981). See also note 19, chap. 1, above.

38. Marchigiana, called a *moredet*, a rebel, for her tactics, is the subject of RJ292. On sexuality in general, see for an introduction, David Feldman, *Marital Relations, Birth Control, and Abortion in Jewish Law* (New York, 1974). Of medieval and Renaissance manuals on sexuality, which still form the basis of contemporary halachic prescription, the most interesting, for its true stress on mutuality and on the achievement thereby of "sanctity," correct behavior, with clearly affect, is Abraham ben David of Posquierres, *Sefer Baʿalei ha-Nefesh*, ed. J. Kafah (Jerusalem, 1964). But see also the variants,

often kabbalistically driven, in *Iggeret ha-qodesh*, ed. Ch. Chavel, *Khitvei ha-Ramban* (Jerusalem, 1969), 316–37, and later, especially Elazar Azqari, *Sefer Haredim* (Venice, 1601), part 3, chap. 2. These are discussed in K. Stow, "The Jewish Family in the Rhineland: Form and Function," *American Historical Review* 92 (1987): 1101.

39. *Notai ebrei*, 2,5,11r, on the appointment of Arpino; and on other women appointed prayer leaders in various places, see Natalie Davis, *Women on the Margins*, 59–60; Giulio Morosini, *Via della fede* (Rome, 1683), 226–27; and Stefanie Siegmund, "La Vita nei ghetti," in Vivanti, ed., *Gli ebrei*, 1:890. Various texts also make it clear that the women were meeting for prayer during the week, at least on Mondays and Thursday mornings when the Torah was read. This would cast some doubt on Siegmund's theory that laws about the early morning opening of stores in Florence were directed against women. More important, the rules of one of the Roman Gemilut Hasadim societies specify that stores are not to be open during prayer time. The emphasis seems consciously, if not wholly, to be on this point, not on possible competition from women.

40. See esp. Christiane Klapisch-Zuber, "The 'Cruel Mother': Maternity, Widowhood, and Dowry in Florence in the Fourteenth and Fifteenth Centuries"; in Cochrane, *Women, Family, and Ritual.*

41. On the education of Christian women, see Elisa Chavarria, "Ideologia e comportamenti familiari nei predicatori italiani tra cinque e settecento: Tematiche e modelli," *Rivista Storica Italiana* 100 (1988): 679–723; and Ottavia Niccoli, "Creanza e disciplina: buone maniere per i fanciulli nell'Italia della controriforma," in Paolo Prodi, ed., *Disciplina del corpo*. And in general on education at this time, see Paul Grendler, *Schooling in Renaissance Italy: Literacy and Learning, 1300–1600* (Baltimore, 1989).

42. The texts regrettably say little about the education of Jewish women, or, in fact, of men. Typical of a young girl is an apprenticeship contract stipulating: "lavori di donna [fine weaving] et insegnarla de leggere Ebraico," and we should note the *leggere*, to read, not just recite; *Notai ebrei*, 11,6,n.113 (23 Jan. 1584). Boys fared not much better, with the average being to know some *haftarot*, weekly reading from the Prophets, and be able to explain the weekly Torah portion, hardly higher Talmudic learning; *Notai ebrei*, 6,2,141r (10 June 1591). To gauge this information, it is important to note that youths of even better families were often apprenticed.

43. For fathers doing just this, *Notai ebrei*, 5,2,115r–120v; and see also 7,2,205r; 1,1,137r; 5,3,5v–9r. See the comment of Moses Isserles on Joseph Karo's *Shulkhan 'Arukh*, *'Even ha-'ezer*, 82:7, and also the comments of Joel Syrkis (Cracow, seventeenth century) *Bayyit hadash*, at the same place, E. H., 82:7, but this time on the *Tur* of the fourteenth century Jacob ben Asher; and for contemporary parallels, see D. B. Sinclair, "Jewish Law in the State of Israel: Custody and the Role of Women in Their Children's Education, *Jewish Law Annual* 9 (1991): 251–57. Among Christians, too, the statute of the "cruel mother" did not absolutely determine practice; on which see Giulia Calvi, "Reconstructing the Family: Widowhood and Remarriage in Tuscany in the Early Modern Period," in *Marriage in Italy, 1300–1650*, ed. Kate Lowe and Trevor Dean (Cambridge, 1998), 275. Calvi shows that the father's family might gain full control over the child's inheritance, but that physical custody might be granted by the courts to the mother. Whether these father surrogates would be encharged, as in the Jewish case, with overseeing their wards' education is another matter.

44. For general considerations of custody in Jewish law, whether in past times or contemporary ones, see Eliav Shochetman, "On the Nature of the Rules Governing Custody of Children in Jewish Law," *Jewish Law Annual* 10 (1992): 115–58, and Pinhas Schifman, "The Welfare of the Child and Religious Considerations," *Jewish Law Annual* 10 (1992): 159–76.

45. The matter is somewhat unclear with respect to Christian women. Chojnacki, "Power of Love," esp. 138–40, speaks of women living between two lineages, patricians in Venice in particular. Christiane Klapisch-Zuber, "Zacharias," 118–19, speaks more in terms of women in Florence "going out" of one lineage, that of their fathers, and entering into that of their husbands. Kuehn, *Law, Family, and Women*, 210, concludes a discussion of *patria potestas* by saying that contrary to general historical opinion, fathers of married daughters did not lose *potestas* and that there were social ramifications, although these mostly have to do with the devolution of property.

46. For Vittoria Zamat, *Notai ebrei*, 2,4,42v (11 June 1570).

47. The matter still requires some research, but the issue of wife beating in the Ghetto often appears as social drama. In some cases, the beating ended tragically, as in the tale of Speranza Capone, RJ 1203, 1210, 1212, 1215. In others, beating alternates with a public berating and cursing by the wife; it is not said whether the berating preceded or followed the beating. Twice,

the beating was administered to the husband by the wife's family. The information comes, however, as part of an agreement, usually two-staged, in which the parties stated their consent to stop their actions, and when they did not, they divorced, with the primary concern being a just financial settlement for both parties; thus the social drama. Everything in the texts is suspect of legal manipulation. It is only when one looks at all the texts together that the formulaic nature comes out: the common clauses, the common stipulations. Read one by one, it may seem that striking women is being allowed. In fact, the women are being allowed to refuse to be struck, leave their husbands, and receive a divorce where the dowry, essential for remarriage, is returned. See here also the cases of Beniamino and Marchigiana, RJ292, 381, 393, Angelo and Perna, RJ451, and Rosetta and Angelo, RJ17, 419, 449, 452, 454, and Berechiah and Fiore, *Notai ebrei*, 9,1,124r. Also Laura Limentani and Sabato d'Uriel, RJ93, 137, 394, a text containing the phrase that there are times when "it is appropriate to hit" (*ha-mitztarekh le-halqotah*), or Beniamino Bonuomo and Ricca, RJ 1066. See also Boksenboim, *Responsa of Diena*, 1:410–19, where the wife is painted as cruel and sadistic. We have no way of knowing whether this was true; but the story shows enormous marital complexity, for the question was one of a second marriage involving the children of a first marriage. On the question, raised above, of permissibility, see Moses Isserles, *Shulkhan 'Arukh, Eben Ha-ezer*, 154 (entire section); Abraham Grossman, "Medieval Rabbinic Views on Wife-Beating, 800–1300," *Jewish History* 5/1 (1991): 53–62; Howard Adelman, "Rabbis and Reality: Public Activities of Jewish Women in Italy During the Renaissance and Catholic Restoration," *Jewish History* 5/1 (1991): 27–40; and idem, "Servants and Sexuality: Seduction, Surrogacy, and Rape: Some Observations Concerning Class, Gender, and Race in Early Modern Italian Jewish Families," in Tamar Rudavsky, ed., *Gender and Judaism* (New York, 1995). See also Various Authors, "Criminal Law, Husband and Wife," *Jewish Law Annual* 9 (1991): 5–170. Finally, an unpublished Hebrew essay of E. Westreich, delivered at Ben Gurion University in the spring of 1998, rigorously demonstrates the differing attitudes of Ashkenazi and Sephardi medieval authorities on the question of wife beating, with the former unanimously forbidding it under all circumstances.

48. Perna Capone, the sister of Sabato di Jeruham, was the effective family head in distributing a legacy in favor of an orphaned niece, which she

did to prevent her brothers from claiming too much for themselves; *Notai ebrei*, 2,1,202r (4 Oct. 1557). On Mazal Tov Zamat suing her father, RJ277, 278, and the case cited here, RJ566. In RJ771, women are protagonists in a dispute among themselves, with the men concerned that a young daughter or granddaughter would not get a sufficient dowry if the older women divided a legacy almost exclusively among themselves. On the related issue of the permissibility of women owning property at all, see the theoretical discussion by Shmuel Morell, "An Equal or a Ward: How Independent Is a Married Jewish Woman according to Rabbinic Law?" *Jewish Social Studies* 44 (1982): 190–200. See also the modes of circumventing the formal, but never enforced, prohibition of ownership that appeared in the very early third-century compilation, the Mishnah, *Nedarim*, 11:8; I thank David Halivini for this reference; and see the medieval ruling about women being responsible for their business dealings, in Finkelstein, *Jewish Self-Government*, 195, 201–2.

49. RJ1852 is the opening text in this drama; see also 1861, 1866, 1878, 2005.

50. For the full story of Ricca, see Stow, "Marriages Are Made in Heaven." See also E. A. Wrigley and R. S. Schonfield, *The Population History of England, 1541–1871* (Cambridge, Mass., 1981), 255, 423–24, on the high age of marriage in seventeenth-century England, twenty-six for women and twenty-eight for men, cited in David Cressy, *Birth, Marriage, and Death*, 234, 534.

51. Recently, it has been said that the formalization of Jewish communities in Italy about this time weakened the powers and standing of Jewish women; Siegmund, "La Vita nei ghetti." This does not seem true for Rome.

52. RJ59.

53. RJ449, 451, 452, 454; and on women taking oaths, for example, RJ189, 980, 1844.

54. This is Siegmund's central thesis, "La Vita," see note 51 above, restated (April 1998) at a conference on Jewish and Protestant Women in England at the University of Reading, that acts of the organized community at Florence, formed after the start of the ghetto, had a negative effect on women's privileges. To be sure, Jewish men make the laws—subject to the Vicar, as Roman Jews say outrightly (see RJ844, acknowledging the need for the Vicar to approve rabbinic bans)—but these laws, among other things, guarantee women's personal (not family) honor (see below on Ricca Soporto) or

ensure their rights to inherit, not diminishing them. It thus remains to be determined whether the absence of formal control was synonymous with the absence of control in fact. Cecil Roth, "The Memoirs of a Sienese Jew (1625–1633)," *Hebrew Union College Annual* 5 (1928): 353–402, suggests that women could defend their rights in Siena. The Sienese mother in the letter concerning the proposed match, a letter in the handwriting of the groom himself, accompanying the notarial act, is clearly a matriarchal figure: *Notai ebrei*, 5,2,93r–95v (29 June 1612), "dil tutto ci ha consentito la mac.ca mia madre, che senza il suo placito Jo non havrei fatto niente." This is far more than what is suggested by Cohn, *Siena.*

55. For Contessa, RJ1218; Menahem Azariah da Fano, *Sefer she'elot ve-teshuvot*, no. 81.

56. Arbi, once actually Parnas of the Catalan-Aragonese synagogue, RJ1966, had clearly fallen on hard times; *Notai ebrei*, 1,1,114v. For the male counterpart of *me'un*, see Jeffrey Woolf, "Toward a Halachic and Intellectual Portrait of Rabbi Elijah Capsali" (in Hebrew), *Tarbiz* 65 (1996): 173–87, and the responsum of Azriel Diena, no. 134, cited in note 34 above. For non-Jews and marital choice, see Houlbrooke, *English Family*, 69–78, Cressy, *Birth, Marriage, and Death*, 255–60, 260–63, and Ferraro, "Power to Decide." The continued emphasis on the conjugal family as the central familial unit among European Jews from the eleventh century and after is discussed in Stow, "The Jewish Family," 1089–93; and see the literature cited there. See also Michael Toch, "The Jewish Community of Nuremberg in the Year 1489, Social and Demographic Structure" (in Hebrew), *Zion* 45 (1980): 60–72.

57. On contrary-to-fact application, see the divorce of Berechiah and Fiore in 1580, noted in note 33 above. After having fled her home, Fiore is told to return "as the law insists." But this is merely a formal statement to allow her to leave permanently, although without receiving support payments from her husband. Fiore was a widow with a son, and independent of Berechiah. About weak rabbinic power in Rome, Bonfil, *Rabbis*, 235–46, leaves no doubt. And see Jacob Katz, "'Da'at Torah'—The Unqualified Authority Claimed for Halakhists," *Jewish History* 11/1 (1997): 41–50, showing how rabbinic power, in any case, need not be equated with the rule of halachah, but all too often was connected with political aspiration.

58. RJ1017, 1082, 1086, 1089, 1090, 1092, and also the sources for the citations immediately following in the text; and see also Stow, "The Knotty

Problem of Shem Tov Soporto: Male Honor, Marital Initiation, and Disciplinary Structures in Mid-Sixteenth Century Jewish Rome," delivered at the annual conference of the Renaissance Society of America, April 1997 (forthcoming in *Italia* 13 (2000), commemorative issue in memory of Joseph B. Sermoneta). On the problem of falsely claimed virginity, or when virginity's apparent absence was justiciable, if ever at all, see Rashi's comment to Deut. 22:19, the site of the primary biblical discussion of virginity and claims about its absence. The notion of *mukat ʿetz*, accidental loss of virginity, or supposed loss, is raised in the Mishnah, *Ketubot*, 1:7, and see the Babylonian Talmud, *Ketubot*, 1:11a, as well as *Responsa of Diena*, ed. Y. Boksenboim, no. 137, and Judah Mintz, *Responsa*, no. 6, both also cited in Adelman, "Rabbis and Reality," nn. 53 and 54; also Maimonides, *Mishneh Torah*, *Hilkhot ʿishut*, 11:3, and *Shulkhan ʿarukh*, *ʿeben ha-ʿezer*, 67:5, 68; I thank Riccardo di Segni for this last reference. See also *Encyclopedia Judaica* (Jerusalem, 1971), s.v. "Virginity."

59. For a thorough discussion of Jewish practices of this kind, see, with caution, Roni Weinstein, "The Jewish Marriage in Italy during the Early Modern Era," (Ph.D. diss., Jerusalem, 1995); and the illuminating but always to be verified claims of the convert Giulio Morosini, *Via della Fede* (Rome, 1683).

60. On the knot, see Emanuel Le Roy Ladurie, "L'aiguillette," *Le territoire de l'historien* (Paris 1973), 136–49; Jacob Bazaq, *Beyond the Senses* (in Hebrew) (Tel Aviv, 1968), 52–56; Peter Burke, "Rituals of Healing in Early Modern Italy," *The Historical Anthropology of Early Modern Italy* (Cambridge, 1987), 212–14; and Stow, *Alienated Minority*, 135–36. But see also the reference in Boksenboim, *Responsa of Diena*, 434, no. 125, on a man married "who for a time . . . was without strength . . . for I was tied . . . magically . . . but then Heaven took mercy. . . ."

61. RJ1092.

62. On the honor of Christian women, see Guido Ruggiero, *The Boundaries of Eros*, esp. 17–18; see also Sandra Cavallo and Simona Cerutti, "Female Honor and the Social Control of Reproduction in Piedmont between 1600 and 1800," in Edward Muir and Guido Ruggiero, eds., *Sex and Gender in Historial Perspective* (Baltimore, 1990), 81: "the woman, whose honor, weaker and more exposed, constituted a threat to the status of her entire community should it be lost . . . one [family] member's fall into dishonor threw

into doubt the authority and power of the family." Cf., too, Elizabeth S. Cohen, "No Longer Virgins: Self-Preservation by Young Women in Late Renaissance Rome," in M. Migiel and J. Schiesari, eds., *Refiguring Woman: Perspectives on Gender and the Italian Renaissance* (Ithaca, 1991), where young women who had been raped, or otherwise ill used at the cost of their maidenhead, went into court self-consciously hoping to improve their situations, to gain a dowry or some payment from their violator. But we do not really know how these cases turned out when they were tried, or at least investigated, before the court of the papal Governor. The sense is that they may have resulted in some succor, but not in a decision based not only on principle but on a purposeful adjustment of even biblical law; that is, there was an ad hoc rather than a consistent basis for determinations. Moreover, the cases Elizabeth Cohen discusses are all of very lower-class women, many of whom seem to have floated on the edge of prostitution. They are likely not exemplary of middle-class women in similar predicaments, or in one like that of Ricca Soporto, malfamed but hardly ill-used. See, too, Ferraro, "Power to Decide," 495.

63. For this trial, see Pier Cesari Ioly-Zorattini, *Processi del S. Uffizio di Venezia contro ebrei e giudaizzanti*, vol. 11 (Florence, 1993), 51–53, "Domenico Temponi." On Chrysostom and the Jews, see Wayne Meeks and Robert Wilkens, *Jews and Christians in Antioch in the First Four Centuries of the Common Era* (Missoula, Mont., 1978).

64. On the synod and Sanasi, see David Gentilcore, *From Bishop to Witch: The System of the Sacred in Early Modern Terra di'Otranto* (Manchester and New York, 1992), 215; and see Muir, *Ritual*, 218.

65. On Christian concepts of the body and its use, or misuse, see, among many others, Peter Brown, *The Body and Society: Men, Women, and Sexual Renunciation in Early Christianity* (New York, 1988); also Dyan Elliott, *Spiritual Marriage: Sexual Abstinence in Medieval Wedlock*; and see Caroline Walker Bynum, *The Resurrection of the Body in Western Christendom, 200–1336* (New York, 1995), 334–41, for a woman's body that is resurrected—perfected—through spirituality while still alive.

66. On Jewish bodily images as linked to Jewish political thought, see K. Stow, "Holy Body, Holy Society: Conflicting Medieval Structural Perceptions," in J. Prawer, R. J. Z. Werblowsky, and B. Z. Kedar, eds., *Sacred Space: Shrine, City, Land* (New York, 1998). At issue here are fundamental ideas

like those of sovereignty and representation on which modern states and statecraft are based, thus far removed from more traditional discussions of matters such as kingship, on which, for example, see Abraham Melamed, "The Perception of Jewish History in Italian Jewish Thought of the Sixteenth and Seventeenth Centuries," *Italia Judaica II, Gli ebrei in Italia* (Rome, 1986), 139–70; or Joseph Sermoneta, "Aspetti del pensiero moderna nell'ebraismo italiano tra Rinascimento e Età Barocca," *Italia Judaica II, Gli ebrei in Italia* (Rome, 1986), 17–35. And see Simone Luzzatto, cited in Introduction, note 33 above. On the problems of Christians separating public from private realms, see Georgio Chittolini, "Il 'privato,' il 'publico,' lo Stato," Angela De Benedictis, "Consociazioni e 'contratti di signoria' nella costruzione della Stato in Italia," and Thomas Kuehn, "Antropologia giuridica dello Stato"—all in Giorgio Chittolini, Anthony Molho, and Pierangelo Schiera, eds., *Origini dello Stato, Processi di formazione Statale in Italia fra medioevo ed età moderna* (Bologna, 1994). See also the discussion and literature cited in chapter 3 and in notes 33 and 34 there.

67. See the essays of Herlihy and Groppi cited in note 36 above.

68. Specifically on these themes in a broad sense, see Milton M. Gordon, *Assimilation in American Life* (New York, 1964), and Peter I. Rose, *They and We: Racial and Ethnic Relations in the United States*, 5th ed. (New York, 1997).

69. Joseph Sermoneta, "Tredici giorni nella Casa dei Conversi—dal diario di una giovana ebrea del 18 secolo," *Michael* 1 (1972): 261–315, and the full version, also Sermoneta, *Ratto della signora Anna del Monte trattenuta a'catecumeni tredici giorni dalli 6 fino alli 19 maggio anno 1749* (Rome, 1989).

70. See note 28 above; and on Christian women, see esp. Eleanor Riemer, "Women, Dowries, and Capital Investment"; and Samuel K. Cohn, Jr., *Death and Property in Siena, 1205–1800: Strategies for the Afterlife* (Baltimore, 1988), 198–209; but see the reservations of Ago, as in note 30 above.

71. I thank Elisabetta Mori of the Archivio Storico Capitolino for the information about Christian lawyers and their ways. On Abramo Scazzocchio's less than precise legal citations, see RJ1215, 1656, but also *Notai ebrei*, 12,1,118v,119v–120v, where he also makes the seemingly astounding statement that Rabbenu Tam directed his regulations only to Jews around Narbonne. Jacob Tam, of course, resided in Champagne, the seat of his power, influence, and teaching. Nevertheless, even so careful a scholar as Henri Gross, *Gallia Judaica* (Paris, 1897), s. v. "Troyes," thought that Narbonne

was (although not exclusively) intended; cited conveniently in Finkelstein, *Jewish Self-Government*, 43, note 2.

72. On the Jews' deteriorated condition, see the *Al'Ill.ma Congr. di Pio VI*, a collection of documents gathered by Roman Jews, sent to Pius VI in 1789, used and referred to often by Milano in *Il Ghetto*. See again Stow, "The Consciousness of Closure: Roman Jewry and Its 'Ghet,'" and "The Good of the Church, The Good of the State: The Popes and Jewish Money." The usage *nostro ghet* or *il ghet* appears no more than four or five times, and the fuller *il ghetto* about five or six times more, beginning about 1600. That is, only ten or eleven references to the Ghetto by this name or its punning variant (*serraglio* or the Hebrew *hazer* appears not infrequently before 1589) in the fifty years between 1589 and 1640, which is surely indicative of hesitancy on some level to evoke the term.

73. On papal programs at this time, see Marina Caffiero, "'Le insidie de' perfidi Giudei,' Antiebraismo e riconquista Cattolica alla fine del settecento," *Rivista Storica Italiana* 105 (1993): 555–81; idem, "Tra Chiesa e Stato: Gli ebrei in Italia nell'età dei Lumi e della Rivoluzione," in Vivanti, ed., *Gli ebrei*, 2:1091–1132; and Mario Rosa, "Tra tolleranza e repressione: Roma e gli ebrei nel '700," *Italia Judaica III* (Rome, 1989). On the level of Jewish study, see Joseph Sermoneta, "Jewish Culture at Rome in the XVIIIth Century as Seen Through New Documentation" (in Hebrew), *Italia Judaica III*.

74. Lois Dubin, "Trieste and Berlin: The Italian Role in the Cultural Politics of the Haskalah," in Jacob Katz, ed., *Toward Modernity: The European Jewish Model* (New York, 1987), 199–209.

75. On the Giudiate, see Milano, *Il Ghetto*, 322–27, and on this *bando*, 84–85, 97, as well as the literature cited in chapter 1, note 49, above.

76. With respect to clothing, Jews also absorbed selectively. Various plates in Therese and Mendel Metzger, *Jewish Life in the Middle Ages: Illuminated Hebrew Manuscripts of the Thirteenth to Sixteenth Centuries* (New York, 1982), e.g., 332, 335, and 347, and the plate in Stow, "Marriages," 448, show Jews dressed exactly as non-Jews in Italy. Milano, *Il Ghetto*, 339–42, implies that Jews continued wearing varicolored garb through at least the early seventeenth century, when sumptuary legislation tried to impose dark colors; and Luciano Allegra, *Identica in bilico: Il Ghetto ebraico di Torino nel Settecento* (Turin, 1996), 262–65, is emphatic about varied colors in even the eighteenth century. Bonfil paints a far more somber picture in *Jewish*

Life, 104–11, arguing that uniform dark colors (as Roman sumptuary laws prescribe) were directed toward achieving distinctiveness even while absorbing culture—the emphasis is on absorption, not a dialectic. There is a further aspect of interest. Sumptuary laws existed throughout Italy, and these regularly prescribe appropriate clothing for diverse social rank. Jewish clothing is uniform, as Jewish sumptuary legislation testifies; see Finkelstein, *Jewish Self-Government*, various places, esp. 285–87 and 292–94; and Milano, above. Hence, we may suggest that Jewish clothing reflects a social homogeneity that is a prime characteristic of Jewish life in fact, at least in Rome; and we await a full comparative study. Jewish women in Venice have been described as extraordinarily bedecked, a hint of which is seen in Calimani, *Ghetto di Venezia*, 247. But which of them? Sumptuary laws are also notorious for their observance in the breach.

77. On the changes in the names of Christian women, see David Herlihy, "Tuscan Names, 1200–1530," in *Women, Family and Society in Medieval Europe* (Providence, 1995), 342.

78. See the index in Stow, "Donne," 107–16, specifying dates, language, and the names of the various notaries. See once more Camargo, *Ars dictaminis*, on the development of the Christian notarial art. Bonfil, "Changes in the Cultural Patterns," would see the change in language as an example of the process of "closure in order to open" that lies at the heart of his extraordinary thesis. But here at least, this thesis would be difficult to establish. In certain spheres it was the pope who decided in which language Jews were to write.

79. See the pioneering studies of Elliott Horowitz, "Coffee, Coffee Houses, and the Nocturnal Rituals of Early Modern Jewry," *AJS Review* 14 (1989): 17–46, esp. 37–40, and his "Jewish Confraternities in Seventeenth Century Verona: A Study in the Social History of Piety" (Ph.D. diss., Yale University, New Haven, 1982). See chapter 1, note 46, for recent works on confraternities at this time.

80. Dagmar Herzog, "Carl Scholl, Gustav Struve, and the Problematics of Philosemitism in 1840s Germany: Radical Christian Dissent and the Reform Jewish Response," *Jewish History* 9/2 (1995): 53–72, and more specifically Herzog's *Intimacy and Exclusion: Religious Politics in Pre-Revolutionary Baden* (Princeton, 1996), 55.

81. One need but see the strictures of W. C. Dohm, *Concerning the*

Amelioration of the Civil Status of the Jews, trans. Helen Lederer (Cincinnati, 1957), and the comments of Stow, "Church, Conversion, and Tradition," 28, to see where even most so-called liberals drew lines based, as Dohm's footnotes leave unambiguous, squarely on traditional Roman law.

82. See Heinrich Graetz, *A History of the Jews*, 6 vols. (Philadelphia, 1939), although this translation is without the weighty notes of the original, and Graetz, *The Structure of Jewish History and Other Essays*, ed. and trans. Ismar Schorsch (New York, 1975). On acculturation without assimilation, without even its possibility, see Steven Zipperstein, *The Jews of Odessa: A Cultural History, 1794–1881* (Stanford, 1981).

83. George L. Mosse, *German Jews Beyond Judaism* (Bloomington, 1985). On specifically women's behavioral modes, see Hyman, *Gender and Assimilation*, 50–92; and, for Germany, Marion A. Kaplan, "For Love or Money: The Marriage Strategies of Jews in Imperial Germany," in Marion A. Kaplan, ed., *The Marriage Bargain* (New York, 1985), and her *The Jewish Feminist Movement in Germany* (Westport, 1979).

84. Mosse, *German Jews*, 8.

85. Ibid., 14 (citing Leo Strauss on Goethe), 12.

86. The only full length study of the entry of Roman Jews into Roman society, from the fall of the Ghetto through the reactions of the 1920s up to the period of fascism, is Stefano Caviglia's *L'identità salvata*.

87. On this noncondemnatory view of Italian fascism, see esp. Daniel Carpi, *Between Mussolini and Hitler: The Jews and the Italian Authorities in France in Tunisia* (Jerusalem, 1994), and the responses of Michele Sarfatti, *Mussolini contro gli ebrei* (Turin, 1994).

88. In particular, see Cecil Roth, *The Jews in the Renaissance* (Philadelphia, 1959), and now the careful "reassessment" of Ruderman, "Cecil Roth, Historian of Italian Jewry." The term *convivenza*, usually associated with Spanish Jewry, is also used by contemporary Italian historians speaking of Jews; for one, Maria Giuseppina Muzzarelli as the title of a collection of essays she has edited: *Verso l'epilogo di una convivenza: gli ebrei a Bologna nel xvi secolo*. Of course, just as in its sometimes overly optimistic application to Jewish life in medieval Spain, so too may the term be applied unduly with respect to Italy. Muzzarelli here means the term literally, in the sense of toward the expulsion, in 1569, of Bolognese Jews.

89. See the penultimate reference in the Afterword, below, to the inter-

view of Henry Louis Gates, Jr., in Peter Applebome, "Can Harvard's Power-house Alter the Course of Black Studies," *New York Times Education Life Supplement*, November 3, 1996, p. 24.

3 / Social Reconciliation, from Within and Without

1. J. Donovan, *Rome, Ancient and Modern and Its Environs* (Rome, 1843), 3:906–8, cited in Benocci and Guidoni, *Il Ghetto*, 84.

2. See Bonfil, *Rabbis*, 209–30, esp. 221; and Bonfil, *Jewish Life*, 204–12, and Stow, *Taxation*, 37–38, on the complexities of Jewish jurisdiction.

3. On this episode, see David Malkiel, "The Tenuous Thread: A Venetian Lawyer's Apology for Self-Government in the Seventeenth Century," *AJS Review* 12 (1987): 223–50; and Benjamin Ravid, "Republica nifredet mikol shilton 'aher," in A. Greenbaum and A. Ivry, eds., *Thought and Action* (Tel Aviv, 1983), 27–53. On the real corporate structure, or its absence in Jewish communities, see K. Stow, "Corporate Double Talk: *Kehillat Kodesh* and *Universitas* in the Roman Jewish Sixteenth Century Environment," *Journal of Jewish Thought and Philosophy*, 8(1999): 283–30.

4. See RJ844, a text revealing the Jewish awareness of the need to circumvent the Vicar, which they do purposefully in compacts to arbitrate, e.g., RJ105–106.

5. See RJ1012, for a widow inheriting an entire estate. On inheritance by Christian women, see notes 26, 28, and 70 in chapter 2 above, and esp. Samuel Cohn, "Women and the Counter-Reformation in Siena." Kuehn, *Law, Family*, 216–35, esp. 235, attributes to widows always a modicum of devolutionary power, although a living woman's husband was her procurator, a real controller, far more than the *mundualdus* who represented a woman in court. Chojnacki, "Marriage Legislation," submits that women had more rights than we attribute them with, especially regarding dowry and inheritance, although cf. Cohn, *Death and Property*, 201. Riemer, "Women, Dowries," note 26 in chapter 2 above, presents the most restrictive aspects of legislation; Ago, note 30 in chapter 2, a most liberal interpretation, and on the basis of severely restrictive legislation.

6. This is the thesis of Bonfil, in his "Changes in the Cultural Patterns."

7. This is again a thesis of Robert Bonfil, "Jewish Attitudes Toward

History and Historical Writing in Pre-Modern Times," *Jewish History* 11/1 (1997): 7–41. Bonfil has also written on Jewish historical writing at this time in "How Golden Was the Age of the Renaissance in Jewish Historiography," *History and Theory* 27 (1988), reprinted in Ruderman, ed., *Essential Papers*; this article is really Bonfil's response to Yosef H. Yerushalmi, "Clio and the Jews: Reflections on Jewish Historiography in the Sixteenth Century," *Proceedings of the American Academy of Jewish Research* 46–47 (1980), also reprinted in *Essential Papers*, but especially to Yerushalmi's *Zakhor* (Seattle, 1982). See also note 8 below. On related intellectual pursuits, especially literary ones, which were also responsive to outside influence, both accepting and rejecting it, see Dan Pagis, "Ha-pulmus ha-shiri ʿal tiv ha-nashim — Babuʿah le-temurot ve-shirah ha—ivrit be-ʿItaliah," in Ezra Fleischer, ed., *Poetry Aptly Explained: Studies and Essays on Medieval Hebrew Poetry* (in Hebrew) (Jerusalem, 1993), concerning poetry written between 1335 and 1530 in praise or denigration of women — mostly a literary exercise — showing how the whole structure, no matter how loaded it was with references to such as Greek mythology, was rooted in traditional rabbinic patterns and halachic principles; see also, Pagis, "Baroque Trends in Italian Hebrew Poetry." On Jewish humanism, see chapter 1, note 14, above.

8. On the question of hesitancy to adopt and also the functioning of social memory as presented here, see K. Stow, "The New Fashioned from the Old: Parallels in Public and Learned Memory and Practice in Sixteenth Century Jewish Rome," in B. Cooperman and B. Garvin, eds., *Memory and Identity: The Jews of Italy* (College Park, Md., 2000), and the penetrating synthesis of Paul Connorton, *How Societies Remember* (Cambridge, 1989), which also has an excellent bibliography.

9. See once again Prodi, *Il Sovranno Pontefice*; Adriano Prosperi, "L'inquisitore come confessore," in Paolo Prodi, ed., *Disciplina dell'anima, disciplina del corpo e disciplina della società tra medioevo ed età moderna* (Bologna, 1994), pp. 187–224; and Prosperi, *Tribunali*.

10. See here, Bonfil, *Jewish Life*, 174–76, 188–91; and K. Stow, "Holy Body, Holy Society: Conflicting Medieval Structural Perceptions."

11. The actual deliberations of communal councils may be found in such works as Daniel Carpi, *The Minute Books of the Jewish Community of Padua* (in Hebrew), 2 vols. (Jerusalem, 1974, 1980), or Yacov Boksenboim, ed., *Minute Books of the Jewish Community of Verona, 1600–1630* (Tel Aviv,

1990). Yet the kind of deliberation there, as in the very brief fascicle 18 of the *Notai ebrei* of the mid-1570s, shows an inconsistency born of the absence of theory. One certainly does not see lawmaking, and, by contrast, one sees texts more appropriate for notarial acts. What political thought there was, really theoretical on such matters as the virtues of monarchies, is discussed by Sermoneta, "Aspetti del pensiero," and Melamed, "The Perception of Jewish History," whose contents may be compared with the contents of the essays of Gaines Post, *Studies in Medieval Legal Thought: Public Law and the State, 1100–1322* (Princeton, 1964). On Roman institutions at this time, especially judicial ones, see note 33 below.

12. On rabbis and rabbinical attitudes and prerogatives, see Bonfil, *Rabbis*, passim, esp. 47–49, 53–55, and Bonfil, *Jewish Life*, 198. On previous rabbinical history, see Mordecai Breuer, *The Rabbinate in Ashkenaz During the Middle Ages* (in Hebrew) (Jerusalem, 1976), and Yisrael Y. Yuval, *Scholars in Their Time: The Religious Leadership of German Jewry in the Late Middle Ages* (in Hebrew) (Jerusalem, 1988).

13. RJ1174; and on deathbed confessions, see Horowitz, "Jewish Confraternities," 71, and Bonfil, *Jewish Life*, 141–42. See also Elliott Horowitz, "The Jews of Europe and the Moment of Death in Medieval and Modern Times," *Judaism* 44 (1995): 271–82, and idem, "Giotto in Avignon, Adler in London, Panofsky in Princeton: On the Odyssey of an Illustrated Hebrew Manuscript from Italy and on Its Meaning," *Jewish Art* 19–20 (1993–94): 99–111. Horowitz argues that the vogue of deathbed confessions began in fifteenth-century Spain and continued to grow in sixteenth-century Italy. By the end of the sixteenth century, there was often a rabbi and a minyan (a quorum of ten) present, whereas earlier the task of confessing was left to a ritual expert. In Rome, it appears that the notary's skill at taking down the confession and other last wishes was the prime requisite for this task. With respect to *niddui*, it is impossible to overemphasize the intrinsic difference between Jewish and Christian, especially Catholic, excommunication. Judaism emphasizes the sacred—indeed never, in any sphere of life, including elementary bodily functions, does it wholly divorce the sacred from the profane. But, unlike Catholicism, Judaism is not sacramental. In particular, a Jew is never dependent on a priest (rabbi) or priestly dispensations at any stage of life or death. The Jew, however, is dependent on the community that provides such services as kosher meat, a ritual bath, and kosher burial. These

are all services that may be furnished by a knowledgeable layman, and in fact often are. But even a layman could not provide them to an excommunicate; on the *scomunica* as discussed here, see Yacov Boksenboim, *Parashiot* (Tel Aviv, 1986), 43.

14. On rabbinic pretense to sacrality, see Jacob Katz, "Da'at Torah." On rabbinical occupations, or where rabbis were supported by wives, see Emanuel Etkes, "Family and Study of Torah" (in Hebrew), *Zion* 51 (1986): 87–106 (English trans. in Paula Hyman, ed., *The Jewish Family*). The various occupations of the noted Leone da Modena are found in Mark R. Cohen, trans. and ed., *The Autobiography of a Seventeenth-Century Venetian Rabbi*, 160–62, 108–09, 118–20. See Bonfil, *Rabbis*, 187–92, on rabbinical incomes, and esp. 190–92 on the income of Leone da Modena.

15. Stow, *Taxation*, passim, on the problems of Jewish taxation by the papacy. On communal organization, its chartering, and its statutes, see the text from 1505 in Simonsohn, *Apostolic See*, no. 1179, where the pope orders that one of the three communal *fattori* be from the *hebreis forensibus*, an order which—perforce—assumes a unified community. Ultramontane Jews could quite obviously not be *fattori* in a community of which they were not a part; thus one could not be simultaneously a member of two communities. On this problem, whether at Rome there were for a short period at the start of the sixteenth century various communities, see note 26 below. On the *Capitoli*, see Milano, "Capitoli." Bonfil, *Jewish Life*, 191–93, proposes a relationship between Jewish communal assemblies and those of the Italian Commune. But any borrowing was partial at best, because of the absence of the political theory, let alone the jurisdiction.

16. Clear evidence on procedural, if not theoretical, unclarity comes from the incident of June 29, 1561, *Notai ebrei*, 1,1,117r and again 117r. The Vicar was called in by certain parties to halt the election of the *fattori*, while others insisted that those *fattori* elected before the Vicarial mandate was delivered were validly elected. More, in texts from October 1611, *Notai ebrei*, 5,1,262–63r, the Quattro Capi synagogue, still in existence, debated which three of its members were to be elected to the Council of Sixty. The *Capitoli* of da Pisa made provision for no such specific synagogal representation. Power thus was distributed in surprising ways. Various texts cited in notes 25 and 26 below, illustrate how limited the communal action really was—rather remarkably, considering the hundreds of years of Jewish communal

life in Europe prior to the sixteenth century. The sole area where the organized community, acting through chosen representatives, the Estimators (of taxes), functioned well was fiscality. Here, there was simply no choice, on which see chapter 2 of my *Taxation*. Besides, the Vicar and the papal Chamberlain, the Cardinal Camererius, had urgent interests here and thus promoted communal activity directly.

17. On confraternities, see chapter 1, note 46, and chapter 2, note 79. Also see the fundamental study of the Venetian *Scuole* made by Brian Pullan, *Rich and Poor in Renaissance Venice* (Cambridge, Mass., 1971); and David Ruderman, "The Founding of a Gemilut Hasadim Society in Ferrara in 1515," *AJS Review* (1976): 233–67.

18. This is the basic problem debated in Prodi, *Disciplina dell'anima*.

19. See Elliott Horowitz, "The Eve of the Circumcision: A Chapter in the History of Jewish Nightlife," *Journal of Social History* 23 (1989), reprinted in Ruderman, *Essential Papers*. Horowitz suggests, 564, that he is describing a second stage in popular cultural patterns at this time, in which the laity was taking charge from the clergy, which in a first phase—later in the sixteenth century and into the beginning of the seventeenth—had made great inroads and achieved control of confraternities; see Peter Burke, *Popular Culture in Early Modern Europe* (New York, 1978), 222, 240. Yet, this description of Christian lay leadership fits Protestant regions, not Catholic ones; Prodi, *Disciplina dell'anima*, various essays. More particularly, on the "clear attempt to gather the fragmented charity of the confraternities under the stringent control of ecclesiastical authorities," that is, to entrench priestly control (in the seventeenth century) of activities once supervised by lay Christian confraternities, see Angela Groppi, "Roman Alms and Poor Relief in the Seventeenth Century," in P. van Kessel and E. Schulte, eds., *Rome-Amsterdam: Two Growing Cities in Seventeenth Century Europe* (Amsterdam, 1997), esp. 181—hence, the contrary of what is being said here about Jewish confraternal life. And it is the Catholic pattern as described by Groppi and others that is better used as a standard to measure conformity (to the majority) or deviance in Italian Jewish practice. As, in fact, I have suggested above, I find no period in which Jewish confraternities were clerically directed; see again Toaff, *Ghetto di Roma*, 31–32.

20. Bonfil, "Changes in the Cultural Patterns," and elsewhere stresses a growing distinction between the sacred and profane, as does Elliott

Horowitz in various studies mentioned in the notes here. But what I perceive as both continued lay dominance and, more important, the continued confraternal function as a vehicle of social reconciliation would suggest a moderation of this picture, a judgment applying also to synagogues, which asked members, see below, to arbitrate disputes intramurally if possible.

21. See Horowitz, "Coffee, Coffee Houses," 17–46, esp. 37–40. The idea of nighttime activity as liberating has been expressed independently of Jews by Elizabeth Crouzet-Pavan, "Recherches sur la nuit vénitienne à la fin du moyen âge," *Journal of Medieval History* 7 (1981): 339–56.

22. See Aurelio Musi, "Lo 'scalco spirituale': un manuale Napoletano di disciplina del corpo (sec. xvii)," in Prodi, ed., *Disciplina dell'anima*; but see also Bossy, *Christianity*, 126–34, on "discipline" as it extended to Protestant practice.

23. See, among others, Brown, *The Body and Society*, and Elliott, *Spiritual Marriage*, cited in note 65, chapter 2, above. On Jewish sanctification achieved through sexuality, see the works cited in chapter 2, note 38: the *Iggeret ha-qodesh*, attributed to the Ramban; Abraham ben David of Posquierres, *Sefer Ba'alei ha-Nefesh*, and Elazar Azqari, *Sefer Haredim*.

24. On extramarital sex, see Howard Adelman, "Finding Women's Voices in Italian Jewish Literature," in Judith Baskin, ed., *Women of the Word: Jewish Women and Jewish Writing* (Detroit, 1992), and his "Servants and Sexuality." See also the text in Riccardo Calimani, *Storia del Ghetto di Venezia* (Milan, 1985), 361–66, esp. 363, on illegitimate births. On the confraternity in Asti, see Elliott Horowitz, "A Jewish Youth Confraternity in Seventeenth Century Italy," *Italia* 5 (1985): 36–97.

25. On the overall problems of strictly synagogal life, see Stow, "Prossimità." On the synagogue as opposed to the community, a study of whose respective activities shows to have been distinct institutions in both perception and performance, see, for example: Community, RJ9, 89, 123, 125, 334, 377, 397, 415, 417, 478, 488, 509, 510, 514, 552, 694, 715, 717, 746, and 818; Synagogues, RJ11, 24, 253, 267, 282, 283, 378, 379, 679, 682, and 742. An important contrast can be seen with Amsterdam, where the synagogue effectively preceded the Community; see Miriam Bodian, "The Escamot of the Spanish-Portuguese Jewish Community of London, 1664," *Michael* 9 (1985): 9–26, although one must especially note with reference to Bodian, Yosef Kaplan, "Political Concepts in the World of the Portuguese Jews of Amsterdam dur-

ing the Seventeenth Century: The Problem of Exclusion and the Boundaries of Self-Identity," in *Menasseh ben Israel and His World,* ed. Henry Méchoulan (Leiden, 1989), 60–61. And for an overall perspective on changes in the role of synagogues about this time, see S. W. Baron, *The Jewish Community* (Philadelphia, 1948), 1:348–50, speaking mostly about Turkey, but with important general implications.

26. Jacob Katz, *Tradition and Crisis: Jewish Society at the End of the Middle Ages* (New York, 1961), 103, warns that the Community is basically a geographical concept. It has been observed that beginning in the early years of the sixteenth century, a number of privileges issued by either the papal chancery or certain notaries at Rome to various Jewish synagogues use interchangeably the terms *scuola* and *universitas*—and, for that matter, *communitas*. The 1511 statutes of the Aragonese synagogue speak of the *Comunità* and then of the *scola* as patently equivalent terms. In 1518, we hear, in one breath, of the *communitas scole Catalanorum . . . universitate predicte* and the *dicta universitas sive communitas* (Esposito, cited here, 185). Moreover, these terms were not temporary ones. A similar usage, the *Università di scola quattro Capi,* may be found as late as July 31, 1614 (13,1,175r). Were, therefore, these terms really so easily interchangeable? And did they mean the same thing for both Christians and Jews? Claims that they did and that in the early sixteenth century there was more than one Community in Rome are expressed by Anna Esposito, "Le 'comunità ebraiche di Roma prima del Sacco (1527): problemi di identificazione," *Henoch* 12 (1990): 185, echoing, in fact, Ariel Toaff, "The Jewish Communities of Catalonia, Aragon and Castile in 16th Century Rome," in A. Toaff and S. Schwarzfuchs, eds., *The Mediterranean and the Jews: Banking, Finance and International Trade (XVI–XVIII Centuries)* (Ramat-Gan, 1989), 262 and 254, in that order. The documents on page 262, dated 9 Nov. 1555 and 14 Oct. 1566, both refer to *Universitate Cathalanorum.* On page 254, we are told that "in 1519 the Catalan Jews were formally recognized by Pope Leo X as a separate community *Universitas judaeorum nationis Cathalanorum.*" Something is awry here, for after 1524 and the statutes of Daniel da Pisa, the existence of one sole Community is undisputed. Hence, either we assume the terms were transvalued by 1555, so that *universitas* now meant something other than a "separate community," or we assume that the term *universitas* itself always meant something else (most likely, simply corporate body, subject, of

course, to the special strictures applying to Jewish quasi corporations) and that there is no ground for assuming that there ever existed at Rome more than one recognized *Comunità*—that is, more than one recognized Jewish Communal body. This second assumption is the correct one, to wit, the persistence of the terminology into the seventeenth century, showing that it is no basis, in itself, for conclusions about the nature of the Community versus the synagogue; *Notai ebrei*, 13,1,175 (1614): *Università di scuola quattro capi*; and *Notai ebrei*, 5,1,220v–221r (1611): *Università degli hebrei*. Also: the Gemilut Hasadim confraternity is listed strictly as a *compagnia*, 4,1,218r– 220v (1615–02–01).

27. No better testimony to this institutional weakness can be brought than fascicle 18 of the *Notai ebrei*, purportedly a book of statutes and deliberations. It is in scope far from the Minute Books like those cited above for Verona and Padua. It was also unique until at least the third decade of the seventeenth century. And it is slim, containing but a handful of taxation provisions and a few texts that look like they belong in the notarial collections. Council meetings were also infrequent, if one may judge by entries that are often weeks, if not months apart. If one judges communal vibrancy on their basis, clearly the seat of communal action was not in the Council as directed by da Pisa; it was in—and through—notarial acts.

28. See Malkiel, "The Tenuous Thread" (note 3 above); Prodi, *Il Sovranno Pontefice*, passim; and Prosperi, *Tribunali*, esp. 57–116.

29. Bonfil, *Jewish Life*, 204–12, and see notes 2, 4, 10, and 12 above. On papal encouragement, see RJ1654, 1656, where a difficult situation finished, surely with Vicarial assent, in the hands of Jewish arbiters; and RJ1954, 1955, 1956, 1986, 1988, 1990, where the Vicar directed the application, as he did in other cases, of R. Tam's Ordinance concerning evictions. The Vicar also became involved in matrimonial matters where halachic interpretation was involved; RJ1794, 1878. Of course, in both instances the Vicar was convinced he was acting to his own advantage. The Jews usually exploited such instances well. Nonetheless, they preferred avoiding them; this may be seen in the case of Raffaele di Sezze, the very case encapsulated in RJ1654 and 1656. See also the acts cited in notes 55 and 57 below, and the accompanying discussion in the text. Papal encouragement was tempered, however. The fees assigned Jewish notaries in the bull *universi agri dominici* of 1612 regulating Roman tribunals were higher than Christian fees, even though per capita

the Jews had less money; on this bull and its effects on Jews, see Simona Feci, "Tra il tribunale e il ghetto: le magistrature, la communità e gli individui di fronte ai reati degli ebrei romani nel Seicento," *Quaderni Storici* 99 (1998): 575–600; for the text and the clauses concerning Jewish notarial fees, see C. Cocquelines, *Bullarum privilegiorum ac diplomatum romanorum pontificium*, Roma 1745, Tome Five, part IV, 189, *Universi agri dominici* (1.3.1612). Were these different fees for Jewish notaries intended to discourage their activities? If so, the ploy did not work. The texts rarely mention fees, but when they do, the fees Jewish notaries were taking in practice were exceedingly small. In addition, the bull complains about notaries usurping judicial functions by acting without first seeking judicial permission for some of the acts they drew. The reference was to Christian notaries, but it might as well have been to Jewish ones, too, admitting, in effect, that the Jewish notary had taken the place of the technically prohibited formal Jewish tribunal.

30. Bossy, *Christianity*, 60. See more recently, idem, ed., *Disputes and Settlements: Law and Human Relations in the West* (Cambridge, 1983), esp. James Casey, "Household Disputes and the Law in Early Modern Andalusia," 189, and Nicole Castan, "The Arbitration of Disputes under the Ancien Regime," 219.

31. Kuehn, *Law, Family*, 19–23, who emphasizes, too, arbitration's flexibility as opposed to the rigidity of formal courts.

32. Indicative of the flexibility of Jewish arbitration is the absence of halachic indications in the acts themselves. That is, halachot surely underlie various decisions, but these laws are not cited, since the decision was generally rendered in the spirit, not the letter, of the law. Sometimes, as in the case of Shem Tov Soporto (see chapter 2), the letter of the law was significantly inverted. Indeed, in the approximately 900 acts concerning litigation out of the total of 6,000 I have calendered from the *Notai ebrei*, actual citations of halachot may be counted on the fingers of one hand. On problems of turning to non-Jewish courts in Italy, see Berachah Rivlin, *Mutual Responsibility in the Italian Ghetto Holy Societies, 1516–1789* (in Hebrew) (Jerusalem, 1991), 191–96; for Islam, see the discussions in Mark Cohen, *Jewish Self-Government in Medieval Egypt* (Princeton, 1980), and S. D. Goitein, *A Mediterranean Society*, vol. 2 (Berkeley, 1971). Ahkenazim prohibited turning to outside jurisdictions almost hermetically, on which see the Ordinance, *Tsats ha-mateh*, in Finkelstein, *Jewish Self-Government*, 159.

33. On these themes, see Michele De Sivo, "Roman Criminal Justice between State and City: The Reform of Paul V," in P. van Kessel and E. Schulte, eds., *Rome-Amsterdam: Two Growing Cities in Seventeenth Century Europe* (Amsterdam, 1997), 280: "If one studies the actual functioning of the tribunals and the careers of their officials together with the use made of the judicial system, also by those who appeared in front of the judges, then this complexity, multiformity and sometimes even complementarity turn out to be consistent with a society where the distinction between private and public was non-existent and where both spheres were so interdependent that they were considered as one." De Sivo seems to be referring, by interpenetrability, to the fluidity with which one might pass from one judicial venue to another. Jews, as we note, might—and did—do the same. Yet that meant avoiding their community, which was far from the case with Christian judicial leapfrogging. Nonetheless, we should not ignore that in its state of liminality between the public and the private, Jewish practice was once again intrinsically Jewish yet reinforced by non-Jewish behavior, our constant theme. Moreover, this liminality was reinforced by the lack of precision in the bull *universi agri dominici* mentioned in note 29 above; the bull leaves the subject of Jewish arbitration untouched. For other literature on this subject, see the works cited in note 66, chapter 2, above.

34. On the *vicinato*, see Christiane Klapisch-Zuber, "Parenti, amici e vicini, Il territorio urbano d'una famiglia mercantile nel XV secolo," *Quaderni Storici* 33 (1976): 953–82, trans. as "Kin, Friends, and Neighbors: The Urban Territory of a Merchant Family in 1400," in *Women, Family, and Ritual in Renaissance Italy*. The reference to the *shekhunah* is *Notai ebrei*, 12,1,80r (1557).

35. Refer again to the Introduction, notes 4–6, for details of the Roman Jewish notary.

36. Yael Granot, "The Notary as Communal Surrogate," Seminar paper, University of Haifa, 1996.

37. For example, in Hebrew, virtually all the texts, and in Italian, for example, *Notai ebrei*, 10,1,197r (1597) 8,1,47r (1609); 10,3,118r (1612); and see below in the text for further discussion of this clause.

38. See Bossy, *Christianity*, 22–26, and Guido Ruggiero, *The Boundaries of Eros*, 25–28. On rabbinic officiating at weddings, see Ze'ev W. Faulk, *Jew-*

ish Matrimonial Law in the Middle Ages (Oxford, 1966), and Freimann, *Seder kiddushin*, 66.

39. RJ1607.

40. By memory, I mean that of the notary, that of witnesses, or that of those coached by lawyers. All are possibilities. For an initial discussion of Jewish social memory and its forms in this period, see Yerushalmi, *Zakhor*, and Stow, "New Fashioned from the Old."

41. See Stow, "Abramo ben Aron Scazzocchio."

42. The absence of formal Jewish jurisdiction was reiterated, by stressing the Jews' obligations to use the *ius commune* in disputes, in the bull *Cum sicut accepimus*, of 22 Feb. 1550, Julius III; see Stow, *Catholic Thought*, 23–24. On new taxes, see Stow, *Taxation*, passim, esp. 30–36.

43. Dagger episode: RJ1598. *Notai ebrei*, 13,1,105v–106r (1569), for Passapaire; and on the need for formal decisions concerning housing the elderly, see 14,1,135r–v.

44. Most of these texts simply report the event. What is important is not that these young women's hymens were really ruptured; the number is too high for this to be true, about 70 over 100 years. Rather, this is what people thought. The question of the innocence of these thoughts, nonetheless, is hard to resolve and put to rest. Thus a text from 12 June 1569 notes that the young child was "kicked by a horse"; and *Notai ebrei*, 2,4,17r,27v–28r (19 Oct. 1569), is about a young girl frightened by a great noise and humming coming from a *cupella* (a beehive?). However, *Notai ebrei*, 2,4,33r (23 Jan. 1570), tells of an engaged girl who wanted to sleep in her parents' bedroom during the night. Possibly, most of the reports are in fact innocent, but this left room for the real offenders to slip in under the wire.

45. Horse issue: RJ1636. Housing disputes: RJ1954,1955,1956,1986,1988, 1990, and various others. The complex rent dispute is discussed in Stow, "Prossimità." If anything testifies to living in a world of illusion, this case is certainly it. If one pretends that at stake was simply a payment for rent, rather than liturgical continuity, and gets away with the pretense, tension is considerably eased.

46. Family issues: RJ451,131–32,292,1066. Synagogues: Stow, "Prossimità," passim. Money: RJ1830,1889,1919. Joshua Abbina: RJ1905.

47. On such as funeral processions and burial, see Samuel K. Cohn, Jr.,

"Burial in the Early Renaissance: Six Cities in Central Italy," in J. Chiffoleau, Lauro Martines, and A. Paravicini Bagliani, eds., *Riti e rituali nelle Società Medievali* (Spoleto, 1994).

48. See for this term, meaning simply "cemetery," at least in Yiddish usage, Sylvie-Anne Goldberg, *Crossing the Jabok: Illness and Death in Ashkenazi Judaism in Sixteenth Through Nineteenth-Century Prague*, trans. Carol Cosman (Berkeley, 1996), 21, and also 20–27, which is a thorough discussion of death, the laws regarding it, and the Gemilut Hasadim society of Prague during this long period.

49. On funeral decorum and orations, see again Cohn, "Burial," and also Diane Owen Hughes, "Mourning Rites, Memory, and Civilization in Premodern Italy," both in Chiffoleau et al., eds., *Riti e rituali*. See also Samuel K. Cohn, Jr., *The Cult of Remembrance and the Black Death: Six Renaissance Cities in Central Italy* (Baltimore, 1992), and Cohn, *Death and Property*. See also Sharon T. Strocchia, "Funerals and the Politics of Gender in Early Renaissance Florence," in M. Migiel and J. Schiesari, eds., *Refiguring Woman: Perspectives on Gender and the Italian Renaissance* (Ithaca, 1991), discussing how funeral pomp might also, among Christians, show gender differences or public status of male officials.

50. On the pomp that might accompany a Jewish funeral, see Bonfil, *Jewish Life*, 267–70, on the funeral of the august Judah Mintz; and the general discussion of Leon Modena, 265–67. For the funeral of the equally eminent Samuel Aboab, see Elliott Horowitz, in a paper delivered in January 1986 at a conference held in Jerusalem, organized by S. N. Eisenstadt (the proceedings were never published): "Confraternal Processions and Social Tensions in the Jewish Communities of the Veneto." This paper, as well as my own (uncited) response to Horowitz at this conference, is used liberally by Miriam Bodian in her "The Portuguese 'Dowry Societies' in Venice and Amsterdam," *Italia* 6 (1987): 52. See in general on funeral rites, Horowitz, "Jewish Confraternities," 105–10.

51. On Giudiate, see note 49 in chapter 1 above, and esp. for funerals, Milano, *Il Ghetto*, 261–68; also Berliner, *Storia*, 221–24. For Aaron Berechiah di Modena, see Abriel Bar-Levav, "Rabbi Aharon Berechia di Modena and Rabbi Naftali Ha-Cohen Katz: 'Abot ha-mehabrerim sifrei holim vameitim," *'Asufot* 9 (1997): 189–234; as well as Goldberg, *Crossing the Jabok*,

passim. On stonings at funerals, which could occur by day as well as by night, see again Milano, *Il Ghetto*, 262–69, and with much detail, Ariel Toaff, *Il Vino e la carne* (Bologna, 1989), 67–68, 224–225. See also Laurie Nussdorfer, "The Politics of Space in Early Modern Rome," *Memoirs of the American Academy in Rome* 42 (1999): 161–86, esp. 172, on Jewish cemeteries, and 172–73, on the *giudiata*.

52. Confession: RJ1138, 1551, 2004. Obligations of burial: RJ890, 1043, 1093, 1266.

53. See Cohn, Hughes, and Strocchia, as cited in note 49 above.

54. RJ1743 and 105, 106.

55. RJ1844; and Bonfil, *Jewish Life*, 204, on the Vicar authorizing the ban as a means to force the payment of taxes.

56. On the claim of the popes directly to judge the Jews for violating aspects of Jewish law and ritual, see B. Z. Kedar, "Canon Law and the Burning of the Talmud," *Bulletin of Medieval Canon Law* 9 (1979): 79–82, for the basic text of Innocent IV; Stow, "Ebrei e inquisitori, 1250–1350," 3–18; and Stow, *The '1007 Anonymous' and Papal Sovereignty*.

57. See note 55 above, as well as RJ1799, and 1720, 1794, 1798, but esp. 1049, where the Vicar is stymied, 1743, 1799.

58. RJ1654, 1656.

59. RJ1209.

60. *Notai ebrei*, 2,3,19r (17 September 1562).

61. *Notai ebrei*, 10,1,197r (17 Feb. 1597) and 8,1,47r (30 June 1609); and 10,3,118r (1612).

62. See Bonfil, *Rabbis*, 221–30, where he suggests that the form of *compromesso* was introduced in other cites, but I imagine following the Roman model.

63. For this imprecision, despite the technical meaning of the word "corporation," see the texts and discussion in note 26 above, and Mack Walker, "Jewish Identity in a World of Corporations and Estates," in Ronnie Po-Chia Hsia and Harmut Lehmann, eds., *In and Out of the Ghetto* (Washington, D.C., 1995), 317–20, who places Jews in the category of urban dwellers who lacked real corporate identity, but one that was modified by intrinsically Jewish cultural continuities. This categorization would fit the loose corporate definitions Roman authorities were applying to Jews; it would also

facilitate the emergence of the Jewish notary. See, too, Laurie Nussdorfer, *Civic Politics in the Rome of Urban VIII* (Princeton, 1992), 128–30, on the juridical status of Roman professional corporations.

64. John Bossy, *Christianity*, 60, might suggest that we should be speaking about "charity" rather than publicity. In discussing activities within various late medieval confraternities and their statutes which insisted that disputes between members go to arbitration, Bossy says, "The activity was clearly a real attempt to fulfil the Augustinian principle that lawsuits were a form of enmity which Christians should avoid; it was surely influential in creating the general consensus in early modern Europe that disputes between neighbours should be settled by arbitration, not taken to court. All these were expressions of charity as people understood it." This point is strengthened remembering that jurists sometimes called *caritas* a principle of justice on which the world stood. Hence, the well-functioning public sphere is one that rests on *caritas*. Nonetheless, *caritas* has a patently fideistic element within the strict Christian confraternal framework that does not fit well with at least my perception of communal-wide Jewish arbitrational procedures. Besides, as said, neither Christian confraternities, however they may have had similar elements, nor Jewish confraternities, however they included in their statutes the idea of internal arbitration, were certified communities, certainly not in the sense that the Jewish Community embodied the totality of Jewish self-regulatory agencies and sovereignty (limited as it was). That the Jews equated publicity and arbitration with justice, public and private, is another matter. And here there is a parallel, a strong one, but not an identity.

65. RJ1654, 1656. By contrast, and stressing our point here, when standing before Christian tribunals, Jews did not seem to show emotional constraint as they confronted accusers; see Irene Fosi, "Criminalità ebraica a Roma fra cinquecento e Seicento: autorappresentazione e realtà," *Quaderni Storici* 99 (1998): 553–74.

66. RJ1565; and see the difficult story of Isach di Segní, RJ1209, whom the Vicar was somehow able to force into a divorce. The text even suggests that Isach may have been pressured to convert.

67. *Notai ebrei*, 2,4,42v (1570); and RJ451.

68. Much work has been done on the question of understanding emotions by understanding their cultural setting. See J. Coulter, "Affect and So-

cial Context: Emotion Definition as a Social Task," in Rom Harré, ed., *The Social Construction of Emotions* (Oxford, 1986), 127: "Types of situation are paradigmatically linked to the emotions they afford *by convention*. The link is neither deterministic, nor biological, but sociocultural"; or Harré's article therein, "An Outline of the Social Constructionist Viewpoint," 81: "to the extent that emotions reflect and sustain the religious, moral, and political beliefs, interests and values of a community, then ... the analysis of these interrelated systems should be prior to our analysis of the emotions which feature in, and support such systems." Emotion thus is viewed as a relative expression, measuring among other things degrees of reaction to various stimuli, reaction that is controlled or unbound, considered legitimate or illegitimate depending on circumstance and specific cultural setting. And see the fundamental anthropological studies of Catherine A. Lutz, *Unnatural Emotion: Everyday Sentiments on a Micronesian Atoll and Their Challenge to Western Theory* (Chicago, 1988); and Catherine Lutz and Lila Abu-Lughod, eds., *Language and the Politics of Emotion* (Cambridge, 1990). Without quarreling with these positions, I suggest a reciprocity rather than a one-way street between setting and emotion; nor do I imagine that the authors just noted would disagree. Namely, I suggest that one may move in the opposite direction as well, at least with public emotion, because of its coded nature. Once one deciphers the code—the conventions bounding emotional expression—one may proceed to analyze social postures. See, too, Barbara H. Rosenwein, "Controlling Paradigms," in Rosenwein, ed., *Anger's Past: The Social Uses of an Emotion in the Middle Ages* (Ithaca, 1998), on anger as a social instrument.

69. RJ1954, 1955, 1956, 1986, 1988, 1990, and various others.

70. Dennis Brissett and Charles Edgley, eds., *Life as Theater*, 119; and see Introduction, note 69, above.

71. On *non dabarà*, especially in the seventeenth century, when ghetto crowding had begun to stimulate brawls, sometimes even with Christians, as well as a greater sense of instability in many areas, see Micaela Procaccia, "'Non dabarà': Gli ebrei di Roma nei primi cinquanta anni del Cinquecento attraverso le fonti giudiziarie," *Italia Judaica VI; Gli ebrei nello Stato pontificio fino al Ghetto (1555)* (Rome, 1998). For the *herem-scomunica* in Rome, RJ1174, 1562; and see Calimani, *Ghetto di Venezia*, 245–51, and also 364 for a parallel use of the *scomunica* in Venice under different conditions

of internal Jewish control. On Rabbenu Gershom, see Finkelstein, *Jewish Self-Government*, 20–35, 110–47.

72. *Notai ebrei*, 2,3,46r (20 March 1563), for the maneuvering of Abramo Scazzocchio.

73. Intriguingly, the *herem* thus functioning fits well the definition of Nancy Struever, *The Language of History in the Renaissance* (Princeton, 1970), 140, that publicity is the taking and carrying on of political life and decision in the open, as opposed to privacy, the taking of self-council, which is tyranny. What is also noticeable is that this concept of consensual *herem* to some extent imitates the idea of social contract and stands opposed to the idea of a unified Christian body politic that imitated in its essence the Corpus Christi. The problem, of course, is that modern political bodies combine and balance both concepts: individual rights and the idea of belonging to a precisely defined political entity. Jews have never achieved this balance.

74. On rabbinic feuding, see Bonfil, *Jewish Life*, 197–203, 210–11, and his "Zutot le-parashat ha-get Tamari-Ventorozzo" ("Some Points about the Affair of the Tamari-Ventorozzo Divorce"), in D. Carpi et al., eds., *Shlomo Simonsohn Jubilee Volume* (Tel Aviv, 1992), 19–28. Also see Yacov Boksenboim, *Responsa Mattanot Ba-Adam* (Tel Aviv, 1983), 197–98.

75. By contrast, see Ronald F. E. Weissman, "From Brotherhood to Congregation: Confraternal Ritual between Renaissance and Catholic Reformation," who speaks of collective public piety at this time being replaced by private interiorized piety, with piety subsumed into the parish cult of sacraments. Wholly at odds with this picture, the Jews' socioreligious structure, their Jewish mode of self-control, was pushing them far away from what at least the Church desired and was pressing for in terms of confraternal (i.e., neighborhood) reform; and, instead, they perceived the Ghetto much as a (confraternal) neighborhood. See also Nussdorfer, note 63 above, on the juridical functions that Roman professional confraternities, non-Jewish ones, did claim. How much they were able to exercise these functions is another matter, overshadowed as they were by the multiplicity of other Roman jurisdictional instances; see De Sivo, "Roman Criminal Justice," note 33 above. Nor, and this is crucial, did these professional confraternities necessarily expect members to undertake to arbitrate all their dissensions within confraternal walls, something that certain Jewish confraternities did pretend to do.

76. On these Christian notaries, see Carmelo Trasselli, "Un ufficio notarile per gli Ebrei di Roma," *Archivio della R. Deputazione Romana di Storia Patria* 60 (1938): 231–44, which describes the notarial registers of Christian notaries whose acts concerned primarily the Jews; there are thousands of documents in these registers. G. Bluestein, *Storia degli ebrei in Roma* (Rome, 1920), gives the date of 1682 for the change from Jewish to Christian notaries, but he may be confusing this date with that of the closing of Jewish banks, indeed, in 1682. Berliner, *Storia*, 359–60, refers to a Jewish notary, Astruc Toscano, in the later seventeenth century; but in fact he acknowledges the main series of *Notai ebrei* running to 1620, then one volume of 1663–98, by Toscano, which requires examining before drawing conclusions. What we must assume is that even if somehow the Jewish notary survived, it was in seriously diminished straits—and fitfully; and this is the point. See again Di Sivo, "Roman Criminal Justice," and his description of the juridical reforms of 1612. Possibly these affected the course of the Jewish notaries. These reforms also partially challenged the Vicar's monopoly on Jewish justice, another possible reason for change in the Jewish notarial system.

77. Donovan, *Rome*, cited in note 1 above.

78. It is beyond my intention to describe Jewish life in these later centuries. Milano's descriptions still have great value, whether for social or cultural life. Apart from his studies already cited, see Milano, "L'impari lotta della Comunità di Roma contro la Casa del Catecumeni," *La Rassegna Mensile di Israel* 16 (1950): 355–68, and 408–19. See, instructively, Joseph Sermoneta, "Jewish Culture at Rome in the XVIIIth Century as Seen Through New Documentation" (in Hebrew), *Italia Judaica III* (Rome, 1989), in which one sees continued study of such subjects as Italian rhetoric, but on a steadily deteriorating level, a deterioration which the late Professor Sermoneta confirmed to me personally. Berliner, too, *Storia*, esp. 214–16, discussing the rabbinate, with the exception of Tranquillo Corcos, 224–38, gives an idea of how low the level of education had become. Also Milano, *Il Ghetto*, 385–89. At the same time, we must remember that the average Jewish youth was never highly educated. On which, see various apprenticeship contracts, which all stipulate what the boy, sometimes the girl, must learn: the girls, to read Hebrew, prayers; the boys, to explain the weekly Torah portion. See, for example, RJ196, 1523 and *Notai ebrei*, 6,2,42v–43r (1590), and 6,2,141r (1591).

79. On renewed papal restriction in the seventeenth century, see the text of the bull of Pius VI (1775) in Berliner, *Storia*, 263–75; and the studies of Caffiero, "'Le insidie de' perfidi Giudei'" and "Tra Chiesa e Stato"; and Mario Rosa, "Tra tolleranza e repressione," cited in chapter 1, note 9. See also, on imprisonment and its dangers, Stow, "Castigo e delitto nello Stato della Chiesa: Gli ebrei nelle carceri romane dal 1572 al 1659." On the plague of 1565, Berliner, *Storia*, 218–20, and Milano, *Il Ghetto*, 92, who indicates that, according to his figures, 800 of 4,127 Jews died, while 14,500 to 22,000 of all of Rome's then 120,000 residents succumbed. The best figures on this plague and a general discussion are in Sonnino and Traina, "La pesta del 1656–57 a Roma: Organizzazione sanitaria e mortalità." On impoverishment, see Milano, *Il Ghetto*, 163–73, 412–13.

80. Donovan, *Rome*, 3:906.

81. See Milano, *Il Ghetto*, 111–12, 397–414; Berliner, *Storia*, 277–79.

82. "Cultural arrest" applies primarily to acculturation, but in fact to all serious cultural advance as well. As for the modernization suggested by Bonfil, "Changes in the Cultural Patterns," one must beware that Bonfil means a wholly internal modernization, not a tendency to acculturate to external behavior or patterns. See the selection from Gregorovius in chapter 1, above.

AFTERWORD

1. For conflicting views of this epoch see Daniel Carpi, *Between Mussolini and Hitler*, and Michele Sarfatti, *Mussolini contro gli ebrei*, both cited in chapter 2, note 87, above.

2. See, in particular, on leaving the American ghetto, Samuel C. Heilman, *Portrait of American Jewry: The Last Half of the Twentieth Century* (Seattle, 1995); also Deborah Dash Moore, *At Home in America: Second Generation New York Jews* (New York, 1981), Jeffrey Gurock, *When Harlem Was Jewish, 1870–1930* (New York, 1979), and Paul Ritterband, in Robert Seltzer and Norman Cohn, eds., *The Americanization of the Jews* (New York, 1995), as well as Ritterband's collection, *Modern Jewish Fertility* (Leiden, 1981). The number of works one might cite here is legion.

3. The most accessible list of Judaeo-Romanesco words is in Milano, *Il Ghetto*, 435–71. And see the literature cited there.

4. The only monograph on the Jews of Rome post-1870 is Stefano Caviglia, *L'identità salvata*. For the Fascist period, see the chapter on the Di Veroli family in Alexander Stille, *Benevolence and Betrayal: Five Italian Jewish Families under Fascism* (New York, 1991). On the overall question of emancipation in Italy, see Francesa Sofia and Mario Toscano, eds., *Stato nazionale ed emancipazione ebraica* (Rome, 1992).

5. We await the publication of the studies made in 1996–97 by the anthropologist Judith Goldstein on these vendors of mementos, known as the *ricordi*.

6. To visualize this scene, which may conjure up the story of the Christian miller who galloped his horse and wagon through the Ghetto and met his death, see Simona Feci, "The Death of a Miller: A Trial *contra hebreos* in Baroque Rome" and consult the extraordinary maps in Benocci and Guidone, *Il Ghetto*, passim, but esp. 36–37.

7. Menahem Azariah da Fano, *Responsa*, no. 81.

8. On Livorno, see Renzo Toaff, *La Nazione Ebrea a Livorno e a Pisa (1591–1700)* (Florence, 1990). We also await the paper of Bernard Cooperman on Jewish communal rule in Livorno delivered at the University College London Conference on Italian Jewry in April 1995.

9. See Klapisch-Zuber, "The 'Cruel Mother'"; and also "The Griselda Complex: Dowry and Marriage Gifts in the Quattrocento," and "Zacharias, or the Ousted Father," all in *Women, Family, and Ritual*; and Chojnacki, "'The Most Serious Duty'" and "The Power of Love."

10. Cohn, "Women and the Counter-Reformation in Siena," in *Women in the Streets*; but see, once more, the reservations of Ago as noted in note 30, chapter 2, above, who believes that Christian women, apparently in Rome in particular, were inheriting somewhat more than is usually thought. But note that her reservations also deal largely with the seventeenth century, when the formal prohibitions in this city were officially restated by Innocent XI (1680); Ago, "The Family," 91.

11. For this restrictive view, see Stephanie Siegmund, "La Vita nei ghetti," 239–61. But see *Notai ebrei*, 5,2,93r–95v (29 June 1612), "dil tutto ci ha consentito la mac.ca mia madre, che senza il suo placito Jo non havrei fatto niente" (cited in chapter 2, note 54, above), a text suggesting the Roman pattern was not limited to Rome.

12. Henry Louis Gates, Jr., in Peter Applebome, "Can Harvard's Power-

house Alter the Course of Black Studies," *New York Times Education Life Supplement*, November 3, 1996, 24. Among the many studies on the Black ghetto in general, see the basic discussion in Joe Darden, *The Ghetto* (Monticello, Ill., 1977).

13. Arnold M. Eisen, "Rethinking Jewish Modernity," *Jewish Social Studies* n.s. 1.1 (1994): 1–22.

14. On the interpenetration of Jewish and African-American culture in the United States, especially among theater and musical artists, in the early decades of the twentieth century, see Stephen J. Whitfield, *In Search of American Jewish Culture* (Hanover, N.H., 1999).

BIBLIOGRAPHY

Archivio di Stato, Modena, Fondo dell'Inquisizione, *busta* 26.

Archivio di Stato, Roma, Camerale I, Diversa Cameralia, *varia*; Tribunale del Governatore, Criminali, Costituti, 37, 38.

Archivio di Stato, Roma, Camerale II, Ebrei, *b*. 1. Il Vero Stato degli Ebrei di Roma.

Archivio della Comunità Israelitica, Roma, IE1, *Libro dei giuramenti per la tassa sul capitale*. 1692.

Archivio Storico Capitolino, Rome, Sezione III, Notai Ebrei, and Sezione I.

Abraham ben David of Posquierres. *Sefer Baʿalei ha-Nefesh*, ed. J. Kafah. Jerusalem, 1964.

Abrahams, I. "Marriages Are Made in Heaven." *Jewish Quarterly Review* 2 (1890): 172–77.

Accati, Luisa. "Matrimony and Chastity, Symbolic Change and Social Control in Northeastern Italy, 1550–1750." *International Journal of Moral and Social Studies* 5 (1990): 23–24.

Adelman, Howard. "Finding Women's Voices in Italian Jewish Literature." In Judith Baskin, ed., *Woman of the Word: Jewish Women and Jewish Writing*. Detroit, 1992.

———. "Rabbis and Reality: Public Activities of Jewish Women in Italy During the Renaissance and Catholic Restoration." *Jewish History* 5/1 (1991): 27–40.

————. "Servants and Sexuality: Seduction, Surrogacy, and Rape: Some Observations Concerning Class, Gender, and Race in Early Modern Italian Jewish Families." In Tamar Rudavsky, ed., *Gender and Judaism*. New York, 1995.

Ago, Renata. *Carriere e clientele nella Roma barocca*. Rome-Bari, 1990.

————. "The Family in Rome, Structures and Relationships." In P. van Kessel and E. Schulte, eds., *Rome-Amsterdam: Two Growing Cities in Seventeenth Century Europe*. Amsterdam, 1997.

Agus, Irving. *Urban Civilization in Pre-Crusade Europe*. New York, 1965.

Ait, Ivana. "Mercanti 'stranieri' a Roma nel secolo XV nei registri della 'dogana di terra.'" *Studi Romani* 35 (1987): 25–30.

Allegra, Luciano. "A Model of Jewish Devolution." *Jewish History* 7/2 (1993): 29–58.

————. *Identica in bilico: Il Ghetto ebraico di Torino nel Settecento*. Turin, 1996.

Altmann, Alexander. "Ars Rhetorica as Reflected in Some Jewish Figures of the Italian Renaissance." In B. Cooperman, ed., *Jewish Thought in the Sixteenth Century*. Cambridge, Mass., 1983.

Arru, Angiolina. "'Donare non è perdere': I vantaggi della reciprocità a Roma tra Settecento e Ottocento." *Quaderni Storici* 98 (1998): 361–63.

Ashtor, E. "Palermitan Jewry in the Fifteenth Century." *Hebrew Union College Annual* 50 (1979): 242–43.

Augustinus Aurelius. *City of God*. Trans. M. Dods. New York, 1950.

————. *Adversus Judaeos*. In *Fathers of the Church*, 27: 391–416. Washington, D.C., 1965.

Avi Yonah, Michael. *The Jews of Palestine: A Political History from the Bar Kokhba War to the Arab Conquest*. Oxford, 1976.

Azqari, Elazar. *Sefer Haredim*. Venice, 1601.

Bachi, Roberto. "The Demographic Development of Italian Jewry from the Seventeenth Century." *Jewish Journal of Sociology* 4/2 (1962): 172–91, which is a condensed version of the unpublished "L'evoluzione demografica degli ebrei italiani dal 1600 al 1937." Florence, 1939.

Baer, Yitzhak. "Ha-megamah ha-datit-ha-hevratit shel Sefer Hasidim." *Studies in the History of the Jewish People*. Jerusalem, 1985.

Bar-Levav, Abriel. "Rabbi Aharon Berechia di Modena and Rabbi Naftali Ha-Cohen Katz: 'Abot ha-mehabrerim sifrei holim va-meitim." *'Asufot* 9 (1997): 189–234.

Baron, S. W. *The Jewish Community.* 3 vols. Philadelphia, 1948.

——. *A Social and Religious History of the Jews.* New York, 1952–. Volume 14.

Barone, Giulia. "Il movimento francescano e la nascita delle confraternite romane. In Luigi Fiorani, ed., *Le confraternite romane: esperienza religiosa, società, committenza artistica* [= *Ricerche per la storia religiosa di Roma* 5 (1984): 71–80].

Battista De' Giudici. *Apologia Iudaeorum.* Ed. and trans. Diego Quaglioni. Rome, 1987.

Beard, Charles. "That Noble Dream." *American Historical Review* 46 (1935): 74–87.

Benocci, Carla, and Enrico Guidoni. *Il Ghetto.* Rome, 1993.

Benvenuti, Paolo. *Il Confortorio.* Film. Italy, 1993.

Berger, Peter. "Sociological Perspectives—Society as Drama." In Dennis Brissett and Charles Edgley, eds., *Life as Theater: A Dramaturgical Source Book.* New York, 1990.

Berliner, Abraham. *Kobez al Yad* 4:27–31.

——. *Storia degli Ebrei di Roma.* Milan, 1992. Trans. of *Geschichte der Juden in Rom.* Frankfurt am Main, 1893.

Bevilacqua, Mario. *Il Monte dei Cenci.* Rome, 1988.

Biale, David. "Confessions of an Historian of Jewish Culture." *Jewish Social Studies* 1/1 (1994): 40–52.

Biale, Rachel. *Women and Jewish Law.* New York, 1984.

Biblioteca Apostolica Vaticana, Cod. Urb. Lat. 1038, 1039.

Biersack, Aletta. "Local Knowledge, Local History, Geertz and Beyond." In Lynn Hunt, ed., *The New Cultural History.* Berkeley, 1989.

Black, Christopher. *Italian Confraternities in the Sixteenth Century.* Cambridge, 1989.

Bluestein, G. *Storia degli ebrei in Roma.* Rome, 1920.

Blumenkranz, Bernard. "Deux compilations canoniques de Florus de Lyon et l'action antijuive d'Agobard." *Revue Historique de Droit Français et Étranger* 33 (1955): 227–54, 560–82.

Bodian, Miriam. "The Escamot of the Spanish-Portuguese Jewish Community of London, 1664." *Michael* 9 (1985): 9–26.

——. "The Portuguese 'Dowry Societies' in Venice and Amsterdam." *Italia* 6 (1987): 52.

Boiteux, Martine. "Espace urbain, pratiques rituelles, parcours symbo-liques: Rome dans la seconde moitié du XVIème siècle." In F. Hinard and M. Royo, eds., *Rome: L'Espace urbain et ses représentations*. Tours, 1993.

———. "Rivaltà festive: rituali pubblici romani al tempo di Sisto V." In M. Fagiolo and M. L. Madonna, eds., *Sisto V*, vol 1. Rome, 1992.

Boksenboim, Yacov, ed. *The Responsa of Rabbi Azriel Diena*. 2 vols. Tel Aviv, 1977.

———. *Responsa Mattanot Ba-Adam*. Tel Aviv, 1983.

———. *The Letters of Rabbi Leon Modena*. Tel Aviv, 1984.

———. *Parashiot*. Tel Aviv, 1986.

———. *Minute Books of the Jewish Community of Verona, 1600–1630*. Tel Aviv, 1990.

Bonfil, Robert. "Toward a Social and Spiritual Portrait of the Jews of the Ve-neto in the Early Sixteenth Century" (in Hebrew). *Zion* 41 (1976): 77.

———. "Società cristiana e società ebraica nell'Italia medievale e rinasci-mentale: riflessioni sul significato e sui limiti di una convergenza." In M. Luzzati, M. Olivari, and A. Veronese, eds., *Ebrei e Cristiani nell'Ita-lia Medievale e Moderna: Conversioni, Scambi, Contrasti*. Rome, 1988.

———. "Changes in the Cultural Patterns of a Jewish Society in Crisis: Italian Jewry at the Close of the Sixteenth Century." *Jewish History* 3/2 (1988): 11–30.

———. "Myth, Rhetoric, History? A Study in the Chronicle of Ahimaʿaz" (in Hebrew). In M. Ben-Sasson, R. Bonfil, and J. Hacker, eds., *Culture and Society in Medieval Jewry*. Jerusalem, 1989.

———. *Rabbis and Jewish Communities in Renaissance Italy*. Trans. J. Chip-man. Oxford, 1990.

———. "Jewish Lenders in Italy During the Renaissance: An Economic Force" (in Hebrew). *Peʿamim* 41 (1990): 58–64.

———. "How Golden Was the Age of the Renaissance in Jewish Histori-ography?" *History and Theory* 27 (1988). Reprinted in David B. Ruder-man, ed., *Essential Papers on Jewish Culture in Renaissance and Baroque Italy*. New York, 1992.

———. "Zutot le-parashat ha-get Tamari-Ventorozzo" ("Some Points about the Affair of the Tamari-Ventorozzo Divorce"). In D. Carpi et al., eds., *Shlomo Simonsohn Jubilee Volume*. Tel Aviv, 1992.

———. *Gli ebrei in Italia nell'epoca del Rinascimento*. Florence, 1991; English trans., *Jewish Life in Renaissance Italy*. Berkeley, 1994.

———. "Jewish Attitudes Toward History and Historical Writing in pre-Modern Times." *Jewish History* 11/1 (1997): 7–41.

Bossy, John. *Christianity in the West: 1400–1700*. Oxford, 1985.

Bossy, John, ed. *Disputes and Settlements: Law and Human Relations in the West*. Cambridge, 1983.

Boyarin, Daniel. *A Radical Jew: Paul and the Politics of Identity*. Berkeley, 1994.

———. "The Married Monk: Babylonian *Aggada* as Evidence of Changes in Babylonian Halacha." In Yael Azmon, ed., *A View into the Lives of Women in Jewish Societies* (in Hebrew). Jerusalem, 1995.

———. *Unheroic Conduct: The Rise of Heterosexuality and the Invention of the Jewish Male*. Berkeley, 1997.

Braude, W. G., and I. J. Kapstein, eds. *Pesikta de-Rab Kahana*. Philadelphia, 1975.

Bresc, Henri. "La famille dans la societé sicilienne médiévale." In *La famiglia e la vita quotidiana*. Rome, 1986.

Bressolles, Mgr. *Saint Agobard, Évêque de Lyon, 760–840*. Paris, 1949.

Breuer, Mordecai. *The Rabbinate in Ashkenaz During the Middle Ages* (in Hebrew). Jerusalem, 1976.

Brissett, Dennis, and Charles Edgley, eds. *Life as Theater: A Dramaturgical Source Book*. New York, 1990.

Brown, Peter. *The Body and Society: Men, Women, and Sexual Renunciation in Early Christianity*. New York, 1988.

Brundage, James. *Law, Sex, and Christian Society in Medieval Europe*. Chicago, 1987.

Bullarium Diplomatum et Privilegiorum Taurensis Editio. Turin, 1857–72. Volume 4.

Burke, Peter. *Popular Culture in Early Modern Europe*. New York, 1978.

———. "Southern Italy in the 1590s: Hard Times or Crisis?" In Peter Clark, ed., *The European Crisis of the 1590s: Essays in Comparative History*. London, 1985.

———. "Rituals of Healing in Early Modern Italy." *The Historical Anthropology of Early Modern Italy*. Cambridge, 1987.

Bynum, Caroline Walker. *The Resurrection of the Body in Western Christendom, 200–1336*. New York, 1995.

Caffiero, Marina. "'Le insidie de' perfidi Giudei,' Antiebraismo e riconquista Cattolica alla fine del settecento." *Rivista Storica Italiana* 105 (1993): 555–81.

———. "Tra Chiesa e Stato: Gli ebrei in Italia nell'età dei Lumi e della Rivoluzione." In Corrado Vivanti, ed., *Gli ebrei in Italia, Storia d'Italia, Annali 11.* Turin, 1996.

Calimani, Riccardo. *Storia del Ghetto di Venezia.* Milan, 1985.

Calvi, Giulia. "Reconstructing the Family: Widowhood and Remarriage in Tuscany in the Early Modern Period." In Kate Lowe and Trevor Dean, eds., *Marriage in Italy, 1300–1650.* Cambridge, 1998.

Camargo, Martin. *Ars dictaminis, ars dictandi.* Turnhout, 1991.

Cannarozzi, Ciro, ed. *Bernardino da Siena, Le prediche Volgare.* Florence, 1958.

Carpi, Daniel. *The Minute Books of the Jewish Community of Padua* (in Hebrew). 2 vols. Jerusalem, 1974, 1980.

———. *Between Mussolini and Hitler: The Jews and the Italian Authorities in France in Tunisia.* Jerusalem, 1994.

Casey, James. *The History of the Family.* Oxford, 1989.

Caviglia, Stefano. *L'identità salvata.* Bari, 1995.

Chavarria, Elisa. "Ideologia e comportamenti familiari nei predicatori italiani tra cinque e settecento: Tematiche e modelli." *Rivista Storica Italiana* 100 (1988): 679–723.

Chazan, Robert. "Review of K. Stow, The '1007 Anonymous.'" *Speculum* 62 (1987): 728–31.

Chittolini, Georgio. "Il 'privato,' il 'publico,' lo Stato." In Giorgio Chittolini, Anthony Molho, and Pierangelo Schiera, eds., *Origini dello Stato, Processi di formazione Statale in Italia fra medioevo ed età moderna.* Bologna, 1994.

Chojnacki, Stanley. "The Power of Love: Wives and Husbands in Late Medieval Venice." In Mary Erler and Maryanne Kowaleski, eds., *Women and Power in the Middle Ages.* Athens, Ga., 1988.

———. "Marriage Legislation and Patrician Society in Fifteenth-Century Venice." In B. Bachrach and D. Nicholas, eds., *Law, Custom, and the Social Fabric in Medieval Europe: Essays in Honor of Bryce Lyon.* Kalamazoo, 1990.

———. "'The Most Serious Duty': Motherhood, Gender, and Patrician

Culture in Renaissance Venice." In Marilyn Migiel and Juliana Schiesari, eds., *Refiguring Woman: Perspectives on Gender and the Italian Renaissance*. Ithaca, 1991.

Cocquelines, C. *Bullarum privilegiorum ac diplomatum romanorum pontificium*, Roma 1745, Tome Five, part IV, 189, *Universi agri dominici*
(1.3.1612).

Cohen, Elizabeth S. "No Longer Virgins: Self-Preservation by Young Women
in Late Renaissance Rome." In Marilyn Migiel and Juliana Schiesari,
eds., *Refiguring Woman: Perspectives on Gender and the Italian Renaissance*. Ithaca, 1991.

Cohen, Elizabeth S., and Thomas V. Cohen. *Words and Deeds in Renaissance
Rome: Trials Before the Papal Magistrates*. Toronto, 1993.

Cohen, Jeremy. *The Friars and the Jews*. Ithaca, 1982.

———. *Living Letters of the Law: Ideas of the Jews in Medieval Christianity*.
Berkeley, 1999.

Cohen, Jeremy, ed. *From Witness to Witchcraft: Jews and Judaism in Medieval Christian Thought*. Weisbaden, 1996.

Cohen, Mark R. *Jewish Self Government in Medieval Egypt*. Princeton, 1980.

Cohen, Mark R., trans. and ed. *The Autobiography of a Seventeenth-Century
Venetian Rabbi: Leon Modena's Life of Judah*. Princeton, 1988.

Cohen, Thomas V. "The Case of the Mysterious Coil of Rope: Street Life
and Jewish Persona in Rome in the Middle of the Sixteenth Century."
Sixteenth Century Journal 19 (1988): 209–22.

Cohn, Samuel K., Jr. *Death and Property in Siena, 1205–1800: Strategies for
the Afterlife*. Baltimore, 1988.

———. *The Cult of Remembrance and the Black Death: Six Renaissance
Cities in Central Italy*. Baltimore, 1992.

———. "Burial in the Early Renaissance: Six Cities in Central Italy." In
J. Chiffoleau, Lauro Martines, and A. Paravicini Bagliani, eds., *Riti e
rituali nelle Società Medievali*. Spoleto, 1994.

———. "Women in the Streets: Women in the Courts in Early Renaissance
Florence," "Last Wills: Family, Women, and the Black Death in Central
Italy," and "Women and the Counter-Reformation in Siena: Authority
and Property in Family," *Women in the Streets: Essays on Sex and Power
in Renaissance Italy*. Baltimore, 1996.

Connorton, Paul. *How Societies Remember*. Cambridge, 1989.

Cooperman, B. D. "Venetian Policy Towards Levantine Jews in Its Broader
Italian Context," in G. Cozzi, ed., *Gli Ebrei e Venezia*. Milan, 1987.

Coulter, J. "Affect and Social Context: Emotion Definition as a Social Task."
In Rom Harré, ed., *The Social Construction of Emotions*. Oxford, 1986.

Cressy, David. *Birth, Marriage, and Death: Ritual Religion, and the Life Cycle
in Tudor and Stuart England*. Oxford, 1997.

Crouzet-Pavan, Elizabeth. "Recherches sur la nuit vénitienne à la fin du
moyen âge." *Journal of Medieval History* 7 (1981): 339–56.

———. "Venice between Jerusalem, Byzantium, and Divine Retribution: The Origins of the Ghetto." *Mediterranean Historical Review*
6 (1991): 164.

D'Alvray, A., and M. Tausche. "Marriage Sermons in *Ad Status* Collections
of the Central Middle Ages." *Archives d'histoire doctrinale et littéraire
du Moyen Âge* 47 (1980): 71–119.

D'Amico, John. *Renaissance Humanism in Papal Rome*. Baltimore, 1983.

Darden, Joe. *The Ghetto*. Monticello, Ill., 1977.

Davidson, N. S. "Northern Italy in the 1590s." In Peter Clark, ed., *The European Crisis of the 1590s: Essays in Comparative History*. London, 1985.

Davis, Natalie Z. "The Sacred and the Body Social in 16th Century Lyon."
Past and Present 90 (1981): 40–70.

———. "Women in the Crafts in Sixteenth-Century Lyon." In B. Hanawalt, ed., *Women and Work in Preindustrial Europe*. Bloomington, 1986.

———. *Fiction in the Archives: Pardon Tales and Their Tellers in Sixteenth-
Century France*. Stanford, 1987. Reprint. Cambridge, 1988.

———. *Women on the Margins*. Cambridge, Mass., 1995.

De Benedictis, Angela. "Consociazioni e 'contratti di signoria' nella costruzione dello Stato in Italia." In Giorgio Chittolini, Anthony Molho, and
Pierangelo Schiera, eds., *Origini dello Stato, Processi di formazione Statale in Italia fra medioevo ed età moderna*. Bologna, 1994.

Delicado, Francisco. *La Lozana Andaluza*. Ed. Claude Allaigre. Madrid, 1985.

Delumeau, Jean. *Vie économique et sociale de Rome dans la seconde moitié du
XVIe siècle*. 2 vols. Rome, 1959. Italian abridgment, *Vita economica e sociale di Roma nel cinquecento*. Florence, 1979.

De Sivo, Michele. "Roman Criminal Justice between State and City: The Reform of Paul V." In P. van Kessel and E. Schulte, eds., *Rome-Amsterdam:
Two Growing Cities in Seventh Century Europe*. Amsterdam, 1997.

Despres, Denise. "Immaculate Flesh and the Social Body: Mary and the Jews." *Jewish History* 12/1 (1998): 45–46.

De Susannis, Marquardus. *De Iudaeis et Aliis Infidelibus.* Venice, 1558.

Diana infedele di Baruccabà, BAV Vatican Library, Racc. Gen. Miscell IV, 94, int. 2.

Dohm, W. C. *Concerning the Amelioration of the Civil Status of the Jews.* Trans. Helen Lederer. Cincinnati, 1957.

Donovan, J. *Rome Ancient and Modern and Its Environs.* Rome, 1843. In Carla Benocci and Enrico Guidoni, *Il Ghetto.* Rome, 1993.

Douglas, Mary. "Deciphering a Meal." *Daedalus* 101 (1972): 61–82.

Dubin, Lois. "Trieste and Berlin: The Italian Role in the Cultural Politics of the Haskalah." In Jacob Katz, ed., *Toward Modernity: The European Jewish Model.* New York, 1987.

Eisen, Arnold M. "Rethinking Jewish Modernity." *Jewish Social Studies* n.s. 1/1 (1994): 1–22.

Elinson, Eliakim. *'Ish ve-'Ishto.* Volume 3 of *Ha-'Ishah ve-ha-mitzvot.* Jerusalem, 1981.

Elliott, Dyan. *Spiritual Marriage: Sexual Abstinence in Medieval Wedlock.* Princeton, 1993.

Esposito, Anna. "Gli Ebrei a Roma nella seconda metà del '400 attraverso i protocolli del notaio Giovanni Angelo Amati." In AA.VV., *Aspetti e problemi della presenza ebraica nell'Italia centro-settentrionale (secoli XIV e XV).* Rome, 1983.

———. "Le 'confraternite' del Gonfalone (secoli XIV–XV)." In Luigi Fiorani, ed., *Le confraternite romane: esperienza religiosa, società, committenza artistica* [= *Ricerche per la storia religiosa di Roma* 5 (1984): 91–136].

———. "Le 'comunità' ebraiche di Roma prima del Sacco (1527): problemi di identificazione." *Henoch* 12 (1990): 178–85.

Esposito, Anna, and Diego Quaglioni. *Processi contro gli ebrei di Trento, 1475–1478.* Padua, 1990.

Etkes, Emanuel. "Family and Study of Torah in Lithuanian Talmudist Circles in the Nineteenth Century" (in Hebrew). *Zion* 51 (1986): 87–106. English trans. in Paula Hyman, ed., *The Jewish Family, Myth and Reality.* New York, 1986.

Faulk, Ze'ev W. *Jewish Matrimonial Law in the Middle Ages.* Oxford, 1966.

Fano, Menahem Azariah da. *Sefer she'elot ve-teshuvot*. Jerusalem, 1963.

Feci, Simona. "The Death of a Miller: A Trial *contra hebreos* in Baroque Rome." *Jewish History* 7/2 (1993): 15–20.

———. "'Sed qua ipsa est mulier. . . .' Le risorse dell'identità giuridica femminile a Roma in età moderna." *Quaderni Storici* 98 (1998): 275–300.

———. "Tra il tribunale e il ghetto: le magistrature, la communità e gli individui di fronte ai reati degli ebrei romani nel Seicento." *Quaderni Storici* 99 (1998): 575–600.

Feldman, David. *Marital Relations, Birth Control, and Abortion in Jewish Law*. New York, 1974.

Ferraro, Joanne M. "The Power to Decide: Battered Wives in Early Modern Venice." *Renaissance Quarterly* 48 (1995): 492–512.

Finkelstein, L. *Jewish Self-Government in the Middle Ages*. New York, 1964.

Flandrin, J. L. *Families in Former Times: Kinship, Household, and Sexuality*. Trans. R. Southern. Cambridge, 1976.

Foa, Anna. "Il gioco del proselitismo: politica delle conversioni e controllo della violenza nella Roma del Cinquecento." In M. Luzzati, M. Olivari, and A. Veronese, eds., *Ebrei e Cristiani nell'Italia Medievale e Moderna: Conversioni, Scambi, Contrasti*. Rome, 1988.

———. "The New and the Old: the Spread of Syphilis (1494–1530)." In Edward Muir and Guido Ruggiero, eds., *Sex and Gender in Historical Perspective*. Baltimore, 1990.

———. "The Witch and the Jew: Two Alikes that Were Not the Same." In Jeremy Cohen, ed., *From Witness to Witchcraft: Jews and Judaism in Medieval Christian Thought*. Weisbaden, 1996.

———. *The Jews of Europe: From the Black Death to Emancipation*. Los Angeles, 2000.

———. "Un vescovo marrano: il processo a Pedro de Aranda." *Quaderni Storici*. 99 (1998): 533–52.

———. "The Marranos' Kitchen." Proceedings of the II Conference on Mediterranean Jewry, Bar Ilan University, December 1993. Forthcoming.

———. "Converts and Conversos in Sixteenth Century Italy: Marranos in Rome." In B. Cooperman and B. Garvin, eds., *Memory and Identity: The Jews of Italy* (College Park, Md., 2000).

———. "The Religious Orders and Conversion." In Stephen McMichael and Larry Simon, eds., *The Friars and the Jews*. Leiden, 2000.

Foà, Simona, ed. *La Giustizia degl'ebrei*. Rome, 1987.

———. ed. *Le "Chroniche" della Famiglia Citone*. Trans. A. A. Piattelli. Rome, 1988.

Fosi, Irene. "Criminalità ebraica a Roma fra cinquecente e Seicento: auto-rappresentazione e realtà." *Quaderni Storici* 99 (1998): 553–574.

Freimann, A. *Seder kiddushin ve-nissuin 'aharei hatimat ha-Talmud*. Jerusalem, 1964.

Friedberg, Emil, ed. *Corpus iuris canonici*. Reprint. Graz, 1959.

Funkenstein, Amos. "The Dialectics of Assimilation." *Jewish Social Studies* 1/2 (1995): 1–15.

Gabel, Leona, et al. *The Renaissance Reconsidered: A Symposium*. Northampton, Mass., 1964.

Gager, Kristin E. *Blood Ties and Fictive Ties*. Princeton, 1996.

Gampel, Benjamin. *The Last Jews on Iberian Soil, Navarese Jewry 1479/1498*. Berkeley, 1989.

Gates, Henry Louis, Jr., in Peter Applebome, "Can Harvard's Powerhouse Alter the Course of Black Studies." *New York Times Education Life Supplement*, November 3, 1996.

Geertz, Clifford. *Negara: The Theatre State in Nineteenth Century Bali*. Princeton, 1980.

Gentilcore, David. *From Bishop to Witch: The System of the Sacred in Early Modern Terra di'Otranto*. Manchester and New York, 1992.

Giannini, G. *La Poesia popolare a stampa nel secolo XIX*. 2 vols. Udine, 1938.

Gilboa, Akiva, ed. and trans. *Agobardi Lugdunensis Archiepiscopi, Epistolae Contra Iudaeos*. Latin text with Hebrew translation. Jerusalem, 1964.

Gilboa, Tidhar. "Dowries in the Roman Ghetto." Seminar paper, University of Haifa, 1997.

Giustiniani, Paolo, and Pietro Quirini. *Libellus ad Leonem Decem*, ed. J. B. Mittarelli and A. Costadoni. *Annales Camuldulenses*, vol. 9. Venice, 1773.

Gnoli, G. "Descriptio urbis, censimento della popolazione di Roma avanti il sacco borbonico." *Archivio della R. Deputazione Romana di Storia Patria* 17 (1905): 365–520.

Goitein, S. D. *A Mediterranean Society*. 3 vols. Berkeley, 1967, 1971, 1974.

Golb, Norman. *The Jews in Medieval Normandy*. Cambridge, 1998; and the review by Kenneth Stow, *The Medieval Review* (electronic), July 1999.

Goldberg, Sylvie-Anne. *Crossing the Jabok: Illness and Death in Ashkenazi Judaism in Sixteenth Through Nineteenth-Century Prague*. Trans. Carol Cosman. Berkeley, 1996.

Goldstein, Judith. *The "ricordi" of Rome*. Forthcoming.

Goody, Jack. *Representations and Contradictions: Ambivalence Towards Images, Theatre, Fiction, Relics and Sexuality*. Oxford, 1997.

Gordon, Milton M. *Assimilation in American Life*. New York, 1964.

Gottlieb, Beatrice. *The Family in the Western World from the Black Death to the Industrial Age*. New York, 1993.

Grabois, A. "The Nassiim of Narbonne" (in Hebrew). *Michael* 12 (1991): 42–66. Hebrew numeration.

Graetz, Heinrich. *A History of the Jews*. 6 vols. Philadelphia, 1939.

———. *The Structure of Jewish History and Other Essays*. Ed. and trans. Ismar Schorsch. New York, 1975.

Granot, Yael. "The Notary as Communal Surrogate." Seminar paper, University of Haifa, 1996.

Grayzel, Solomon. *The Church and the Jews in the Thirteenth Century*. Vol. 1. Philadelphia, 1933 (reprint, New York, 1966); and vol. 2, ed. K. Stow. New York, 1989.

Gregorovius, Ferdinand. *Der Ghetto und die Juden in Rom*. Reprint. Berlin, 1935. Translated, *The Ghetto and the Jews of Rome*. New York, 1948.

Grendler, Paul. *Schooling in Renaissance Italy: Literacy and Learning, 1300–1600*. Baltimore, 1989.

Groppi, Angela. "Il lavoro delle donne: un questionario da arricchire." In Simona Cavaciocchi, ed., *La donna nell'economia Secc. XIII–XVIII*. Florence, 1990.

———. "Roman Alms and Poor Relief in the Seventeenth Century." In P. van Kessel and E. Schulte, eds., *Rome-Amsterdam: Two Growing Cities in Seventeenth Century Europe*. Amsterdam, 1997.

———. "Ebrei, donne, soldati e neofiti: l'esercizio del mestiere tra esclusioni e privilegi (Roma XVI–XVIII secolo)." Unpublished.

Grossman, Abraham. "Medieval Rabbinic Views on Wife-Beating, 800–1300." *Jewish History* 5/1 (1991): 53–62.

———. "Shorshav shel kiddush ha-shem be-ʿashkenaz ha-qedumah." In

I. Gafni and A. Ravitzky, eds., *Kiddush haShem and the Suffering of the Soul: Studies in Memory of Amir Yekutiel*. Jerusalem, 1992.

———. "The Bond between Halachah and Economics Regarding the Status of Jewish Women in Early Ashkenaz." In Menahem Ben-Sasson, ed., *Religion and Economy, Connections and Interactions* (in Hebrew). Jerusalem, 1995.

Gunzberg, Lynn. *Strangers at Home: Jews in the Italian Literary Imagination*. Berkeley, 1992.

Gurevitch, Aaron. *Medieval Popular Culture*. Trans. J. Bak and P. Hollingsworth. New York and Cambridge, 1990.

Gurock, Jeffrey. *When Harlem Was Jewish, 1870–1930*. New York, 1979.

Ha-Meiri, Menahem. *Beit ha-Behirah*. Ed. Abraham Sofer. Jerusalem, 1963.

Hanawalt, Barbara A. "Peasant Women's Contribution to the Home Economy in Late Medieval England." In B. Hanawalt, ed., *Women and Work in Preindustrial Europe*. Bloomington, 1986.

Harris, Alan C. "La demografia del ghetto in Italia, 1516–1797 circa." *Rassegna Mensile di Israel*. Supplement. Rome, 1967.

Heilman, Samuel C. *Portrait of American Jewry: the Last Half of the Twentieth Century*. Seattle, 1995.

Herculano, *History of the Origin and Establishment of the Inquisition in Portugal*. Reprint. New York 1972.

Herlihy, David. "The Making of the Medieval Family: Symmetry, Structure, and Sentiment." *Journal of Family History* 8 (1983): 116–130.

———. "Women's Work in the Towns of Traditional Europe." In Simona Cavaciocchi, ed., *La donna nell'economia Secc. XIII–XVIII*. Florence, 1990.

———. *Women, Family and Society in Medieval Europe: Historical Essays, 1978–1991*. Intro. Anthony Molho. Oxford, 1995.

Herlihy, David, and Christiane Klapisch-Zuber. *Les Toscans et leurs familles*. Paris, 1978. Abridged English, *Tuscans and Their Families: A Study of the Florentine Catasto of 1427*. New Haven, 1985.

Herzog, Dagmar. "Carl Scholl, Gustav Struve, and the Problematics of Philosemitism in 1840s Germany: Radical Christian Dissent and the Reform Jewish Response." *Jewish History* 9/2 (1995): 53–72.

———. *Intimacy and Exclusion: Religious Politics in Pre-Revolutionary Baden*. Princeton, 1996.

Hood, John Y. B. *Aquinas and the Jews*. Philadelphia, 1995.

Horowitz, Elliott. "Jewish Confraternities in Seventeenth Century Verona: A Study in the Social History of Piety." Ph.D. dissertation, Yale University, 1982.

———. "The Way We Were: Jewish Life in the Middle Ages." *Jewish History* 1/1 (1986): 75–90.

———. "Nuptial Practices in the Venetian Ghetto" (in Hebrew). *Tarbiz* 56 (1987): 347–71.

———. "Jewish Confraternal Piety in the Veneto in the Sixteenth and Seventeenth Centuries." In G. Cozzi, ed., *Gli Ebrei e Venezia*. Venice, 1987.

———. "Coffee, Coffee Houses, and the Nocturnal Rituals of Early Modern Jewry." *AJS Review* 14 (1989): 17–46.

———. "Speaking of the Dead: The Emergence of the Eulogy among Italian Jewry of the Sixteenth Century." In David B. Ruderman, ed., *Preachers of the Italian Ghetto*. Berkeley, 1992.

———. "The Eve of the Circumcision: A Chapter in the History of Jewish Nightlife." *Journal of Social History* 23 (1989). Reprinted in Ruderman, ed., *Essential Papers*. New York, 1992.

———. "Giotto in Avignon, Adler in London, Panofsky in Princeton: On the Odyssey of an Illustrated Hebrew Manuscript from Italy and on Its Meaning." *Jewish Art* 19–20 (1993–94): 99–111.

———. "The Jews of Europe and the Moment of Death in Medieval and Modern Times." *Judaism* 44 (1995): 271–82.

———. "Mondi Giovanili Ebraici in Europa, 1300–1800." In Giovanni Levi and J-C Schmitt, eds., *Storia dei Giovani*. Vol. 1. Bari, 1994. Translation, *History of Young People in the West*. Cambridge, Mass., 1997.

Houlbrooke, Ralph A. *The English Family, 1450–1700*. London, 1984.

Hsia, Ronnie Po-Chia. *The Myth of Ritual Murder*. New Haven, 1988.

———. *Trent 1475*. New Haven, 1992.

———. *In and Out of the Ghetto*. Cambridge, 1995.

———. *The World of Catholic Renewal, 1540–1740*. New York, 1998.

Hudson, William. "Religion and Society in Early Modern Italy." *American Historical Review* 101 (1996): 783–804.

Hughes, Diane Owen. "Distinguishing Signs: Ear-Rings, Jews and Franciscan Rhetoric in the Italian Renaissance City." *Past and Present* 112 (1986): 3–59.

———. "Mourning Rites, Memory, and Civilization in Premodern Italy." In J. Chiffoleau, Lauro Martines, and A. Paravicini Bagliani, eds., *Riti e rituali nelle Società Medievali*. Spoleto, 1994.

Hunt, Lynn, ed. *The New Cultural History*. Berkeley, 1989.

Hurwitz, Yeshaiah. *Shenai luhot ha-berit*. Furth, 1764.

Hyman, Paula E. *Gender and Assimilation in Modern Jewish History: The Roles and Representation of Women*. Seattle, 1995.

Ibn Verga, Shelomo. *Sefer Shebet Yehudah*. Ed. Y. F. Baer and A. Shohat. Jerusalem, 1947.

Ibn Zerah, Menahem. *Zedah la Darekh*. Jerusalem, 1977.

Idel, Moshe. "Particularism and Universalism in Kabbalah, 1480–1650. In Ruderman, ed., *Essential Papers*. New York, 1992.

———. "Major Currents in Italian Kabbalah Between 1560 and 1660." In Ruderman, ed., *Essential Papers*.

Infessura, Stefano. *Diario della Città di Roma*. Ed. O. Tommasini. Rome, 1890.

Ingram, Martin. *Church Courts, Sex, and Marriage in England, 1570–1640*. Cambridge, 1987.

Ioly-Zorattini, Pier Cesari. *Processi del S. Uffizio di Venezia contro ebrei e giudaizzanti*. 14 vols. Florence, 1980–97.

Jellinek, Aharon, ed. "Haqirot ʿal ʿinyanei ha-nozrim meʿet R. Yishmaʾel Haninah." *Ha-Shahar* (1871), 17–23.

Johnson, Willis. "Before the Blood Libel: Jews in Christian Exegesis After the Massacres of 1096." M. Phil., Cambridge, 1994.

Jordan, Wm. C. "Jews on Top: Women and the Availability of Consumption Loans in Northern France in the mid-Thirteenth Century." *Journal of Jewish Studies* 29 (1978): 39–56.

Kaplan, Marion A. "For Love or Money: The Marriage Strategies of Jews in Imperial Germany." In Marion A. Kaplan, ed., *The Marriage Bargain: Women and Dowries in European History*. [= *Women and History* 10 (1985)].

———. *The Jewish Feminist Movement in Germany*. Westport, 1979.

———. "Priestess or Hausfrau: Women and Tradition in the German-

Jewish Family." In S. Cohen and P. Hyman, eds., *The Jewish Family*. New York, 1986.

Kaplan, Yosef. "Political Concepts in the World of the Portuguese Jews of Amsterdam during the Seventeenth Century: The Problem of Exclusion and the Boundaries of Self-Identity." In Henry Mechoulan, ed., *Menasseh ben Israel and His World*. Leiden, 1989.

Katz, David, and Yosef Kaplan, eds. *Exile and Return: Anglo-Jewry Through the Ages* (in Hebrew). Jerusalem, 1993.

Katz, Jacob. *Tradition and Crisis: Jewish Society at the End of the Middle Ages*. New York, 1961.

———. *Exclusiveness and Tolerance: Studies in Jewish-Gentile Relations in Medieval and Modern Times*. New York, 1961.

———. "Leaving the Ghetto." *Commentary* 101/2 (1996): 29–33.

———. "'Daʿat Torah'—The Unqualified Authority Claimed for Halakhists." *Jewish History* 11/1 (1997): 41–50.

Kedar, B. Z. "Canon Law and the Burning of the Talmud." *Bulletin of Medieval Canon Law* 9 (1979): 79–82.

Kelly-Gadol, Joan. "Did Women Have a Renaissance." In Claudia Koonz and Renata Bridenthal, eds., *Becoming Visible*. Boston, 1977.

Kingdon, Robert M. *Adultery and Divorce in Calvin's Geneva*. Cambridge, Mass., 1995.

Klapisch-Zuber, Christiane. "Parenti, amici e vicini, Il territorio urbano d'una famiglia mercantile nel XV secolo." *Quaderni Storici* 33 (1976): 953–82. Trans. as "Kin, Friends, and Neighbors: The Urban Territory of a Merchant Family in 1400," in Lydia Cochrane, trans., *Women, Family, and Ritual in Renaissance Italy*. Chicago, 1985.

———. "The 'Cruel Mother': Maternity, Widowhood, and Dowry in Florence in the Fourteenth and Fifteenth Centuries"; "The Griselda Complex: Dowry and Marriage Gifts in the Quattrocento"; "Zacharias, or the Ousted Father: Nuptial Rites in Tuscany between Giotto and the Council of Trent." All in Lydia Cochrane, trans., *Women, Family, and Ritual in Renaissance Italy*. Chicago, 1985.

———. "Kinship and Politics in Fourteenth Century Florence." In David Kertzer and Julius Kirschner, eds., *The Family in Italy, from Antiquity to the Present*. New Haven, 1991.

Klar, B. *The Scroll of Ahimaaz* (in Hebrew). Jerusalem, 1974.

Kuehn, Thomas. *Law, Family, and Women: Toward a Legal Anthropology of Renaissance Italy*. Chicago, 1991.

———. "Antropologia giuridica dello Stato." In Giorgio Chittolini, Anthony Molho, and Pierangelo Schiera, eds., *Origini dello Stato, Processi di formazione Statale in Italia fra medioevo ed età moderna*. Bologna, 1994.

Ladurie, Emanuel Le Roy. "L'aiguillette." *Le territorie de l'historien*. Paris, 1973.

Landes, Richard. "The Massacres of 1010: On the Origins of Popular Anti-Jewish Violence in Western Europe." In Jeremy Cohen, ed., *From Witness to Witchcraft: Jews and Judaism in Medieval Christian Thought*. Weisbaden, 1996.

Lederhendler, Eli. *Jewish Responses to Modernity: New Voices in America and Eastern Europe*. New York, 1994.

Levi, Leo. "Canti tradizionali e tradizioni liturgiche giudeo-italiane." *Rassegna Mensile di Israel* 23 (1957): 433–45.

Lewy, Hans. ʿ*Olamot Nifgashim*. Jerusalem, 1960.

Linder, Amnon. *The Jews in the Legal Sources of the Early Middle Ages*. Jerusalem and Detroit, 1997.

Little, Lester. "Una confraternità di giovani in un paese bergamasco, 1474." *Società, Istituzioni, Spiritualità: studi in onore di Cinzio Violante*. Spoleto, 1994.

Loevinson, Ermano. "La Concession de banques de prêtes aux Juifs par les papes." *Revue des Études Juives* 92 (1932): 1–20; 93 (1933): 27–52; 157–78; 94 (1934): 57–72, 167–83; 95 (1935): 23–43.

Lombardo, Maria Luisa. *La Dogana Minuta a Roma nel primo quattrocento*. Viterbo, 1983.

Lutz, Catherine A. *Unnatural Emotion: Everyday Sentiments on a Micronesian Atoll and Their Challenge to Western Theory*. Chicago, 1988.

Lutz, Catherine, and Lila Abu-Lughod, eds. *Language and the Politics of Emotion*. Cambridge, 1990.

Luzzati, Michele. "Alle radici della 'juedische Mutter': note sul lavoro famminile nel mondo ebraico italiano fra Medioevo e Rinascimento." In Simona Cavaciocchi, ed., *La donna nell'economia Secc. XIII–XVIII*. Florence, 1990.

Luzzatto, Simone. *Discorso*. Ed. A. Z. Ascoli. Hebrew trans., *Ma'amar 'al Yehudaei Veneziah*, Riccardo Bacchi and Moshe Shulvass. Jerusalem, 1951.

Maimonides. *Mishneh Torah*, *'Ishut*, 4:1,7, and 8; and *Gerushin*, 11:3.

Maire Vigueur, J. C. "Les Juifs à Rome dans la seconde moitié du XIVe siècle: informations tirés d'un fonds notarié," in AA.VV., *Aspetti e problemi della presenza ebraica nell'Italia centro-settentrionale secoli XIV e XV*. Rome, 1983.

Malkiel, David. "The Tenuous Thread: A Venetian Lawyer's Apology for Self-Government in the Seventeenth Century." *AJS Review* 12 (1987): 223–50.

Marcus, I. G. *Piety and Society*. Leiden, 1981.

———. "Kiddush haShem in Ashkenaz and the Story of Rabbi Amnon of Mainz." In I. Gafni and A. Ravitzky, eds., *Kiddush haShem and the Suffering of the Soul: Studies in Memory of Amir Yekutiel*. Jerusalem, 1992.

Marcus, J. R. *The Jew in the Medieval World*. New York, 1965.

Marsh, Peter. "Identity, an Ethnogenic Perspective." In Richard C. Trexler, ed., *Persons in Groups*. Binghamton, 1985.

Martin, John. "Inventing Sincerity, Refashioning Prudence: The Discovery of the Individual in Renaissance Europe. *American Historical Review* 102 (1997): 1309–42.

Martines, Lauro. "Ritual Language in Renaissance Italy." In J. Chiffoleau, Lauro Martines, and A. Paravicini Bagliani, eds., *Riti e rituali nelle Società Medievali*. Spoleto, 1994.

McGinness, Frederick. *Right Thinking and Sacred Oratory in Counter-Reformation Rome*. Princeton, 1995.

Meeks, Wayne, and Robert Wilken. *Jews and Christians in Antioch in the First Four Centuries of the Common Era*. Missoula, Mont., 1978.

Melamed, Abraham. "The Perception of Jewish History in Italian Jewish Thought of the Sixteenth and Seventeenth Centuries." *Italia Judaica, Gli Ebrei in Italia tra Rinascimento ed Età Barocca, Atti del II Convegno Internazionale, Genova 10–15 giugno 1984*. Rome, 1986.

Mendelsohn, Sara. "The Weightiest Business: Marriage in an Upper-Gentry Family in Seventeenth Century England." *Past and Present* 85 (1979): 126–35.

Metzger, Therese and Mendel. *Jewish Life in the Middle Ages: Illuminated*

Hebrew Manuscripts of the Thirteenth to Sixteenth Centuries. New York, 1982.

Milano, Attilio. "I 'Capitoli di Daniel da Pisa' e la comunità di Roma." *La Rassegna Mensile d'Israel* 10 (1935–36): 409–26.

———. "L'impari lotta della Comunità di Roma contro la Casa dei Catecumeni." *La Rassegna Mensile di Israel* 16 (1950): 355–68, and 408–19.

———. *Storia degli ebrei in Italia.* Turin, 1963.

———. *Il Ghetto di Roma.* Rome, 1964.

Minty, Mary. "Kiddush HaShem in German Christian Eyes in the Middle Ages" (in Hebrew), *Zion* 59 (1994): 233–44.

Modena, Leone da. *Historia de' riti Hebraici.* Paris, 1637. Translation, *Rites of the Jews.* London, 1650.

Molho, Anthony. *Marriage Alliance in Late Medieval Florence.* Cambridge, Mass., 1994.

Moore, Deborah Dash. *At Home in America: Second Generation New York Jews.* New York, 1981.

Morell, Shmuel. "The Constitutional Limits of Communal Government in Rabbinic Law." *Jewish Social Studies* 33 (1971): 91–100.

———. "An Equal or a Ward: How Independent Is a Married Woman According to Rabbinic Law?" *Jewish Social Studies* 44 (1982): 190–97.

Morosini, Giulio. *Via della Fede.* Rome, 1683.

Moses ben Nahman, Nahmanides (pseudo?). *Iggeret ha-qodesh.* In Ch. Chavel, ed., *Khitvei ha-Ramban.* Jerusalem, 1969.

Mosse, George L. *German Jews Beyond Judaism.* Bloomington, 1985.

Muir, Edward. "The Virgin on the Street Corner: The Place of the Sacred in Italian Cities." *Religion and Culture in the Renaissance and Reformation.* Kirksville, Missouri, 1989.

———. *Ritual in Early Modern Europe.* Cambridge, 1997.

Musi, Aurelio. "Lo 'scalco spirituale': un manuale Napoletano di disciplina del corpo (sec. xvii)," in P. Prodi, ed., *Disciplina dell'anima, disciplina del corpo e disciplina della società tra medioevo ed età moderna.* Bologna, 1994.

Muzzarelli, M. G. *Ebrei e Città d'Italia in Età di transizione: Il Caso di Cesena dal XIV al XVI secolo.* Bologna, 1983.

———. "Ebrei, Bologna e sovrano-pontifice: la fine di una relazione tra verifiche, restrizioni e ripensamenti." In M. G. Muzzarelli, ed., *Verso l'epilogo di una convivenza: gli ebrei a Bologna nel xvi secolo*. Florence, 1996.

Myers, David N. "'Distant Relatives Happening onto the Same Inn': The Meeting of East and West as Literary Theme and Cultural Ideal." *Jewish Social Studies* 1/2 (1995): 75–100.

Natali, Ettore. *Il Ghetto di Rome*. Rome, 1887.

Niccoli, Ottavia. "Creanza e disciplina: buone maniere per i fanciulli nell'Italia della contrariforma." In Paolo Prodi, ed., *Disciplina dell'anima, disciplina del corpo e disciplina della società tra medioevo ed età moderna*. Bologna, 1994.

Nirenberg, David. *Communities of Violence: Persecution of Minorities in the Middle Ages*. Princeton, 1996.

Nussdorfer, Laurie. *Civic Politics in the Rome of Urban VIII*. Princeton, 1992.

———. "The Politics of Space in Early Modern Rome." *Memoirs of the American Academy in Rome* 42 (1999): 161–86.

O'Malley, John. *Rome of the Renaissance*. London, 1981.

Ozment, Steven. *When Fathers Ruled: Family Life in Reformation Europe*. Cambridge, Mass., 1983.

Pagis, Dan. "Baroque Trends in Italian Hebrew Poetry." *Italia Judaica, Gli Ebrei in Italia tra Rinascimento ed Età Barocca, Atti del II Convegno Internazionale, Genova 10–15 giugno 1984*. Rome, 1986.

———. "Ha-pulmus ha-shiri ʿal tiv ha-nashim—Babuʿah le-temurot ve-shirah ha–ivrit be-ʿItaliah." In Ezra Fleischer, ed., *Poetry Aptly Explained: Studies and Essays on Medieval Hebrew Poetry* (in Hebrew). Jerusalem, 1993.

Parente, Fausto. "La Chiesa e il Talmud." In C. Vivanti, ed., *Gli ebrei in Italia, Storia d'Italia, Annali 11*. Turin, 1996.

Pavan, Paola. "Permanenze di schemi e modelli del passato in una società in mutamento." In Massimo Miglio, Francesca Niutta, Diego Quaglioni, and Concetta Ranieri, eds., *Una Pontificato ed una città: Sixto IV (1471–1484)*. Città del Vaticano, 1984.

———. "La confraternità del Salvatore nella società romana del Tre-Quattrocento." In Luigi Fiorani, ed., *Le confraternite romane: esperienza religiosa, socieà, committenza artistica* [= *Ricerche per la storia religiosa di Roma* 5 (1984): 81–91].

Pavoncello, Nello. *I Toponimi del vecchio Ghetto di Roma*. Rome, 1978.

Perani, Mauro. "Documenti sui processi dell'Inquisizione contro gli ebrei di Bologna e sulla loro tassazione alla vigilia della prima espulsione (1567–1568)." In M. G. Muzzarelli, ed., *Verso l'epilogo di una convivenza: gli ebrei a Bologna nel xvi secolo*. Florence, 1996.

Pin, Emile J., and Jamie Turndorf. "Staging One's Ideal Self." In Dennis Brissett and Charles Edgley, eds., *Life as Theater*, 163–81. New York, 1990.

Post, Gaines. *Studies in Medieval Legal Thought: Public Law and the State, 1100–1322*. Princeton, 1964.

Procaccia, Micaela. "'Non dabarà': Gli ebrei di Roma nei primi cinquanta anni del Cinquecento attraverso le fonti giudiziarie." *Italia Judaica VI; Gli ebrei nello Stato pontificio fino al Ghetto (1555)* (Rome, 1998).

Prodi, Paolo. *Il Sovranno Pontefice*. Bologna, 1982. Translation: Susan Haskins, *The Papal Prince*. Cambridge, 1978.

Prosperi, Adriano. "New Heaven and New Earth: Prophecy and Propaganda at the Time of the Discovery and Conquest of the Americas." In Marjorie Reeves, ed., *Prophetic Rome in the High Renaissance Period*. Oxford, 1992.

———. "L'inquisitore come confessore," in P. Prodi and A. Prosperi, eds., *Disciplina dell'anima, disciplina del corpo e disciplina della società tra medioevo ed età moderna*. Bologna, 1994.

———. *Tribunali della conscienza: Inquisitori, confessori, missionari*. Turin, 1996.

Pullan, Brian. *Rich and Poor in Renaissance Venice*. Cambridge, Mass., 1971.

———. "A Ship with Two Rudders: 'Righeto Marrano' and the Inquisition in Venice." *Historical Journal* 20/1 (1977): 25–58.

———. *The Jews of Europe and the Inquisition of Venice, 1550–1670*. Oxford, 1983.

Quaglioni, Diego. "Propaganda Antiebraica e Polemiche di Curia," in Massimo Miglio, Francesca Niutta, Diego Quaglioni, and Concetta Ranieri, eds., *Un Pontificato ed una città: Sixto IV (1471–1484)*. Città del Vaticano, 1984.

———. "Fra tolleranza e persecuzione: Gli ebrei nella letteratura giuridica del tardo Medioevo," in C. Vivanti, ed., *Gli ebrei in Italia, Storia d'Italia, Annali 11*. Turin, 1996.

Queller, D. E., and T. F. Madden. "Father of the Bride: Fathers, Daughters, and Dowries in Late Medieval and Early Renaissance Venice." *Renaissance Quarterly* 46 (1993): 685–711.

Rav, Babylonian Talmud. *Qiddushin*, 41a.

Ravid, Benjamin. "Republica nifredet mikol shilton 'aher." In A. Greenbaum and A. Ivry, eds., *Thought and Action*. Tel Aviv, 1983.

———. "The Religious, Economic, and Social Background and Context of the Establishment of the Ghetti of Venice." In G. Cozzi, ed., *Gli Ebrei e Venezia*. Milan, 1987.

———. "From Geographical Realia to Historiographical Symbol: The Odyssey of the Word *Ghetto*." In David B. Ruderman, ed., *Essential Papers on Jewish Culture in Renaissance and Baroque Italy*. New York, 1992.

Riemer, Eleanor S. "Women, Dowries, and Capital Investment in Thirteen-Century Siena." In Marion A. Kaplan, ed., *The Marriage Bargain: Women and Dowries in European History* (= *Women and History* 10 [1985]).

Rinaldi, Rosella. "La giustizia in città: Indagini sulla comunità ebraica di Bologna tra '400 e '500." In M. G. Muzzarelli, ed., *Verso l'epilogo di una convivenza: gli ebrei a Bologna nel xvi secolo*. Florence, 1996.

Rivlin, Berachah. *Mutual Responsibility in the Italian Ghetto Holy Societies, 1516–1789* (in Hebrew). Jerusalem, 1991.

Romagnoli, G. Franco. "Rome's Jewish Quarter: A Rich Culinary Heritage." *Gourmet Magazine*, August 1995, 52–55, 90–94.

Ronciére, Charles de la. "Les confréries en Toscane aux XIV et XV siècles d'aprés les travaux récents." In Luigi Fiorani, ed., *Le confraternite romane: esperienza religiosa, società, committenza artistica* [= *Ricerche per la storia religiosa di Roma* 5 (1984): 50–64, esp. 61–62].

Roper, Lyndal. "'Going to Church and Street': Weddings in Reformation Augsburg." *Past and Present* 106 (1985): 67.

Rosa, Mario. "Tra tolleranza e repressione: Roma e gli ebrei nel '700." *Italia Judaica III*. Rome, 1989.

Rose, Peter I. *They and We: Racial and Ethnic Relations in the United States.* 5th ed. New York, 1997.

Rosenwein, Barbara H. "Controlling Paradigms." In Barbara H. Rosenwein, ed., *Anger's Past: The Social Uses of an Emotion in the Middle Ages*. Ithaca, 1998.

Roth, Cecil. "La festa per l'istituzione del Ghetto a Verona." *Rassegna Mensile di Israel* 3 (1928): 33–39.

———. "The Memoirs of a Sienese Jew (1625–1633)." *Hebrew Union College Annual* 5 (1928): 353–402.

———. "Forced Baptisms in Italy." *Jewish Quarterly Review* 27 (1936): 117–36.

———. *The House of Nasi: Dona Gracia.* Philadelphia, 1948.

———. *The Jews in the Renaissance.* Philadelphia, 1959.

Ruderman, David B. "The Founding of a Gemilut Hasadim Society in Ferrara in 1515." *AJS Review* 1 (1976): 233–67.

———. "An Apologetic Treatise from Sixteenth Century Bologna." *Hebrew Union College Annual* 50 (1979): 253–75.

———. *The World of a Renaissance Jew.* Cincinnati, 1981.

———. *Kabbalah, Magic, and Science: The Cultural Universe of a Sixteenth Century Jewish Physician.* Cambridge, Mass., 1988.

———. "The Italian Renaissance and Jewish Thought." In A. Rabil, ed., *Renaissance Humanism: Foundations and Forms.* Philadelphia, 1988.

———. "The Impact of Science on Jewish Culture and Society in Venice." In Ruderman, ed., *Essential Papers.* New York, 1992.

Ruderman, David B., ed. *Preachers of the Italian Ghetto.* Los Angeles, 1992.

———, ed. *Essential Papers on Jewish Culture in Renaissance and Baroque Italy.* New York, 1992.

———. *Jewish Thought and Scientific Discovery in Early Modern Europe.* New Haven, 1995.

———. "Cecil Roth, Historian of Italian Jewry: A Reassessment." In David N. Myers and David B. Ruderman, eds., *The Jewish Past Revisited: Reflections on Modern Jewish Historians.* New Haven, 1998.

Ruggiero, Guido. *The Boundaries of Eros: Sex Crime and Sexuality in Renaissance Venice.* Oxford, 1985.

———. *Binding Passions: Tales of Magic, Marriage, and Power at the End of the Renaissance.* Oxford, 1993.

———. "Constructing Civic Morality, Deconstructing the Body: Civic Rituals of Punishment in Renaissance Venice." In J. Chiffoleau, Lauro Martines, and A. Paravicini Bagliani, eds., *Riti e rituali nelle Società Medievali.* Spoleto, 1994.

Rusconi, Robert. "Confraternite, compagnie e devozioni." In G. Chittolini and G. Miccoli, eds., *La Chiesa e il potere politico dal Medioevo all'età contemporanea, Storia di Italia, Annali 9*. Turin, 1986.

Rutgers, Leonard V. *The Jews in Late Ancient Rome: Evidence of Cultural Interaction in the Roman Diaspora*. Leiden, 1995.

Sarfatti, Michele. *Mussolini contro gli ebrei*. Turin, 1994.

Schechner, Richard. "From Ritual to Theater and Back." *Essays on Performance Theory*. New York, 1977.

Schifman, Pinhas. "The Welfare of the Child and Religious Considerations." *Jewish Law Annual* 10 (1992): 159–76.

Schmelz, U. O., S. Della Pergola, and U. Avner. *Ethnic Differences Among Israeli Jews: A New Look*. Jerusalem, 1991.

Schwarzfuchs, Shimon. "Controversie nella Communità di Roma agli inizi del secolo XVI." *Scritti in Memoria di Enzo Sereni*. Jerusalem, 1970.

Segre, Renata. *The Jews in Piedmont*. 3 vols. Jerusalem, 1986.

———. "Sephardic Settlements in Sixteenth Century Italy: A Historical and Geographical Survey." In Alisa Meyuhas Ginio, ed., *Jews, Christians, and Muslims in the Mediterranean World after 1492*. [= *Mediterranean Historical Review* 7 (1992)].

Sermoneta, J. B. "Tredici giorni nella Casa dei Conversi—dal diario di una giovana ebrea del 18 secolo." *Michael* 1 (1972): 261–315.

———. "Aspetti del pensiero moderna nell'ebraismo italiano tra Rinascimento e Età Barocca." *Gli Ebrei in Italia tra Rinascimento ed Età Barocca, Atti del II Convegno Internazionale, Genova 10–15 giugno 1984*. Rome, 1986.

———. "The Liturgy of Sicilian Jews" (in Hebrew). In Haim Beinart, ed., *Jews in Italy*. Jerusalem, 1988.

———. "Jewish Culture at Rome in the XVIIIth Century as Seen Through New Documentation" (in Hebrew). *Italia Judaica*. Rome, 1989.

———. *Ratto della signora Anna del Monte trattenuta a'catecumeni tredici giorni dalli 6 fino alli 19 maggio anno 1749*. Rome, 1989.

Shochetman, Eliav. "On the Nature of the Rules Governing Custody of Children in Jewish Law." *Jewish Law Annual* 10 (1992): 115–58.

Shulvass, M. A. *The Jews in the World of the Renaissance*. Trans. E. Kose. Leiden, 1973.

Siddurim. Hebrew Union College, Klau Collection, ms. 396, and also nos. 243, 245, 247, 248, 264, 290.

Siegmund, Stefanie. "La Vita nei ghetti." In C. Vivanti, ed., *Gli ebrei in Italia, Storia d'Italia, Annali 11*. Turin, 1996.

Simonsohn, Shlomo. *The Jews in the Duchy of Milan*. 4 vols. Jerusalem, 1982.

———. "Divieto di trasportare ebrei in Palestina: New Documentation" (in Hebrew). Gli Ebrei in Italia tra Rinascimento ed Età Barocca, Atti del II Convegno Internazionale, Genova 10–15 giugno 1984. Rome, 1986.

———. *The Apostolic See and the Jews*. 8 vols. Toronto, 1988–91.

———. *The Jews in Sicily*. Vol. 1. Leiden, 1997.

Sinclair, D. B. "Jewish Law in the State of Israel: Custody and the Role of Women in Their Children's Education." *Jewish Law Annual* 9 (1991): 251–57.

Smith, Jonathan Z. *To Take Place*. Chicago, 1987.

Sofia, Francesa, and Mario Toscano, eds. *Stato nazionale ed emancipazione ebraica*. Rome, 1992.

Sonne, Isaiah. *Mi-Pavolo ha-Reviʿi ʿad Pius ha-Hamishi*. Jerusalem, 1954.

Sonnino, Eugenio, and Rosa Traina. "La pesta del 1656–57 a Roma: organizzazione sanitaria e mortalità." In *La demografia storica delle città italiane*. S.I.D.E.S. Bologna, 1972.

———. "The Population in Baroque Rome." In P. van Kessel and E. Schulte, eds., *Rome-Amsterdam: Two Growing Cities in Seventeenth Century Europe*. Amsterdam, 1997.

Sorani, Giustino, "Appunti storici." *Il Vessillo Israelitico* 56 (1908): 171–73, 235–37.

Sorkin, David. "The Impact of Emancipation on German Jewry: A Reconsideration." In Jonathan Frankel and Steven Zipperstein, eds., *Assimilation and Community*. Cambridge, 1992.

Stacey, Robert C. "From Ritual Crucifixion to Host Desecration: Jews and the Body of Christ." *Jewish History* 12/1 (1998): 9–25.

Starr, Joshua. "The Mass Conversion of Jews in Southern Italy, 1290–1293." *Speculum* 21 (1946): 203–211.

Stille, Alexander. *Benevolence and Betrayal: Five Italian Jewish Families under Fascism*. New York, 1991.

Stinger, Charles L. *The Renaissance in Rome*. Bloomington, 1985.

Stow, Kenneth. "The Burning of the Talmud in 1553, in the Light of Sixteenth Century Catholic Attitudes Toward the Talmud." *Bibliothèque d'Humanisme et Renaissance* 34 (1972): 435–59.

———. *Catholic Thought and Papal Jewry Policy*. New York, 1977.

———. "Jewish Approaches to the Papacy and the Papal Doctrine of Jewish Protection, 1050–1150" (in Hebrew). *Studies in the History of the Jewish People and the Land of Israel* 5 (1981): 75–90.

———. "Papal and Royal Attitudes Toward Jewish Lending." *AJS Review* 6 (1981): 161–84.

———. *Taxation Community and State: The Jews and the Fiscal Foundations of the Early Modern Papal State*. Stuttgart, 1982.

———. *The '1007 Anonymous' and Papal Sovereignty: Jewish Perceptions of the Papacy and Papal Policy in the High Middle Ages*. Cincinnati, 1984.

———. "Castigo e delitto nello Stato della Chiesa: gli ebrei nelle carceri romane dal 1572 al 1659." *Italia Judaica, Gli Ebrei in Italia tra Rinascimento ed Età Barocca, Atti del II Convegno Internazionale, Genova 10–15 giugno 1984*. Rome, 1986.

———. "The Jewish Family in the Rhineland: Form and Function." *American Historical Review* 92 (1987): 1085–1110.

———. "Expulsion Italian Style: The Case of Lucio Ferraris. *Jewish History* 3/1 (1988): 51–64.

———. "Life and Society in the Roman Community in the Sixteenth Century" (in Hebrew). *Pe'amim* 37 (1989): 57.

———. "Sanctity and the Construction of Space: The Roman Ghetto," in S. Boesch and L. Scaraffia, eds., *Luoghi sacri e spazi della santità*. Turin, 1990; and revised in M. Mor, ed., *Jewish Assimilation, Acculturation and Accommodation*. Lanham, 1992.

———. "The Papacy and the Jews: Catholic Reformation and Beyond." *Jewish History* 6 (1991): 268.

———. "La Storiographia del ghetto romano: problemi metodologici." In M. G. Muzzarelli and Giacomo Todeschini, eds., *La Storia degli ebrei nell'Italia medievale: tra filologia e metodologia*. Bologna, 1991.

———. "The Consciousness of Closure: Roman Jewry and Its *Ghet*." In Ruderman, ed., *Essential Papers*. New York, 1992.

———. "Prossimità o distanza: etnicità, sefarditi e assenza di conflitti etnici nella Roma del sedicesimo secolo." In A. Foa, M. Silvera, and K. R. Stow, eds., *Oltre il 1492* [= *La Rassengna Mensile di Israel* 58 (1992): 61–74].

———. "Ethnic Rivalry or Melting Pot: The 'Edot' in the Roman Ghetto." *Judaism* 163 (1992): 286–96.

———. "The Good of the Church, The Good of the State: The Popes and Jewish Money." In Diana Wood, ed., *Christianity and Judaism* [= *Studies in Church History* 29]. Oxford, 1992.

———. *Alienated Minority: The Jews of Medieval Latin Europe*. Cambridge, Mass., 1992; rev. (paper), 1994.

———. "A Tale of Uncertainties: Converts in the Roman Ghetto." In D. Carpi, M. Gil, and Y. Gorni, eds., *Shlomo Simonsohn Jubilee Volume*. Tel Aviv, 1993.

———. "Ebrei e inquisitori, 1250–1350. In M. Luzzati, ed., *L'inquisizione e gli ebrei in Italia*. Bari, 1994.

———. "By Land or by Sea: The Passage of the Kalonymides to the Rhineland in the Tenth Century." In M. Goodich, S. Menasche, and S. Schein, eds., *Cross Cultural Convergences in the Crusader Period, Studies in Honor of Aryeh Grabois*. New York, 1995.

———. "Marriages Are Made in Heaven: Marriage and the Individual in the Roman Jewish Ghetto." *Renaissance Quarterly* 48 (1995): 445–91.

———. *The Jews in Rome*. 2 vols. Leiden, 1995, 1997.

———. "The Avignonese Papacy, or After the Expulsion." In Jeremy Cohen, ed., *From Witness to Witchcraft: Jews and Judaism in Medieval Christian Thought*. Weisbaden, 1996.

———. "Church, Conversion, and Tradition: The Problem of Jewish Conversion in Sixteenth Century Italy." *Dimensioni e problemi della ricerca storica* 2 (1996): 26–35.

———. "Holy Body, Holy Society: Conflicting Medieval Structural Perceptions." In J. Prawer, R. J. Z. Werblowsky, and B. Z. Kedar, eds., *Sacred Space: Shrine, City, Land*. New York, 1998.

———. "Abramo ben Aron Scazzocchio: Another Kind of Rabbi." Proceedings of the II Conference on Mediterranean Jewry, Bar Ilan University, December 1993. Forthcoming.

———. "Corporate Double Talk: *Kehillat Kodesh* and *Universitas* in the Roman Jewish Sixteenth Century Environment." *Journal of Jewish Thought and Philosophy* 8(1999): 283–301.

———. "The New Fashioned from the Old: Parallels in Public and Learned Memory and Practice in Sixteenth Century Jewish Rome." In B. D. Cooperman and Barbara Garvin, eds., *Memory and Identity: The Jews of Italy*. College Park, Maryland, 2000.

———. "Papal Mendicants or Mendicant Popes: Continuity and Change in Papal Policies toward the Jews at the End of the Fifteenth Century." In Stephen McMichael and Larry Simon, eds., *The Friars and the Jews* (Leiden, 2000).

———. Review of Amnon Linder, *The Jews in the Legal Sources of the Early Middle Ages*. In *Jewish Quarterly Review* 89 (1999): 432–37.

———. "The Knotty Problem of Shem Tov Soporto: Male Honor, Marital Initiation, and Disciplinary Structures in Mid-Sixteenth Century Jewish Rome." *Memorial Book for Joseph B. Sermoneta* [= *Italia* 13–14, forthcoming, 2000].

Stow, Kenneth R., and S. Debenedetti Stow. "Donne ebree a Roma nell'età del ghetto." *Rassegna Mensile di Israel* 52 (1986): 107–16.

Strocchia, Sharon T. "Funerals and the Politics of Gender in Early Renaissance Florence." In Marilyn Migiel and Juliana Schiesari, eds., *Refiguring Woman: Perspectives on Gender and the Italian Renaissance*. Ithaca, 1991.

Struever, Nancy. *The Language of History in the Renaissance*. Princeton, 1970.

Tacitus. *Histories*. Trans. Kenneth Wellesley. Harmondsworth (Penguin), 1972.

Terpstra, Nicholas. *Lay Confraternities and Civic Religion in Renaissance Bologna*. Cambridge, 1995.

Tirosh Rothschild, Hava. "In Defense of Jewish Humanism." *Jewish History* 3/2 (1988): 31–58.

Toaff, Ariel. "Nuova Luce sui Marrani di Ancona, 1556. *Studi Sull'Ebraismo Italiano*. Rome, 1974.

———. *Il Ghetto di Roma nel Cinquecento, conflitti etnici e problemi socio-economici* (in Hebrew, Italian summary). Ramat Gan, 1984.

———. "Jewish Banking in Central Italy, Thirteenth Through Fifteenth Centuries." In H. Beinart, ed., *Jews in Italy*. Jerusalem, 1988.

———. "The Jewish Communities of Catalonia, Aragon and Castile in 16th Century Rome." In A. Toaff and S. Schwarzfuchs, eds., *The Mediterranean and the Jews: Banking, Finance and International Trade (XVI–XVIII Centuries)*. Ramat-Gan, 1989.

———. *Il Vino e la carne*. Bologna, 1989.

———. "Ebrei spagnoli e marrani nell'Italia del Cinquecento: una presenza contestata." In A. Foa, M. Silvera, and K. R. Stow, eds., *Oltre il 1492*. [= *La Rassegna Mensile di Israel* 58 (1992): 47–60].

———. *The Jews in Umbria*, 3 vols. Leiden, 1993–94.

———. "Gli ebrei a Roma," and "La vita materiale." In C. Vivanti, ed., *Gli ebrei in Italia, Storia d'Italia, Annali 11*. Vol. 1, Turin, 1996.

Toaff, Renzo. *La Nazione Ebrea a Livorno e a Pisa (1591–1700)*. Florence, 1990.

Toch, Michael. "The Jewish Community of Nuremberg in the Year 1489, Social and Demographic Structure" (in Hebrew). *Zion* 45 (1980): 60–72.

Toschi, Paolo. *Le origine del teatro italiano*. Turin, 1955.

Trasselli, Carmelo. "Un ufficio notarile per gli Ebrei di Roma." *Archivio della R. Deputazione Romana di Storia Patria* 60 (1938): 231–44.

Trexler, Richard C. *Public Life in Renaissance Florence*. New York, 1980.

Turner, Victor. *Dramas, Fields, and Metaphors: Symbolic Action in Human Society*. Ithaca, 1974.

———. *From Ritual to Theatre: The Human Seriousness of Play*. New York, 1982.

Various Authors. "Criminal Law, Husband and Wife." *Jewish Law Annual* 9 (1991): 5–170.

Vogelstein, H., and P. Rieger. *Geschichte der Juden in Rom*. 2 vols. Berlin, 1895.

Walker, Mack. "Jewish Identity in a World of Corporations and Estates." In Ronnie Po-Chia Hsia and Harmut Lehmann, eds., *In and Out of the Ghetto*. Washington, D.C., 1995.

Wasserfall, Rahel. "Menstruation and Identity: The Meaning of Niddah for Moroccan Women Immigrants to Israel." In Howard Eilberg-Schwartz, ed., *People of the Body: Jews and Judaism from an Embodied Perspective* (Albany, 1992), 309–29.

Weinberg, Joanna. "Azariah de' Rossi and the Forgeries of Annius Viterbo." In Ruderman, ed., *Essential Papers*. New York, 1992.

Weinstein, Roni. "The Jewish Marriage in Italy during the Early Modern Era." Ph.D. dissertation, Jerusalem, 1995.

Weisner, Merry E. *Women and Gender in Early Modern Europe*. Cambridge, 1993.

———. "Family, Household, and Community." In T. Brady, Jr., H. Oberman, and J. D. Tracy, eds., *Handbook of European History, 1400–1600*. Leiden, 1994.

Weissman, Ronald F. E. *Ritual Brotherhood in Renaissance Florence*. New York, 1982.

———. "From Brotherhood to Congregation: Confraternal Ritual between Renaissance and Catholic Reformation." In J. Chiffoleau, Lauro Martines, and A. Paravicini Bagliani, eds., *Riti e rituali nelle Società Medievali*. Spoleto, 1994.

Werner, Eric. *The Sacred Bridge*. New York, 1959.

Whitfield, Stephen J. *In Search of American Jewish Culture*. Hanover, N.H., 1999.

Wirszubski, Chaim. *Three Studies in Christian Kabbala*. Jerusalem, 1975.

———. *A Christian Kabbalist Reads the Law* (in Hebrew). Jerusalem, 1977.

Wistinetski, Jehuda, ed. *Sefer Hasidim*. Frankfurt am Main, 1924.

Woolf, Jeffrey. *The Life and Responsa of Rabbi Joseph Colon b. Solomon Trabotto Maharik*. Ann Arbor, 1991.

———. "Toward a Halachic and Intellectual Portrait of Rabbi Elijah Capsali," in Hebrew. *Tarbiz* 65 (1996): 173–87.

Wrigley, E. A. "Fertility Strategy for the Individual and the Group," in C. Tilly, ed., *Historical Studies of Changing Fertility*. Princeton, 1978.

Wrigley, E. A., and R. S. Schonfield. *The Population History of England, 1541–1871*. Cambridge, Mass., 1981.

Yerushalmi, Yosef H. *From Spanish Court to Italian Ghetto*. New York, 1971.

———. *Zakhor: Jewish History and Jewish Memory*. Seattle, 1982.

———. "Clio and the Jews: Reflections on Jewish Historiography in the Sixteenth Century." *Proceedings of the American Academy of Jewish Research* 46–47 (1980). Reprinted in Ruderman, ed., *Essential Papers*. New York, 1992.

Yuval, Yisrael J. "Vengeance and Damnation, Blood and Defamation: From Jewish Martyrdom to Blood Libel Accusations." *Zion* 58 (1993): 33–90.

———. *Scholars in Their Time: The Religious Leadership of German Jewry in the Late Middle Ages* (in Hebrew). Jerusalem, 1988.

Zacour, Norman. *Jews and Saracens in the Consilia of Oldradus da Ponte*. Toronto, 1990.

Zedekiah ben Abramo Anaw. *Shibolei ha-leqet*. Venice, 1546.

Zipperstein, Steven. *The Jews of Odessa: A Cultural History, 1794–1881*. Stanford, 1981.

INDEX

Jehudah, Rosa di (fiancée of Sabato Capone), 81

Jesuit Order, 62. *See also* Loyola, Ignatius

Jewish communities, ancient: in medieval Rome, 14; of Lombardy and Tuscany, 20; theoretical concepts of, 150*n*78. *See also* Political thought

Jewish community organization: laity versus rabbis, 22; political friction in, 26; and women's rights, 85; lay dominance, 103; confraternities, 104; decentralization of, 106; and funerals, 112–15; corporate status of, 117, 201; and debt, 125; membership, 128; taxation, 138; the Congrega, 146–47*nn*63, 64

Jews, German: educational ideals of, 96–97. See also *Bildung*

Jews, Italian, 98

Jews, Portuguese: in Venice and Ancona, 24

Jews in Rome, 24–25, 94; history of, 13–22; communal composition of, 23, 27–28. *See also* Demography, of Jews in Rome

John XXII, Pope, 18

Judaeo-Romanesco. *See* Language

Judah Romano, 18

Judaism, as threat to Christian society, 152

Julius Caesar, 13

Jurisdiction, Jewish, 9, 14, 99; arbitration of, 23

Kabbalah, 96; and magic and alchemy, 45; and modernity, 100

Klapisch-Zuber, Christiane, 12, 79, 178*n*40

The knot: curse of impotence, 86–90

Language: of Jews, 9, 92; Jewish use of Italian, 36; natale, 51; and Italian grammar, 69–70, 74; Judaeo-Romanesco, 128, 170*n*5

Law, Roman and canon, 18

Laws of racial purity, in Italy, 127

Lawyers, Jewish, 93, 110

Lending, Jewish, 19, 21–22, 60; Paul IV and Sixtus V on, 143*n*45

Libellus ad Leonem Decem, 165*n*56

Liberals, Protestant, 96–97, 169*n*82

Litigation: Jewish women as instigators of, 82, 83. *See also* Arbitration

Livorno, Jews of, 131

Loyola, Ignatius, 62

Luzzatto, Simone, 141*n*33

Magic, 89. *See also* Kabbalah

Mahberot (Immanuel ha-Romi), 18

Marranos, 23, 59, 166*nn*59,60; in Rome, 144*n*51

Marriage: of Roman Jews, 29, 74, 75, 147–48*n*68; sacramental or civil, 52; Christian, 53, 56; role of priests in, 160*n*38. *See also* Family

Martin IV, Pope, 16

Martin V, Pope, 17, 18, 19

Martyrdom: of Jewish women, 53

Massa Gei Hizayyon (Benjamin de Abramo Anaw), 18

Memory, historical, 33, 100–101; social, 38, 101

Meʿor ʿeinayyim (Azariah de Rossi), 12

Mercantilist theory, 143*n*45

Methods of social history, 6